Anne-Lise H. Macdonald
10 Pilmour Links
St. Andrews
Fife KY16 9JG
Tel. (0334) 72942

On becoming a psychotherapist

On becoming a psychotherapist

Edited by

Windy Dryden

and

Laurence Spurling

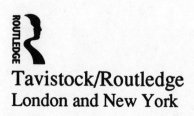

Tavistock/Routledge
London and New York

First published in 1989
Reprinted 1991, 1992 by Routledge
11 New Fetter Lane, London EC4P 4EE

Simultaneously published in the USA and Canada
by Routledge
a division of Routledge, Chapman and Hall, Inc.
29 West 35th Street, New York, NY 10001

Typeset by LaserScript Limited, Mitcham, Surrey
Printed and bound in Great Britain by
Mackays of Chatham PLC, Chatham, Kent

British Library Cataloguing in Publication Data

On becoming a psychotherapist.
  1. Psychotherapy
  I. Spurling, Laurence, *1950-*   II. Dryden, Windy
  616.89'14

Library of Congress Cataloging in Publication Data

On becoming a psychotherapist / edited by Laurence
  Spurling and Windy Dryden.
  p.   cm.
  Includes bibliographies and index.
  1. Psychotherapists – Attitudes.   2. Psychotherapists – Psychology.
  3. Psychotherapists – Mental health.   4. Psychotherapy – Vocational
  guidance. I. Spurling, Laurence, 1950-   . II. Dryden, Windy.
  [DNLM: 1. Psychotherapy. WM 21 058].
  RC480.5.049   1989
  616.89'14023—dc19
  DNLM/DLC
  for Library of Congress
                                              89-3566
                                                CIP

ISBN 0–415–01933–8 (hbk)
ISBN 0–415–03611–9 (pbk)

Contents

Contributors   vii

Preface   ix

Part I: Introduction

1 **The therapist as a crucial variable in psychotherapy**   3
   Paul Gilbert, William Hughes, and Windy Dryden

Part II: The contributions

2 **The object of the dance**   17
   Michael J. Mahoney with Stuart C. Eiseman

3 **Through therapy to self**   33
   Irene Bloomfield

4 **The blessing and the curse of empathy**   53
   Brian Thorne

5 **Chance and choices in becoming a therapist**   69
   P. Paul Heppner

6 **Living vs. survival: a psychotherapist's journey**   87
   Marcia Karp

7 **My career as researcher and psychotherapist**   101
   Hans H. Strupp

8 **A fight for freedom**   116
   Fay Fransella

9 **Challenging the 'White Knight'**   134
   Eddy Street

Contents

10 **A late developer**   148
   John Rowan

11 **Rhythm and blues**   169
   Jocelyn Chaplin

Part III: Commentaries

12 **The self and the therapeutic domain**   191
   Laurence Spurling and Windy Dryden

13 **Ten therapists: the process of becoming and being**   215
   John C. Norcross and James D. Guy

   Appendix   240
   Author index   244
   Subject index   246

Contributors

Irene Bloomfield:	Psychotherapist in private practice, London, England
Jocelyn Chaplin:	Psychotherapist in private practice, London, England
Windy Dryden:	Department of Psychology, Goldsmiths' College, London, England
Stuart C. Eiseman:	Department of Education, University of California, Santa Barbara, California, USA
Fay Fransella:	Centre for Personal Construct Psychology, London, England
Paul Gilbert:	Department of Clinical Psychology, Pastures Hospital, Derby, England
James D. Guy:	Rosemead School of Psychology, Biola University, La Mirada, California, USA
Puncky Paul Heppner:	Department of Psychology, University of Missouri – Columbia, Missouri, USA
William Hughes:	Department of Psychiatry, David Rice Hospital, Norwich, England
Marcia Karp:	Holwell Centre for Psychodrama, North Devon, England
Michael J. Mahoney:	Department of Education, University of California, Santa Barbara, California, USA
John C. Norcross:	Department of Psychology, University of Scranton, Pennsylvania, USA

John Rowan:	Institute of Psychotherapy and Social Studies, London, England
Laurence Spurling:	Psychotherapist in private practice, London, England
Eddy Street:	Child and Family Centre, Cardiff, Wales
Hans H. Strupp:	Department of Psychology, Vanderbilt University, Tennessee, USA
Brian Thorne:	Student Counselling Service, University of East Anglia, Norwich, England

Preface

Recently in the psychotherapy literature there has been renewed interest in the personal lives of psychotherapists and in the personal experiences that have led them to pursue their chosen profession and that characterize their continuing work in that profession (Goldberg 1986; Guy 1987; Kottler 1986). This emphasis perhaps reflects a similar trend in the psychotherapy research literature which has found little differential effectiveness in different approaches to psychotherapy (the 'technical'). As a result, researchers are turning again to more 'personal' therapist variables such as the capacity to form and maintain a therapeutic alliance with clients, in their search for explanations of differential therapeutic outcome (Stiles, Shapiro and Elliott 1986).

In the present book we continue this emphasis on the 'personal' rather than the 'technical' and seek to explicate the process of becoming a psychotherapist. We considered that the best way of approaching our task was to invite a number of therapists to write on this theme from their own experience. The sample of contributing therapists is quite broad. They include both men and women from different therapeutic orientations who are at different stages of their respective careers. Furthermore, they come from both sides of the Atlantic and while some have achieved great eminence in the profession of psychotherapy, others are less well known.

The book is divided into three parts. In Part I, Gilbert, Hughes and Dryden set the scene by laying the foundations of the view that the person of the therapist is a 'crucial variable' in the psychotherapeutic process. In Part II each therapist contributes an autobiographical essay on the theme 'On becoming a psychotherapist'. The content and style of each contribution is essentially personal and individual, but in order to give shape to this section of the book and to focus on some important issues, contributors were asked to use a common chapter structure and to address themselves to specific questions (these are reproduced in the Appendix). Part III contains two commentaries – one by ourselves in which we consider the themes that emerge from the autobiographical essays, and one by Norcross and Guy who consider the contributions in the light of current research knowledge on the personal experiences of psychotherapists.

It is our hope that this text will help experienced and novice therapists to compare their experiences 'on becoming a psychotherapist' with those outlined by the ten contributors. Further, we hope that the book will also encourage those seeking to enter the profession of psychotherapy to reflect on the personal dimensions of their decisions.

Windy Dryden
Laurence Spurling

July 1988
London

References

Goldberg, C. (1986) *On Becoming a Psychotherapist*, New York: Gardner Press.

Guy, J. D. (1987) *The Personal Life of the Psychotherapist*, New York: Wiley.

Kottler, J. A. (1986) *On Being a Therapist*, San Francisco: Jossey-Bass.

Stiles, W. B., Shapiro, D. A., and Elliott, R. (1986) 'Are all psychotherapies equivalent?' *American Psychologist* 41: 165–80.

Part one

Introduction

Chapter one

The therapist as a crucial variable in psychotherapy

Paul Gilbert, William Hughes, and Windy Dryden

Introduction

Strupp in chapter 7 argues that the conduct of effective therapy depends on the person of the therapist *and* the skilful execution of professional craft. Since this book deals with the former, in this chapter we focus on the therapist as a crucial variable in psychotherapy. This chapter should be seen then as providing a context for the autobiographical chapters that follow.

Some historical remarks

Psychotherapeutic encounters are well recorded throughout human history. What counts as such an encounter and how it unfolds reflect historical and cultural processes (Ellenberger 1970). For example, in some cultures, mental distress is viewed as a problem with 'spirit forces' which possess a soul, a situation requiring the intervention of a powerful shaman. Throughout the Middle Ages mental illness was often regarded as the result of transgression and sin (Zilboorg and Henry 1941) requiring punitive treatment. Even today the dividing line between psychotherapy and spiritual guidance can become blurred (London 1986). Hence the human predisposition to engage in a relationship for the purpose of overcoming psychological distress is not a twentieth-century invention but stretches back many centuries.

In non-Western and pre-twentieth century therapeutic approaches, there was often a tendency to regard the personality of the 'healer' as the key factor in therapeutic effectiveness. For example Franz Anton Mesmer (1734–1815), whose approach was the forerunner of hypnosis, was effective as a healer not because of any real force of 'magnetism' but because he had an extraordinarily compelling personality (Ellenberger 1970). With some exceptions, however, we live in an age dominated by the miracles of physical medicine and a fascination with the techniques of the healer. While there is some wisdom to this, there is also need for caution. Can anyone who learns the techniques of their trade be as effective as anyone else? What leads a person to adopt and feel more

3

comfortable with one set of techniques rather than another? What maintains and motivates a therapist in working with distress over many years? What decides whether an individual is able to work with serious psychiatric or borderline clients or stays with mild anxiety conditions? In an ideal world we would say that science chooses and people take up techniques according to their proven efficiency. But we doubt this is often the case. In order to answer these questions one needs to return to the issue of therapist variables (McConnaughty 1987). This is the purpose of this chapter: who becomes a psychotherapist and what affects their way of working?

Who becomes a therapist?

Although it is common to hear young children express professional aims in terms of train driver, doctor or pilot, psychotherapy as a profession is probably considered rather later in life. To some degree the decision to enter training relates to many complex social and personal variables. As Pilgrim points out: 'it is social class of origin rather than individual psychopathology that is more likely to determine whether a person becomes a nurse in Rampton or a psychoanalyst in Hampstead' (1987: 101). Further he cites evidence that social classes tend to recruit from their own. The number of therapists with working class origins is rather less than those of middle or upper class origins. The profession of psychotherapy, like other professions, operates subtle but significant power control over entrants. For example, it is virtually impossible in Britain to become a consultant psychotherapist in the National Health Service, without a medical training, yet there is no evidence that a medical training gives rise to the best therapists. Different professions (e.g., medicine and psychology) have fought more than the odd battle over trying to prescribe who is able to do what to whom. Professionalism always runs a risk of élitism in its efforts to ensure good practice.

These social factors apart, personal factors are also extremely important. Many are drawn towards psychotherapy as a career because of their own personal difficulties. These may be worked through during training, or projected on to patients as a way of resolving personal distress (Kottler 1986). In medicine people may choose psychiatry for its better promotion prospects rather than any particular desire to become a 'mind healer'. In psychology students may commence their clinical or counselling training with only the vaguest idea of what is involved. Nevertheless it is our experience that students are often too ready to attach themselves to a particular school of practice and boldly claim a title for themselves, such as behaviourist or humanist, etc. This may reflect a degree of uncertainty and a desire to project oneself as having positive views, but it can lead to a premature closure on various psychotherapy approaches and in extreme cases to dogmatism. As cognitive science shows, people tend to attend to things they already identify with and reject things they do not.

What therapy?

If it is not scientific criteria that decide what kind of therapy a person chooses to practise (and it often is not) then what other factors might be involved? The first is as serendipitous as historical accident. During training a person may encounter a particularly charismatic teacher who is able to inspire his or her students with ideas and concepts. They may wish to be like him or her and are persuaded as much on the basis of the personality and effectiveness of the teacher as they are from statistics or theory. The fact that the teacher may claim to be, for example, a behaviourist yet achieve therapeutic results using the most lax of techniques is often unnoticed. As Yalom (1980) points out, despite the passivity that psychoanalytic theory insists upon, Freud was not passive, but would often speak with a patient's family, encourage them to behave in certain ways to the patient (e.g. facilitating exposure in cases of agoraphobia) and was not averse to inviting patients to tea with his family or even making personal friends of them.

The second kind of historical accident reflects the availability of learning experiences. If one studies at an institution where the only philosophy to mental life is, for example, behaviourist or psychoanalytic, then it is not surprising if this becomes the dominant orientation for the therapist to adopt. Indeed, as for life in general, the explanation and theoretical axioms one adopts in large part relate to the culture to which one is exposed. This is as true for psycho-therapy as it is for religion and politics. The adoption of psychotherapeutic techniques reflects as much a social process as a scientific one.

The third historical accident relates to personal experiences and needs. Kottler (1986) cites the case of the therapist who had lost her mother from cancer in childhood and sees all psychopathology in terms of mother-child deprivation; or the case of the social worker who had problems in dealing with authority and chose to work with rebellious adolescents. Many examples can be noted from history. Alfred Adler (1870–1937) grew in the shadow of an older brother. In his work we see the issues of sibling rivalry and his introduction of the concepts, inferiority and superiority complexes (Ellenberger 1970). Jung's deeply religious orientation, his interest in Gnosticism and spirituality arose from his religious upbringing (his father and grandfather both being pastors). Hence psychotherapists are not decontextualized beings who, as *tabulae rasae*, are ready to be stamped with learnt technique. Rather they are individuals in search of a method which fits with their personal experiences.

In other cultures and times in history the shaman or healer was expected to have undergone some personal experience of suffering which changed his/her perception of the world (Ellenberger 1970). In our culture, however, there is an implicit assumption that therapists should be psychologically strong, and strenuous efforts may be made to hide personal experiences of suffering. Psychotherapists and mental health workers are not supposed to get depressed or anxious and those who do are often regarded by colleagues as somehow inferior or weak. Like it or not Western culture is obsessed with macho-like images of psychological health and perpetuates a collusion of denial (Rippere and Williams 1985).

Who is suitable to be a therapist?

Whenever this question is raised it inevitably leads one to ask this question of oneself. Many traditional training institutions (e.g. medical and psychology departments) continue to regard intellectual ability as central in the selection of clinicians and the assumption is often made that successful applications have the right qualities for the helping professions or can be helped to acquire them. But, as for music, artistic or writing ability, training may only partly compensate for lack of, in this case, empathy, openness, lack of hostility, etc. Although one may be able to teach someone how to use empathy, it may be much more difficult to train someone to *have* empathy.

To what extent people can learn to be empathic rather than mimic empathic behaviour is a debatable point. True empathy may only be possible through openness to oneself and teaching is then concerned with how to use a talent the person already possesses. The lower the capacity for true empathy, the greater the possibility of projection (Goldstein and Michaels 1985).

There is general agreement that certain types of people are not suited for the profession of psychotherapy. These are individuals who are compulsively self-reliant, emotionally defended, or with severe narcissistic difficulties. There is little evidence as to whether such people are harmful to their clients but general impressions are that they may well be. A psychiatrist in training recently admitted that she could not stand depressives because 'they were so wimpish'. She prided herself on the importance of emotional control. People with autocratic personalities find their way into psychotherapy training as do other types, but the nature of their defences may make their understanding of some patients very difficult. Of course, some patients may gain some relief from autocrats; especially those who seek a collusion of denial.

In psychotherapy there are particular kinds of therapist thinking and evaluating which may interfere with therapy. Ellis (1983) has reviewed many of these, but they include making it a 'must' to follow the right technique or to get someone better, and various forms of negative self-criticism, if this does not happen. Therapists who are prone to personalize ('it's my fault my patient killed himself') or to project blame ('it's the patient's fault, he was just inadequate') quickly run into problems.

The degree of perceived control over another's suffering or recovery is an important question of attribution which requires further research. Therapists who 'personalize' tend to model a style they are trying to educate patients away from, and this can also lead to defensive caring. Here the therapists' main concern is to avoid making a mistake which would lower self-esteem.

They become more concerned with what they are doing rather than listening to, and 'being with', the patient. Therapists who project, however, are more likely to be rigid in therapeutic encounters and see difficulties in therapy as relating to a patient's 'resistances'. In all forms of psychotherapy, good therapists are encouraged to be sceptical and check for alternatives without self- or other-downing. Many of these styles, especially personalization and projection, will have significant bearing on the transference and countertransference. As McConnaughty (1987) points out, there are many therapist variables that are important ingredients in the therapeutic process, e.g. cognitive style, current state of health, level of fatigue, burn out, to name but a few.

What training?

The type of psychotherapeutic training a person obtains is, as we have seen, partly a matter of historical accident relating to social and personal factors. Increasingly, short courses in particular techniques are being offered. Hence various professionals can go on two or three day courses where counselling, cognitive therapy or existential therapy workshops are offered. This allows therapists to learn a variety of techniques from different perspectives – no bad thing perhaps. On the other hand there is probably no suitable substitute for learning at least one approach to therapy well, and being aware of its strengths and weaknesses. Furthermore, training must include education in the kinds of difficulties for which the approach is not suitable, at least not without extensive training on the part of the therapist. On many occasions when I (Paul Gilbert) have invited students to bring cases for discussion, they tried to discuss people who by most criteria have personality problems (see Rutter 1987) and who are best seen by experienced professionals rather than beginning therapists.

The second point about training pertains to the issue of personal experience of therapy. In psychoanalytic therapy personal analysis is required. At present we know of no good evidence to show that a personal therapy does increase effectiveness. Indeed many clinical trials of the newer therapies use relatively novice therapists trained in a particular technique. There is, of course, anecdotal evidence that people do change their way of practice after a personal therapy. However, much may depend on whether therapy is voluntarily undertaken or simply engaged in as a required part of accredited training. In our experience, many therapists who undertake therapy for themselves, rather than to meet professional requirements, have commented that they obtained a different insight into the power of affect when they themselves were having to work through problems. The ability to deal more effectively and honestly with one's own affect is probably central to the development of caring. Coming to know oneself is not always a joyful experience.

Mair poses three questions that therapists should ask themselves: 1) Who or what do I trust? 2) How can I enter into another's way of experiencing?

and 3) How much of myself or others am I willing to know? As he points out, our knowing is about focusing: 'Every way of knowing is, at the same time, a way of ignoring, of turning a particular blind eye, or seeking not to know' (Mair 1987: 118). If a therapist turns a blind eye to things in himself so may the client; dark areas are projected or denied. Therapists may care for their clients as they themselves would like to be cared for, unaware that this is not what their clients need.

So long as technique becomes the new touchstone of psychotherapeutic practice these issues remain secondary concerns. As trainers, we are increasingly under pressure to 'pass on skills' (which is not without its financial benefits). Comparatively little attention is given to the 'people' these skills are imparted to.

Finally we should point out that therapists often do not keep to techniques, even when they are credited as being the originators of techniques. Freud is a well-known example, but there are many others, where observers have noted how their teachers depart in their *actual* practice from what they claim to do. Thus what may start out as an intention to apply a method to a client may be modified to retain the conditions of openness and genuineness. Often therapy is as much about facilitating changes that allow the client to 'start to work' as it is about the work itself. Therapists who fail to see this may become disheartened at lack of progress and fail to recognize that there was nothing wrong with the technique, but the ground (e.g. the working alliance) had not been well enough prepared for the techniques of change to take root.

To this working alliance the client brings transference beliefs (the therapist will make me better; tell me off like mother; will think I'm useless,' etc.) and the therapist will have countertransference beliefs ('this client is an attention-seeker, I must get this client better, this client makes me feel good/bad', etc.). How client and therapist see each other has an important impact on the capacity to develop a therapeutic alliance, especially for the more narcissistically damaged people.

We have seen patients for whom the process of therapy has been prolonged over many years by a process of cautious searching and seeking, trying a bit of this and a bit of that, until, often, perhaps after a phase of symptom control, the conditions finally come together to 'do the work'. Under these conditions change can be remarkably rapid.

The dangers of technique

The more insecure a therapist, the more likely it is that he or she will hide behind technique, dogmatically pursuing it without it necessarily being in the best interests of the client. As someone keen on technique in my younger days (Paul Gilbert), it gradually dawned on me in my practice of cognitive psychotherapy that I did not have to pursue rigorously inference chains or to identify dysfunctional thoughts. As I became more relaxed I was also able to become more passive and to encourage exploration via listening (Margulies 1984). At a recent workshop in England, Aaron Beck, the founder of cognitive therapy recounted an amusing story. He showed a therapy video in which he listened to a client and gently probed her thinking for opportunities to explore and experiment. On the surface it looked like a pleasant therapeutic chat. Behind a one-way mirror were experienced therapists who were training in cognitive therapy. At the end of the interview he asked these therapists what they thought. There was stunned silence before one said, 'Well, that was okay, but it wasn't cognitive therapy.' Maybe listening is the first skill we should try to teach (Margulies 1984).

Technique really can be a hindrance if it becomes a substitute for being in a psychotherapy relationship. Eagle (1987) has recently examined why Kohut's self-psychology has had such an impact on traditional psychoanalysis. There are many reasons, not least because it emerged from within rather than from outside psychoanalysis. But additionally, Kohut's stress on empathy and getting rid of the passive, blank screen position of the analyst provided a theoretical rationale for a style of therapy that many had intuitively felt more reasonable. The impression is that the gradual removal of 'the person of the therapist' in psychoanalysis resulted from an autocratic concern with technique, to which many felt allegiance. At the present time we can only speculate concerning who are the most vulnerable to fall into the tyranny of technique.

In one case of ours, a client had recently seen a behaviour therapist for relationship problems. The therapist had done a good behavioural analysis and suggested homework and although this had been helpful to some degree it had not removed the problem. Rightly or wrongly a new treating therapist (Paul Gilbert) decided to minimize the use of techniques, just to chat about things in general with a focus on her feelings and life history. Eventually she confided a history of sexual abuse, fears that she had been degraded for ever and significant rage and fear of men. The many 'techniques' of a therapy can only come into play once the problem is clear, and this can take a number (sometimes a large number) of sessions.

Increasingly there is a recognition within psychotherapy that clients do not seek help as decontextualized subjects ready for corrective education as one might approach a malfunctioning machine. People experience life as a process (Goldstein 1984) and it is within the context of making sense of one's personal history and of reconceptualizing past events and relationships that change occurs (Mahoney and Gabriel 1987). There is also increasing awareness of the importance of 'working through' and allowing various psychological processes within the person to get under way. For example, consider the client who had never fully grieved the loss of his mother some ten years earlier. Facilitating the process of grief allowed him to rework deep-seated beliefs that if he loved someone they would surely leave him or even die. The importance of working with affect rather than with cognitions *per se* has recently become a central issue in the development of psychotherapy (Greenberg and Safran 1987).

So far in this chapter we have touched briefly on a number of areas which pertain to becoming a therapist. These include social and personal factors, issues of training and the degree to which some therapists may become preoccupied with technique. In the next section we wish to address more fully the question of therapeutic style.

Therapeutic style

The orientation of a therapist reflects complex personal construct systems and ways of appraising life in general. This reflects one's personal philosophy. If one evaluates life as an essentially meaningful and spiritual process then one's orientation to therapy is going to be different from those who regard life as essentially meaningless apart from the positive reinforcers one can control. As Goldstein (1984) points out, there is a distinction to be made between those whose philosophy is essentially positivistic and those who adopt a teleological view. The positivists see humans as objects whose sources of change are external and regard change as subject to control and manipulation of external contingencies. The teleological position, however, views humans subjectively, as beings whose sources of change are related to growth, development and the alteration of internal processes, be these insights or changes in cognitive schemata. (See also Karasu 1986; Mahoney and Gabriel 1987).

A therapist's orientation to therapy will depend essentially on which side of the fence he or she lies (although in fact these need not be mutually exclusive philosophies – see Gilbert 1989). There is, however, an essential difference between those who focus on the subjective life of the client (the personal construction of meaning, memory and past experience) and those who focus on here-and-now objective events. The former tend to choose to work with affect and process and the latter with behaviour.

The other distinction we suggest is that therapists, according to their own personal philosophies of life, will tend to vary in terms of whether they are basically 'facilitators' or 'regulators'. This distinction was first put forward by Raphael-Leff (1986), in regard to infant-mother interactions. Adapting her distinctions, facilitators and regulators differ in a) conceptualization of problems: noted in the conscious attitudes and expectations of the therapeutic role; b) practice: noted in the observable behaviour and practices of the therapist; and c) unconscious processes: noted in the fantasies and defences underlying practices. At present there is little evidence to support this distinction since this model has not yet been applied to therapist behaviour. However, in regard to infant-mother interaction this distinction of role behaviour is supported by some evidence (Raphael-Leff 1986). We suggest that extreme facilitators and regulators orientate themselves to clients in a style that has some similarity to maternal behaviour. Facilitators focus on the subjective life of the client, see therapy as exploratory, involving the gaining of insight and involving growth, tend to focus on 'being with' rather than 'doing to', are concerned with the expression of affect and being in touch with feelings and with the process of 'becoming'. Regulators on the other hand focus on specific dysfunction and problems, on educating and correcting and 'doing to' rather than 'being with'. Regulators are more concerned with performance-based therapy and enactments via exposure or learning skills. Regulators are less interested in history or issues related to process.

We do not believe that one style is more or less valid than the other, but the salient factor is the therapist's ability to comprehend when to guide the therapy in one direction or another. Too strong an adherence to one style, due to a rigidly held personal philosophy, is more likely to be a problem. Extreme facilitators run the risk of becoming 'contaminated' by patients and thus being unable to maintain a helpful therapeutic distance. They may have difficulty in setting limits and are prone to over-identification with patients. Extreme regulators, however, do not make enough contact with patients and are prone to fail to provide a sufficiently trusting environment which will allow patients with deep shame-based disturbances of the self to express and work through these feelings. The regulator may set expectations of the 'right way' and this may inhibit the patient's ability to reveal 'shameful' material.

In addition to the facilitator and regulator types are the styles of containment and confronting. Containment involves a focus on empathy and a communication that whatever the patient says, does or feels, these can be 'contained' within the therapeutic encounter. Clients learn not to feel at risk from the expression of undesired aspects of themselves. This is the basis of positive unconditional regard. Confronting, however, is a therapist-led process where pressure is put on clients to talk about some area of themselves or their lives they would rather keep hidden, or to approach various feared situations or stimuli. Again, as is clear from current conceptualizations of therapy (Karasu 1986), therapists must not hold too rigidly to one pole or another. Some clients are able to confront issues very quickly and will find too much containment pointless or threatening. On the other hand, other clients require a long period of testing the security of a relationship before they are ready to begin the real issue of revealing and reworking various self-beliefs and traumatic episodes from the past. The more narcissistically damaged, the longer this process may take (Russell 1985).

Movement towards either confronting or containing needs to be kept fluid to promote safety for the client. Dryden (1985) has aptly coined the phrase 'challenging but not overwhelming', to refer to homework setting and behavioural tasks. However, this concept can be applied to the therapeutic context such that clients can be challenged but not overwhelmed by the pace, level of interpretation or homework. Without this matching, clients may rightly ask for whose benefit the techniques of therapy are being used, theirs or the therapists'?

Conclusion and summary

We believe that in common with much anecdotal evidence the person of the therapist matters (Kottler 1986; McConnaughty 1987). Why people end up practising psychotherapy, their choice of approach, and the way they put this approach into practice are important research questions. Therapists require a certain kind of interpersonal intelligence and to be able to apply science. But like musicians or artists, technique will only carry a person so far. Those therapists who are probably the more successful are able to marry pragmatically different sets of styles and approaches which are not a mish-mash of eclecticism but a carefully considered application of approaches to suit different clients at different points on their journey. Therapists who are themselves heavily defended will tend to focus on what they are doing and on their techniques. There will, of course, always be some clients who will be helped even by the most defended of therapists. Nevertheless many clients and professionals have expressed the view that the success of a therapy depends on finding the right person (i.e. therapist) as much as in finding the right school of therapy.

One of our clients became so angry and fearful of an interpretation of sexual difficulty at his first encounter with a therapist that he retreated for years before trying for psychiatric help again. When first seen it was necessary to treat him with drugs (William Hughes) until enough trust had been developed to move him into psychotherapy. One of us (Paul Gilbert) has seen some patients who have delayed seeking help for phobic conditions because they had seen hastily made television programmes emphasizing the technique of exposure and were sure they could not go through that.

Finally it is worth remembering that the use of techniques is best viewed within the context of a therapeutic relationship. We have met students who have carried out techniques to the letter and are dismayed that their clients have not improved. The advice we normally give is, do not do anything, listen to them, show a caring interest and curiosity (Gilbert 1989), develop a trusting relationship, then slowly introduce your techniques and see what the patients think about the experiment or homework. If there is a block, go back to listening.

In regard to therapy, therefore, it is as important to focus on the style of the therapist as it is on the techniques of therapy; we need both the singer and the song.

References

Dryden, W. (1985) 'Challenging but not overwhelming: a compromise in negotiating homework assignments', *British Journal of Cognitive Psychotherapy* 3(1): 77–80.

Eagle, M. (1987) 'Theoretical and clinical shifts in psychoanalysis', *American Journal of Orthopsychiatry* 57: 175–85.

Ellenberger, H. (1970) *The Discovery of the Unconscious*, New York: Basic Books.
Ellis, A. (1983) 'How to deal with your most difficult client – you', *Journal of Rational-Emotive Therapy* 1(1): 3–8.
Gilbert, P. (1989) *Human Nature and Suffering*, London: Lawrence Erlbaum.
Goldstein, A. P. and Michaels, G. Y. (1985) *Empathy: Development, Training and Consequences*, Hillsdale NJ: Lawrence Erlbaum.
Goldstein, H. (1984) *Social Learning and Change*, London: Tavistock.
Greenberg, L. S. and Safran, J. D. (1987) *Emotion in Psychotherapy: Affect, Cognition and the Process of Change*, New York: Guilford Press.
Karasu, T. B. (1986) 'The specificity versus non specificity dilemma: toward identifying therapeutic change agents', *American Journal of Psychiatry*, 143: 687–95.
Kottler, J. A. (1986) *On Being a Therapist*, San Francisco: Jossey-Bass.
London, P. (1986) *The Modes and Morals of Psychotherapy* (2nd edn), New York: McGraw-Hill.
McConnaughty, E. A. (1987) 'The person of the therapist in psychotherapeutic practice', *Psychotherapy: Theory, Research, Practice and Training* 24: 303–14.
Mahoney, M. J. and Gabriel, T. J. (1987) 'Psychotherapy and cognitive sciences: an evolving alliance', *Journal of Cognitive Psychotherapy: An International Quarterly*, 1: 39–60.
Mair, M. (1987) 'Pretending to care', in E. Karas (ed.) *Current Issues in Clinical Psychology*, vol. 3, New York: Plenum Press.
Margulies, A. (1984) 'Toward empathy: the uses of wonder', *American Journal of Psychiatry*, 141: 1025–33.
Pilgrim, D. (1987) 'Some psychodynamic aspects of helping: a critical overview', in E. Karas (ed.) *Current Issues in Clinical Psychology* vol. 3, New York: Plenum Press.
Raphael-Leff, L. (1986) 'Facilitators and regulators: conscious and unconscious processes in pregnancy and early motherhood', *British Journal of Medical Psychology* 59: 43–56.
Rippere, V. and Williams, R. (eds.) (1985) *Wounded Healers*, Chichester: Wiley.
Russell, G. A. (1985) 'Narcissism and the narcissistic personality disorder: a comparison of the theories of Kernberg and Kohut', *British Journal of Medical Psychology*, 58: 137–48.
Rutter, M. (1987) 'Temperament, personality and personality disorder', *British Journal of Psychiatry* 150: 443–58.
Yalom, I. D. (1980) *Existential Psychotherapy*, New York: Basic Books.
Zilboorg, G. and Henry, G. W. (1941) *The History of Medical Psychology*, New York: W. W. Norton.

Part two

The contributions

Chapter two

The object of the dance

Michael J. Mahoney with Stuart C. Eiseman

Although what follows is a reconstruction of the first author's personal history
and process of becoming a psychotherapist, it emerged out of a series of
discussions with the second author, who is currently an apprentice in the
profession. As will be apparent, our discussions rendered a presentation that
is both personal and reflective – characteristics that we felt would be
compatible with the objectives of this book. We hope that the dialectic between
mentor and apprentice – here rendered in the first person of the former – has
lent itself well to serving the purpose of this volume.

Prefatory remarks

Writing about myself is a very difficult thing for me to do, perhaps because
there is often a gap between my identity as I experience it and the identities
frequently projected on to me by my readers. As a result, and sometimes to
my dismay, I have become much more self-conscious when I now write than
I used to be ten or fifteen years ago. To be candid, my early writings were
as much for me as for anyone else. They were my meditations, my musings,
and often my private medium of self-teaching and self-therapy. When my first
professional works were published, I relished the opportunities to write, but I
was naively unprepared for the fact that people would actually read what I
had written. I was, in fact, embarrassed by the amount of attention those words
attracted.

Needless to say, I was and am grateful for the readership and affirmation
my writings have enjoyed, and I feel very fortunate in having found an
ecological niche in which my lifelong love of writing can not only survive,
but be generously encouraged. Notwithstanding this welcome good fortune, the
task of writing about myself and my becoming a psychotherapist is a
formidably personal challenge. I have undertaken it with a commitment to
share what I can about a process that – in me as, I believe, in others – is
often long, complex, painful, inspiring, and never completed. This process has
taught me much – most importantly how much more I have yet to learn.

Why did I become a psychotherapist?

My early aspirations did not include becoming a psychologist or psychotherapist. I was the third-born son in a thoroughly Irish-Catholic family. My father was a farmhand in northern Illinois, and my mother managed the kids, the house, the books, and the chickens. My brothers attended a one-room, one-teacher schoolhouse. In those early years, I spent my days conversing with the cows, exploring the fields, or acting out my cowboy/athlete fantasies in our large farmyard. Before I was six, I saw the 'big city' (Joliet) only on special occasions or when we needed supplies. We moved there when my father became a truck mechanic, and I entered first grade.

I don't remember being taught to read or write, but I entered the public school not only writing, but writing poetry. Indeed, my most poignant memory from first grade was being asked to stay after school one day in the spring. I was (and am) shy, and I wondered if I had done something wrong. The teacher told me that she needed to talk to me, and that she would give me a ride home in her big, black Buick. I recall that my frame was so small that my feet didn't reach the floor, and I felt anxious when she said that I mustn't tell anyone that she had given me a ride because it was against the rules. She pulled the Buick over to the curb around the corner from (and out of sight of) my house, and looked down at me like some benevolent sponsor. Her words are still etched in my memory:

> Michael, I'm not sure how to say this, and I am risking getting myself
> in trouble, but it needs to be said. Young man, you have a gift with
> words, and you should know that. I don't know what your life holds for
> you, but treasure that gift – don't let it go to waste.

She wiped tears from her big hazel eyes. I somehow managed a muffled 'Thank you, ma'am', and she had to help me open the heavy Buick door. I stood in bewilderment as she drove away, sensing that something very important in my life had just happened. Those few minutes and that teacher's courage were to stay with me thereafter, often serving as my primary anchor in many later storms of life. Whenever I have the opportunity to address a group of educators, I share that story – the tears now my own – to emphasize the potential power of a well-chosen moment and a core message.

I continued to write throughout grade school – mostly poems and short stories. My first book was begun when I was in sixth grade. The topic, botany, was inspired by my having read biographies of Luther Burbank and George Washington Carver. It was in reading about their lives that I also first experienced my own fascination with the 'inner life' of life.

As a sophomore in high school I had an eerily similar experience to my earlier affirmation in the Buick. My young English teacher asked me to stay after school; I was sure I was in trouble. She said she couldn't teach me and that I was obviously bored in class. I silently avoided her gaze, perhaps hoping

I could conceal my adolescent 'crush' on her. An unconventional idealist herself, she jeopardized her contract (in this, her first year out of college) and exempted me from the entire year's course work and class attendance. My assignment was, instead, to 'read Hemingway and write – write anything you want, just write'. She met with me once a week after school and generously encouraged my short stories and poems, a satire here and there, and scattered reflections on life and existence.

My life goal became very clear to me that year – I wanted to make my living as a writer, preferably a novelist. I wanted to travel and to render my experiences in words; to sculpt the 'insides' of characters in well-turned forms, and to convey the profundity and paradox of the fully-lived life. That was my nascent identity, and it remains a core feature of the scientist-practitioner now writing.

A significant turn of events diverted me from college and studies in literature or journalism, however. During my junior year in high school my first 'real' romance came to a painful demise – an end made more 'tragic' by parental intrusion. I was forbidden to see the young woman thereafter, and her parents threatened legal action if I did not comply. Already struggling with adolescence and strained relations in my own family, I recoiled in pain and bewilderment. What followed was a period of several years of angry rebellion and existential searching. I engaged in a struggle of wills with the high school principal, my parents, the wrestling coach, and several teachers. The ultimate results were painfully real: a broken shoulder blade, ejection from high school on graduation day, avoidance or rejection by former friends, several close-calls with injury and death, and an intensification of my sensed isolation.

When my high school peers went off to college, I set out to see the world. Lacking the money to travel, I joined a small group of fellow 'outcasts' and enrolled in the Marine Corps. My tour of duty was brief, however; it became immediately clear to me that the 'few good men' they were looking for were also supposed to be unthinking and callous. Although I did well on their physical skills requirements, I did poorly on not questioning authority. After a particularly bloody dialogue with a drill instructor, I decided to 'resign' (which I naively thought would be easy). I was threatened, belittled, and interrogated for weeks, until it apparently became clear to them that I was firm in my decision, at which point I was given an honourable discharge and sent home. I did not realize how fortunate I was until months later, when the Marines began using conscription (the 'draft'), refusing resignations like mine, and sending the bulk of their recruits to Vietnam.

When I returned to Illinois, I worked in construction for a while – driving trucks, shovelling concrete – and lived out of a '56 Chevy and a skidrow hotel room. A former patron on my childhood paper route landed me a job as a part-time sports writer for the local newspaper, but I soon grew weary of writing about local high school football rivalries. In desperation, I went to the library and opened a world atlas at a two-page spread of the planet. With my eyes closed, I vowed to leave town – to go wherever my finger first touched – and to write my first novel there. When I opened my eyes, my finger rested on an obscure island off the west coast of Baja California. The next day I sold my few remaining belongings to a pawn dealer and set out for my island.

I did eventually make it to the island of Cedros, but it was not on that first attempt in the winter of 1964–65. Indeed, I shall reserve the story of that journey for the novel itself (which is well into its own process). More pertinent here is the fact that my late adolescent journey to Mexico brought me face-to-face with my own vulnerabilities (again), and I returned to Illinois exhausted, penniless, and struggling with pneumonia. A severe episode of bronchitis deteriorated into acute asthma, and my former athletic vigour was reduced to wheezing bronchospasm at the slightest movement. It was frightening and frustrating. I went to a physician for help; he informed me that there was no cure and that I should expect to die a young invalid.

I convalesced with my parents for a while and sought other opinions on my fate. They varied in their pessimism, but all agreed that my condition was serious and likely to be chronic. They suggested a quiet life – a 'desk job' without physical exertion. Lacking a high school diploma, I enrolled on a probationary basis in night school at Joliet Junior College and worked when I could get it: janitor, security guard, stockboy, switchboard operator, cashier, printer, etc. Three formative events then introduced new twists to my struggling hopes for health and a writing career. Jim Pumphrey, a friend returning from his tour of duty in the Air Force, offered to teach me Olympic-style weightlifting (an anaerobic sport). Within months I had entered regional competitions and emerged with trophies. My self-image as a vigorous, able-bodied athlete had been salvaged. Next, with some trepidation about what I might discover, I took an introductory psychology course in night school. The instructor was inspiringly human and self-disclosing; she singled me out and strongly encouraged that I consider a major in psychology. Finally, I landed a full-time (night shift) job as an aide on the psychiatric unit of a local hospital. Besides allowing me to attend day classes full time, my experiences as a psychiatric aide left some very strong impressions on me (both positive and negative) about the mental health professions.

The chronology of my personal and professional development continues below, but I want to return here to the question of why I became a psychotherapist. The answer does not seem simple or straightforward. Part of it may have been wanting to become the counsellor I had never had during my own stormy adolescence. Some of it came from my fascination with the richness of real, everyday 'inner life' struggles. My years of part-time menial labour had also exposed me to frequent injustices against the poor and minorities, and my aspirations to help seemed to draw from those sources as well. Finally, my early coursework in psychology and my experiences as a psychiatric aide fostered some kind of resonance in me – a deep-felt recognition that I was on the track of my future and that it somehow involved helping. But my career goals were still unclear, and I soon faced some pivotal decisions in their clarification.

How did I become a psychotherapist?

In 1967 I graduated as a co-valedictorian from Joliet Junior College and received a $200 scholarship to continue my studies. My respiratory problems had been exacerbated by the bitter winter and hot, humid summers of northern Illinois. On a physician's recommendation, I decided to continue college in Arizona, choosing Arizona State over the University of Arizona on a coin toss. When I arrived that summer, I was told I would have to declare a major in order to be assigned an adviser. Majors had not been a problem in Illinois: I had concentrated on English and literature. Now I had to make a commitment, and I naively construed it as dichotomous: either I would choose to become a writer or a psychologist. I struggled painfully for several weeks before resorting to professional help.

My savings were scant, and I knew I could only afford one session of counselling to help me make my decision. Looking through the Phoenix *Yellow Pages*, I chose the specialist with the most options after his name: individual and family psychotherapy, vocational counselling, etc. His office was in his home, a small bungalow just off Central Avenue. I explained to his receptionist over the phone that I could only come once – so perhaps we could meet for two hours – and that it had to do with choosing what I wanted to be. She was kind and understanding, and turned out to be his wife. When I arrived, she ushered me through their dining room and back to his office. He was a small man with an intriguing face: tough and yet tender. I didn't notice at first that he sat in a wheelchair behind his large desk.

Like so many of my own clients in later years, I began by not addressing my real concerns; he ended up talking more than I did, filling almost two hours with stories and anecdotes that had no theme I could identify. With only a few minutes left, I screwed up my courage and blurted out my dilemma:

Doctor, I have to decide whether to become a writer or a psychologist.
I love writing, but I don't know if I can make a living at it.
Psychology fascinates me, but ... well ... well, I get nervous and
depressed sometimes, and, well ... what right would I have to tell other
people how to live their lives if I still struggle with my own ...?

He let my impassioned query hang for a long moment while he rubbed the stubble on his bony chin. Then, shifting his weight so that his whole frame leaned into my eyes, he said softly, 'You know, Michael, some of the best football coaches in this country have never played the game.'

I left that session with my head spinning. It would be several years before I appreciated the psyche-logic (rather than formal logic) in his response, but I was sure that he meant I should commit myself to psychology. It would also be several years before I would learn that my 'randomly-selected' counsellor was well known for his uncommon style and advice. To this day I remain respectful and grateful to the person and process that were Milton Erickson.

I was assigned to David C. Rimm as an advisee: he and John Masters had just joined the Arizona State faculty after graduating from Stanford. I was so incredibly compulsive about *really* committing to the profession that I arrived at my first advising session with an outline of a dissertation proposal. Dave Rimm grinned at my over-preparedness, and assured me that I would have plenty of time to think about a dissertation when I got to graduate school. He was very patient and affirming during the next two years, and we collaborated on what turned out to be my first professional publication in 1969.

At that time Arizona State was aptly called 'Fort Skinner' due to its radically behaviouristic psychology department: Art Bachrach was chair and the faculty included Fred Keller, Tom Verhave, J. Gilmore Sherman, Lee Meyerson, and Aaron Brownstein. Skinner and Rogers had staged one of their debates there, and Montrose Wolf, who had just graduated, had helped found the operant *Journal of Applied Behavior Analysis*. The academic atmosphere was an invigorating mixture of almost-religious fervour and Inquisition-like repression. The fervour came from the enthusiasm people felt about science – which then and there meant 'behaviouristic' science – and that equation was also the source of the repression.

I remember how impressed I was with the power and persuasion of Keller's programmed self-instructional (PSI) laboratory courses in animal behaviour (then taught by Sherman). The first semester we worked with rats; the second with pigeons. In the final exam for the latter, a cumulative response curve was randomly selected from a file and each student's task was to reproduce it with their pigeon. Most succeeded, of course (as Keller intended), and such predictability and control were strong enticements to join the faithful. To a large extent, I did: I came to appreciate the need for rigour in scientific language and thinking, and I read everything I could find by Skinner, Watson, Wolpe, Ullmann, Krasner, and 'the Kansas group' (Wolf, Risley, and Baer). Their precision and, more importantly, their firm commitment to science were valuable models for me, and I remain indebted to their teachings.

But the radical behaviourism I encountered was also intolerant and repressive. Students were criticized for using 'mentalistic' terms even in informal conversation (e.g. 're*mind* me'), and my nascent interests in cognition and self-control were met with outright consternation. I managed, however, to extricate myself enough to take the equivalent of a minor in philosophy with special emphasis on epistemology, religion, and belief systems. Just before it was time to apply to graduate school, Albert Bandura came to campus and gave a colloquium. His combination of a clear scientific grounding and an interest in symbolic and self-regulatory processes evoked a deep resonance in me, and I set my sights and hopes on graduate work with him.

By that time, I knew I wanted to be a *scientist* in a deeply *philosophical* sense of that term – an inquirer in the Socratic tradition. I also knew that I wanted to pursue research that had *practical relevance* and accountability. My hope, at that point barely conscious, was to contribute to some kind of attempt to integrate the philosophical domain of inquiry with the nuts-and-bolts experience of daily life. This I could do, of course, only as a career scientist – a member of what Richard Armour has called 'the academic bestiary'. It meant being *both* a scientist and a practitioner, and straddling the unfortunate chasm that continues to separate the purists in both fields. I knew that being an academic meant financial sacrifice, but I felt powerfully drawn to the generous freedom and opportunities of an academic environment, and – sweetest of all for me – the invitation to think and write.

Stanford had regrettably discontinued its clinical programme after the graduation of some creative scientist-practitioners and scholarly researchers, including Gerald Davison, Donna Gelfand, Don Hartmann, John Masters, David Rimm, and Ted Rosenthal. I applied to their new programme in Experimental Psychopathology and Personality, trusting that I would somehow find a means to address the clinical features necessary to create a sensitive two-way bridge between research and practice. After months of waiting I learned that I had been accepted to work with Bandura – an experience and an honour that I shall always treasure.

During my first year of study there Bandura was on sabbatical, and Gerald C. Davison, his former student, had come back for the year from his appointment at the State University of New York at Stony Brook. We were thrown together by fate, and we were a good mix. 'Jerry', as he came to be affectionately known to me, offered an invaluable role model – a bright and energetic mind, a sense of humour, and a deep sensitivity to his clients and his students. He taught me more than I can probably remember about the honour of inquiry and the politics of science. During that same year Walter Mischel introduced me to George Kelly's constructivism, and Carl Thoresen and I launched a series of studies into what was later called 'cognitive behaviour modification' and 'behavioural self-control.'

When Al Bandura returned from his sabbatical, he and I also began to collaborate on a series of studies into cognitive and self-regulatory domains. I was using weight control as a convenient and measurable challenge, partly due to my experience (and struggles) with weight control in high school wrestling and weightlifting. I also began to seek out experiences that were grounded in real-world attempts to help people change. After discussing the matter with both Bandura and Mischel, I accepted an evenings-and-weekends job as a live-in 'teaching parent' in a community-based, family-style treatment programme for 'pre-delinquent youth'. I also began an unpaid internship at the Palo Alto Veterans' Hospital, where I worked with a *sympatico* mentor, John Marquis, and interacted with such peers as Orin Bolstad, Steve Johnson, Steve Koppel, and Michael Spiegler.

With the generous support of Al Bandura, I was also able to live out an incredible dream as a graduate student. I had gone to his office to discuss some research we were doing, and I ended up talking about some of the frustrations emerging from the 'live-in lab' that was my home. The 'children' whose anti-social behaviour I was supposed to alter were not pliant pigeons: they were wilful, thinking people with designs quite at variance to my own. I mentioned that I would love to watch Jerry Patterson or the Kansas team work with their clients. Al suggested that I visit them, and he offered to cover the expenses of my travel. I remember being very moved by both his generosity and his commitment to my development.

I *did* visit Patterson in Eugene, Oregon, and I travelled to Lawrence, Kansas, to visit and learn from the works of Lonnie and Elaine Phillips at the foremost site of the behavioural attempt at surrogate-family-based treatment of delinquency, Achievement Place. Lonnie had been a graduate student with Montrose Wolf, whom I finally got to meet. It was, in fact, an offhand question from 'Mont' that sparked by curiosity about evidence in science. After several days of patiently listening to my descriptions of research at Stanford on self-control, Mont asked if I thought there was 'really anything there'. I was convinced that there was, of course, but I was puzzled as to how to convince him. That puzzle led me into further collaborations with Al Bandura on animal analogues to self-control.

The more I worked with individuals, whether they were children in the delinquency project or patients at the Veterans Administration, the more intrigued I was, not only by each individual case, but also by the complexity of what we were trying to do in the 'real world' relative to what the textbooks had fabricated. To the best of my knowledge, that was the point in my career when I became most convinced about, and committed to, a scientist/practitioner approach to psychology, where research is informed by practice, and practice by research. Simultaneously, I became more aware of the strength of my desire to be a skilled psychotherapist. In the midst of my research in the library and laboratory, I found myself deeply moved by the struggles people reported in their own attempts to adapt.

The domain of self-control became personally meaningful to me, and it was this domain that led me still deeper, not only inside myself, but inside the people that I was working with. The issues they were presenting, as well as the experiences they were sharing, made more clear over time the idea that I could not address several key issues around self-control without getting involved with both cognitive and self psychology.

The impact of my clinical and practical experience on my research was (and is) substantial. Although I have learned a great deal from other professionals, there is no question in my mind that my most important lessons have come from my clients. Often painful and puzzling, those experiences influenced the direction of my research, the nature of my theorizing, and both the content and process of my teaching of psychotherapy. An early example of such a lesson took place with an individual whom I saw one summer at the Veterans Administration Hospital in Palo Alto. Alex was 62 years old, stubborn, diabetic, and anorectic. Although there was no evidence of purging, he was preoccupied with his weight, which had dropped to a level so low that the doctors had become alarmed. The question I asked myself was, 'What could be done, in the context of a token economy, to encourage this man to gain some weight?' I was aware of the behavioural techniques of Stunkard, Bachrach, and others, making hospital privileges contingent upon gaining a quarter of a pound a day. Many of these same contingencies had already failed to increase Alex's weight; I knew that to be successful I would have to find something that was very important to him.

In our conversations, the only things that seemed to matter to him were his wife's visits, which he hated. She was not, shall I say, a positive stimulus in his life. To hear him describe her, she was the bane of his existence. Drawing on my experience in contingency management, I decided to manipulate her presence in his life, or his exposure to her, hoping that this might motivate his eating. I implemented the plan by suggesting to Alex that he might be due for a home visit (which he had avoided for over a year and hated even more than his wife's visits). Although he fervently objected to the idea, I explained that perhaps he would eat more at home than he was eating at the hospital. He blanched.

'If I gain some weight,' Alex pleaded, 'do I not have to go home?' 'Well, if I see evidence that you're taking care of yourself,' I responded, 'that you're making an active attempt to gain weight, it's possible that you wouldn't have to go.' He started to gain, and when he had increased his weight by 8 pounds, an interesting thing happened: I arrived on the ward one day and was promptly informed that Alex's wife had been hospitalized for depression. It did not require much reflection for me to realize that I may have been partly responsible. I had entered into the system dynamics of this couple's relationship in a very naive and insensitive way. Clearly, Alex's wife had valued those contacts with him. She became very distraught when she learned that he had been willing to eat in order to avoid seeing her. It was a hard-learned lesson for both of them and me about the complexities and dynamic balance of relationships and the hubris of manipulation.

When did I become a therapist?

Although I feel good about myself in the role of a psychotherapist, I increasingly sense that my understanding and skills are undeniably primitive and in need of continual refinement. My 'becoming' a therapist, which thus continues, has involved a series of *in vivo* refutations of my beliefs about human change. The vast majority of those beliefs were tacit or unconscious until they were well on their way to refutation. Early in my career, for example, I had equated 'applied science' with 'intervention', and I had assumed that intervention was aimed at removing a problem. As Western rationality would have it, I took on the therapist's role as that of the 'problem solver'. Nothing was impossible, I thought; it was just a question of diligence, skills, and the formidable powers of science in action.

The lessons that disabused me of this myth were offered most powerfully by my clients. Indeed, I find it very painful to reflect back to my days as a beginning therapist and to the naive pragmatism with which I approached other people's lives. Fifteen years ago I would have been much more preoccupied with presenting problems than I am today. My role as expert would have been to do an extensive behavioural and cognitive assessment of the determinants of 'the' problem, its antecedents and consequences, and then to train the client in carrying out some fairly mechanical programme designed to eradicate that problem. If a client presented more than one problem (which most, of course, do), then we would tackle them piecemeal, one at a time. I shudder to think how much I (and my clients) missed with our attention thus displaced to problems rather than to processes and persons. Were I seeking professional help, there is no doubt in my mind that I would prefer the counsel of Mike Mahoney in 1988 over that of 1973.

When I graduated from Stanford in 1972 I accepted a position as an assistant professor of clinical psychology at the Pennsylvania State University. It was an exciting time to be there: Ed Craighead and Alan Kazdin had already begun to build an experimental emphasis in the programme, John Horan was studying thought regulation, and Dan Landers and Dorothy Harris had developed programmes of research in sport psychology. My interests in basic developmental processes and their relevance for psychotherapy were encouraged by Dale Harris, David Palermo, Don Ford, Hugh Urban, and Richard Lerner. Most importantly, perhaps, I met Walter Weimer, who was to become a major influence on my future work in cognitive psychology, science studies, and evolutionary epistemology.

Between 1974 and 1980 I spent many a sleepless night, and my insomnia wasn't exclusively from pondering esoteric points in philosophy or controversial issues in cognitive psychology. There were real, live existential dilemmas in my own life, and they demanded priority. In 1973 my first marriage came to an end. It was a painful but mutual decision, reflecting the fact that we were developing in different directions. I remarried in 1974 and in 1975 became the father of a blue-eyed treasure named Sean Michael: a welcome joy who brought precious experiences and deep-felt responsibilities. Unfortunately, my second marriage had started disintegrating almost before it began. My work (or, more precisely, my love for my work) was experienced as a threat and a competitor by my new wife, who was then considering a career in academic psychology. The amount of professional attention being directed toward me exacerbated our marital problems, and I was given the ultimatum either to stop writing (which was thought to be drawing the disproportionate attention) or face divorce. In anguish, I tried to preserve the marriage by proposing the compromise of my writing anonymously under a pseudonym. My proposal was declined, however, and although my wife abandoned her aspirations for a research career, she tried to use my productivity as evidence against me in later legal battles over the custody and residence of our son. That whole process offered some painful lessons about trust and integrity, not to mention the complexities of life.

The professional attention directed towards me during those years had also amplified a self-conscious shyness that had characterized me since early childhood, and my anxiety about public speaking became very painful. Having failed to overcome the anxiety by myself and still struggling with the emotional fall-out of shattered dreams and a 'broken' home, I entered personal therapy. That was a big step for me; I had been compulsively self-sufficient all of my life. It was therefore a frightening concession for me to seek help, and yet doing so effectively paved the way for much of my later personal and professional development. During and after my own therapy, for example, I began to explore professional workshops, retreats, and opportunities to learn more about myself and about how other professionals dealt with their own and their clients' struggles. My explorations included body work, meditation, gestalt therapy, Arica training, transpersonal psychology, a solo motorcycle pilgrimage to 'my island' off Baja California, and what I would call 'therapeutic philosophy' (readings and dialogues). My friendships with Aaron T. Beck and Walter B. Weimer were valuable sources of support during that time.

In 1980 I felt myself emerging from the preceding period in my life with a much broader and deeper base from which to operate. My divorce had been finalized (although the legal traumas had yet to begin), 5-year-old Sean was healthy and happy, and I was beginning to feel strengthened by all that I had been through. I spent a formative two weeks in the Mojave desert with Brugh Joy, and – thanks to transpersonalists Frances Vaughan and Roger Walsh – I was invited to a secluded weekend retreat in Minneapolis to dialogue with a small group of scientists about consciousness, evolution, world peace, and the inseparability of personal and planetary transformations. It was also in 1980 that I first met Vittorio F. Guidano in Rome and launched another treasured friendship and an ongoing professional collaboration.

Sean and I spent half a year in Rome in 1984 with Vittorio Guidano and Mario Reda. During that time I worked extensively on the theoretical integrations that now form my conceptual base camp. Although I had been aware of John Bowlby's work on attachment, I am indebted to Guidano, Reda, and Teresa Nezworski (a newly-hired child clinician at Penn State) for helping me realize the broader clinical implications of attachment theory. I became particularly (and happily) attached to Teresa Nezworski that same year in Italy. We eloped, honeymooned in Venice and San Marino, and – after a final year at Penn State – moved with Sean to the University of California, Santa Barbara, just before the birth of our daughter, Maureen, in 1985. Beyond our strong bond of love and the quality of life it affords, Teresa has also had a significant impact on my thinking and practice as a clinician.

Although I cannot point to a specific year or a concrete experience 'of passage', my response to the question 'when did you become a psychotherapist?' is straightforward: when I first began to appreciate the complexities of change and the mysteries of helping human relationships. In a sense, then, I became a therapist when I stopped being a technician and, ironically, when I literally adopted the client's role. My own clients taught me to relate to them, rather than just to their problems, and – in their own unique ways – they forced me to reappraise my most basic assumptions about human nature, the nature of change, myself, and my own role as a facilitator. The process and outcome of those reappraisals have been exciting, and I am just now completing a book (*Human Change Processes*) that attempts to pull them together at both theoretical and applied levels.

What sustains me as a psychotherapist?

I smile now when I reflect on the urgent question I had asked Milton Erickson in 1967: 'should I become a therapist or a writer?' Much to my delight, it was possible for me to become both and, indeed, to develop a creative synergy between the two. Writing has been an ongoing love and art form. The practice of psychotherapy has also become an art form for me, as well as a deeply-felt privilege and responsibility. I continue to maintain a small private practice and to dialogue actively with other practitioners. What sustains me in this, in part, is the balance it lends to my more abstract endeavours. I have no doubt that my research questions have been refined by my clients, and that they, in turn, have been well served by some of the skills I have developed in the course of becoming a scientist. I am thus (still) a strong advocate of the scientist-practitioner spirit in graduate training (even though its enactment often leaves much to be desired).

For the past ten years I have worked primarily with individuals whose problem patterns have become chronic and for whom other episodes of therapy have been unsuccessful. Besides my intent to help them, I chose this subgroup with the idea that they would teach me most about the difficulties and complexities of change. They have, indeed, taught me much. In some cases our work together has spanned more than three years, and I now have longitudinal information on their psychological development for periods of four to ten years. Their presenting complaints and diagnoses would cover all but the organic categories, and yet the patterns in their changes have reflected some very basic developmental processes. Besides formatively influencing what I have rendered in my writings, these clients have helped me develop a number of exercises for assessing and facilitating personal psychological development (e.g. stream of consciousness reporting, intensive personal journal work, mirror time, and a variety of movement meditations).

Beneath and beyond this harvest of lessons relevant to my research and writing, though, I have been sustained in my work as a therapist by the powerful privilege of intimately witnessing another human being in their struggle to survive and develop. It is in trying to describe that experience that the research scientist and existential-humanist within me stage their most captivating dialogues. The scientist speaks a language of public and practical effects, while the humanist speaks a language of privacy and process; the scientist speaks mainly from his head, the humanist from his heart. I do not experience them as being at war with one another, and I hold firm to the hope that head and heart can be integrated. Meanwhile, I open my door not to a client or case, but to another human being, and I offer to walk a few minutes and miles with them as confidant, counsellor, and caregiver in their uniquely personal pilgrimage.

In addition to my work with these private clients, I also lead a few workshops and retreats for therapists every year. Although these take place in small groups, they are not 'group work' in the traditional sense, but intensely 'personal process work'. I enjoy that involvement immensely, in part due to the efficiency of working with groups of people who, themselves, work with other individuals. Theoretically, I feel there is more 'return' for my time and energy. That it tends to be work at another level is an additional reason that I find it so satisfying: as clients, psychotherapists tend to be very sophisticated about change, complexity, and coping with life's conflicts. They know, for example, from extensive personal experience, that 'insight is not enough' and that feelings change much more slowly than thoughts.

Perhaps because of my own experiences as a psychotherapist in therapy, I can also relate to many of their concerns and issues about roles and resolution. I derive a lot of pleasure from interacting with other helping professionals in this way, and I often rely on the feedback of full-time practitioners to evaluate the real-world relevance of my work. The bottom line in my writing about human change is its resonance with what my clients and therapist/clients experience. If both groups reflect to me that it makes sense or is helpful, I feel reassured that what I am offering is not just 'ivory tower' speculation. For it to be meaningful, it must speak to those working in the experiential 'trenches' of life, where the real 'work' gets done.

Implications for other psychotherapists

I am hesitant to suggest that my personal experience of becoming a therapist has any clearcut relevance or implications for other psychotherapists, except perhaps at an abstract level. In this section I will therefore briefly address some of those abstractions and attempt to personalize them in the context of examining current policies in research, training, and practice. Before delving into such abstractions, however, let me offer some closure-to-date on the personal side of this narrative. The boy writer is alive and well, and writing remains a primary task and treasure in my life. Although the bulk of my products are scientific and professional, I continue to enjoy writing poetry and an ever-in-process novel. I love teaching, and – despite the salient frustrations of some aspects of academia – I love being a scientist *and* a practitioner. My students and clients are inexhaustible teachers, and my love for learning has never been so deep. Speaking of love, I have been fortunate enough to find and share that precious dimension with my family and friends. I am happier now than might have been dreamed by that Illinois farmboy or the bewildered adolescent who once saw through these eyes. At times I worry about having stretch marks on my consciousness, but I can usually smile at the audacity of that thought. With few qualifications, I feel very good about 'where I am' in my life, in my relationships, and in my activities as a psychotherapist, research scientist, and educator.

Moving now beyond my own personal and professional development, let me address a few abstractions that bear concrete relevance for the field, and particularly for practising therapists and therapy apprentices. The first has to do with the meaning and value of psychotherapy as an activity. Despite efforts to inform and demystify, a stigma about being in therapy stubbornly persists. Though complex, I think part of that tenacity comes from the legacy of the Dark Ages and primitive fears that psychological problems reflect spiritual or moral flaws. Thomas Szasz and Michel Foucault have offered valuable historical reconstructions of the use of insane asylums and psychologizing to deny or quarantine the things we are most frightened of, often within ourselves. Though much headway has been made towards gaining a greater awareness of these biases, it concerns me that many psychotherapists are, themselves, still reluctant to enter psychotherapy today. Their need to be (or appear to be) a 'paragon of adjustment' and their embarrassment at having problems may collude in an unsavoury manner to perpetuate myths and dualisms that would keep psychotherapy in the Dark Ages.

To help rectify this situation, I strongly advocate that we examine the quality of training that our students are receiving. Very few contemporary graduate programmes encourage students to explore personal counselling; indeed, the clear but implicit message in most non-analytic training programmes is that personal difficulties are to be hidden. At the same time, we confront the statistics that first-year graduate students are second only to freshmen in using campus psychological services. The message to the psychotherapy apprentice is, thus, not unlike that rendered to the consumer public: if at all possible, avoid psychotherapy. Is it, then, any wonder that our clients sometimes feel like failures just because they have become clients? I believe that students should be informed about and encouraged to explore the benefits and limitations of the services their own profession offers. Until we have some impact on the traditionally prohibitive message, however, the quality and public image of psychotherapy are not likely to shift significantly.

A second theme of focus has to do with the importance and legitimacy of private experience and the phenomenology of psychological change. I find it reassuring that, over the last fifteen years, more and more psychotherapy researchers have acknowledged the importance of phenomenological and qualitative research, as well as the significance of their own personal experience. It is also encouraging that many of them became more interested in psychotherapy process research not only due to their clients' experiences, but also out of their own experiences as clients. Phenomenological and qualitative research is essential for refining our understanding of self system development, which, I believe, lies at the core of personal meanings and, hence, significant psychological change.

Another pet issue of mine is something I call the 'tyranny of technique' – by which I mean the overemphasis on technique as the source of power in psychotherapy. Techniques are important as structured methods of communication, usually expressed in the different 'languages' of the various theoretical orientations. Those 'languages' should not be mistaken for some very fundamental messages that are conveyed in a variety of ways in the helping relationship. At the core of optimal psychotherapy is a respect for the power and complexity of human development, and, therefore, a respect for the individuality of clients and their capacities with, or without, formalized techniques. Their capacities are often unacknowledged or unappreciated by the clients themselves, and, hence, one of the major contributions a psychotherapist can make is to encourage individuals to step forward to some kind of empowerment of self: who they are, what they are capable of, what they have survived in their lives up to this point, and, perhaps, that one does not have to understand something completely in order to harvest its lessons.

I believe that the power for change in therapy lies primarily in the realm of the client, and secondarily, in the realm of the therapeutic relationship and the psychotherapist as a human being. Only in a tertiary sense do theoretical orientations and ritualized techniques become an important factor. This is not to say that we do not need techniques, or that their teaching should not be an important part of apprenticeship. My point is that a language is a means for conveying a message, but it is not the message itself. Without some conceptual scaffolding about human change processes, techniques are little more than mindless rituals – the modern voodoo of applied science. With a scaffolding, however – which is a source of meaningful messages – familiarity with a wide array of techniques (languages) can help the therapist communicate with many different clients in many different ways.

I shall close with a response to a question posed to me in the course of this writing: namely, what contributions (if any) do I feel I have made to the field of psychotherapy? In brief, I don't know. I have tried to add a voice to a small *a cappella* group of thinkers and therapists who have been seeking the 'big picture' of basic principles and processes of human development. As a group, they have tended to be independents and eclectics whose interests took them beyond the parochial rivalries of the various therapies. They have been trans-theoretical and integrative, often belonging to such organizations as the Society for Psychotherapy Research and the Society for the Exploration of Psychotherapy Integration. These individuals – people like Jerome Frank, Hans Strupp, and Victor Raimy – have remained sensitive to both philosophical and scientific issues. They are strong advocates of the scientist/practitioner model, not because it is perfect, but because it respects the preciousness of inquiry and exploration in science *and* personal development.

I feel honoured and privileged to have had the opportunity to lend a voice to that ensemble, and to join in the struggle to understand the complexity of this endeavour called psychotherapy. Such is the life mission that I most identify with; it is my reference beam for journeying. In the final analysis, I hope to contribute something towards helping psychotherapy move beyond the early isolationism that had characterized it in the middle of the twentieth century, and I hope to offer some heuristic integrations that point towards the basic principles and processes that underlie our efforts to help.

In the meantime, I continue encouraging a coalition between celebrations of the human spirit and refinements of human inquiry. An adequate theoretical psychology will have to address the gap we have created between our heads and our hearts – between our formal mental maps and the complex, dynamic terrain of everyday experience. As our students learn to appreciate the challenging privileges and responsibilities of our profession, they will carry forward 'the work' of bridging that gap. Then, perhaps, with less dogma, science will be practised as open-ended, multi-method inquiry, and psychology will be more adequate to the challenge of studying the complex depths and dynamics of every human life. There will then be more commerce across the bridge between public and private knowing, and the constructs of 'inner life' and 'science' will finally dance together in synergy. And, as Ram Dass and others so aptly remind us, the object of the dance is not to finish: the object of the dance is to dance.

Chapter three

Through therapy to self

Irene Bloomfield

Why I became a psychotherapist

When I was 9 years old, I knew that I was going to be a brain surgeon. My father had a colleague and friend, Bruno, in this profession whom he clearly admired and respected. It seemed evident, therefore, that by becoming like Bruno I would gain my father's approval. At 11 I was going to be an eye specialist, because there was another friend of my father's who was then frequenting our home. My father spoke very highly of Max who was a hospital consultant, and it seemed sensible therefore to change my future profession, although this did not have the same appeal as brain surgery. Perhaps it was just as well that this phase did not last, because Max committed suicide together with his wife when the Nazis came to power in Germany, and he was no longer allowed to carry on practising. Max's suicide hit my father very hard. He was a friend and a colleague and in a very similar position to that of my father.

There were a number of other vocations I aspired to and tried before I ended up as a psychotherapist. At age 15 I left my German school, which had by then become intolerable, and went to work on a farm to prepare myself for life in an Israeli kibbutz. I still have a very vivid picture of my parents' expression of incredulity when they found me sitting by what must have looked like a very large cow, trying to persuade it to part with its surplus of milk. It seemed a far cry from brain surgery.

At home much of the conversation at meal-times revolved around the profession of either of my parents. My father was a lecturer at Berlin University and a psychotherapist. He taught medical psychology which was a highly popular subject among students from most faculties. My father was regarded as a superb teacher, and his classes and seminars were always crowded out.

My mother was a writer and journalist who was beginning to make a name for herself because of her original style, her interviews with some of the famous scientists of the time and her subject. She was writing about scientific discoveries in behavioural and pure science for people who were not scientists themselves.

We, that is my sister and I, learned quite a bit about the worlds of university faculties and journalism. But there were also discussions on the likelihood of man being able to get to the moon in our lifetime, about human rights, justice, religion, philosophy, literature, and politics. Many of my subsequent attitudes, values and philosophy of life were born and nurtured around the dinner table. It seems now that the ultimate choice of my profession of psychotherapy also goes back to those times, because even though I did not understand very much of the theory or practice of psychotherapy at that time, I caught the sense of excitement and enthusiasm with which my father talked of his work, his discoveries, and his ideas, many of which were new and original.

My mother played a less important part in my choice of psychotherapy as a profession, but without her constant material and moral support it would have remained an idle dream. She did, I think, play a very important part in the kind of psychotherapist I have become, for I have internalized a great many of her values and her way of being with people.

Writing has also been an important aspect of my existence as a therapist, and writing was my mother's profession. Although it is always a great struggle to get anything down on paper I feel restless and discontented if I have not got a piece of writing in preparation. It helps me to conceptualize what I do, and stops habits from becoming hardened.

When I returned to England after the war I realized that nothing I had done so far had brought me that same sense of excitement which my parents communicated in their talks about therapy. But it took many years, several blind alleys and a very circuitous route to bring me finally back to the decision to become a therapist.

It was necessary to differentiate myself and separate myself off from my father. I had to do something totally different, something he would never have dreamed of for one of his offspring, like milking cows and digging asparagus at 4 a.m., and later working in a pathology laboratory looking for the causes of various tropical diseases such as malaria, sand-fly fever, bilharzia, etc. Soon after my arrival in Palestine in January 1940 I found I could not live in a kibbutz for the rest of my life. I still admired it more than anything and totally accepted the concept and ideals of the kibbutz movement, but I needed to be free to make my mistakes, to explore and experiment, to take responsibility for myself. I also needed solitude, and living at such close quarters – even with people I admired and some of whom I loved – was too much of a constraint. Perhaps I was also too selfish to take up such a life of considerable hardship, in which the welfare of the *community* was always the first consideration.

Having spent some time studying bacteriology and working in military hospitals, I returned to England to take up my interrupted studies, but I was no longer so interested in the organisms which cause physical symptoms of disease. Something fundamental had changed for me.

My father had died during the war. He was only 56 years old, but the traumas of the Nazi period, of losing everything he had struggled so hard to build up, of having to start again in a strange country with a new language and with great financial hardship, had left him shattered and heartbroken. His heart had begun to give out even before he arrived in England, but he managed to complete a book on his theory and practice of psychotherapy. The book was entitled *Active Psychotherapy* (Herzberg 1945) and was a forerunner of behavioural methods and of short-term psychotherapy long before these became more generally accepted. It was his last gift to psychotherapy and, in a sense, to me.

Apart from the external changes in my life there had been internal ones too. The brief encounters I had had with patients in the army hospitals I had worked in no longer satisfied me. I wanted to know more about people than that they suffered from TB or malaria. The same illness could affect people in such different ways. People's behaviour was often very astonishing and unpredictable. When the men had to be given their TAB (typhoid, anti-tetanus) injections, they formed up in a line and received a tiny prick in the arm which was barely noticeable, but almost invariably one of the toughest and biggest of the men would pass out. It did not make much sense after some of the horrors they had witnessed and experienced. Then there was the senior officer who had always been the life and soul of the social events in the unit. He was not one of the obviously promiscuous men, but he had contracted a venereal disease from a casual contact and went into a lasting depression as a result.

Earlier on I had been amazed and appalled by the brutality which some of the Palestine police used on a small group of women who were demonstrating in what seemed quite an orderly manner against the restrictions which stopped their relatives who had managed to escape from Germany and German-occupied countries from entering Palestine.

I had met English policemen and had come to trust and like them, and on the two-week journey to Palestine I had got to know some who were going to join the force. They had been kind, nice, ordinary people, but here they were, these same men, laying into the women with their truncheons, as if they were fighting the Nazi hordes on the battlefield.

Yes, people's behaviour was strange and often incomprehensible. I thought that the study of psychology would help me to understand more, but it was already clear to me that better understanding of human behaviour was not enough. I wanted to use my understanding in the way my father had done. The decision was made for me from the moment I was accepted for my psychology course in London, but there was a long, long way to go.

There was very little in the degree course which had much to do with people. There was a certain amount about aspects of behaviour, such as memory, learning, cognition and more about experiments, especially with rats in mazes, but it did not teach me much about people. The only lectures which were different were those by Professor J. C. Flugel – a well-known psychoanalyst who had written about *Man, Morals and Society* – and some lectures by Dr Hadfield on psychopathology. Professor Flugel displayed his humanness through his lectures and this helped me to see him as a person with attachments of his own.

Most lecturers seemed to shudder at words like feelings or unconscious. They were unscientific, bad, naughty, taboo words, and to be scientific seemed to be much more important than to understand human beings. However, I was not that easily put off. I took my courage in both hands and asked Professor J. C. Flugel if he would take me on for analysis as a first step in the direction I planned to go. To my amazement he agreed, and so I was on my way.

J.C.F. was both paternal and maternal. He was kind and gentle and occasionally willing to step out of his role of orthodox analyst. My financial resources were non-existent, and J.C.F. helped to get me an assignment to write articles on psychological subjects for a journal to enable me to pay for my analysis. Unfortunately, the kind of knowledge that my psychology course provided was not quite what the editor had in mind, and my side-line of journalism did not last very long. I was nevertheless grateful to my analyst for not being like the proverbial blank screen. There was another way in which he differed from the stereotype. I had a rival for my place on the couch. It was a miniature, rather neurotic female poodle, which yelped pitifully when it had to make way for me on the analytic couch. I had a fantasy that I had interrupted its analytic session!

Encouragement received from family and others

I knew hardly anyone in London when I returned from my sojourn in Palestine and my years in the army hospitals in Jerusalem, Beirut and Cairo, except for my mother and my sister who had stayed in London throughout the war. My mother had been through very hard times. She had not been able to go back to her writing career, and the total amount of money with which she had arrived in England to start a new life was 10 Deutschmarks, which was the equivalent of about £1.00 sterling. She and my sister arrived in England a year after my father; my parents had decided to separate, and not to emigrate together. My mother, therefore, had to make her own way and take responsibility for my sister, her 89-year-old mother and a nephew who would have been in great danger had he stayed behind in Germany. She did this by opening a home for other refugees and, later, a café and a restaurant where refugees could meet and find a little of the atmosphere they had cherished in the cafés of Vienna and Berlin and which they had had to leave behind. But in spite of the popularity of these enterprises, my mother was not business-minded, and never made enough money to be free from pressure and worries. Despite that, she helped, supported and encouraged my wish to become a therapist in every way she could. She was not without some knowledge of what it entailed, since my father had started off as a general practitioner, then changed to psychotherapy and finally to lecturing at the university. My mother also knew quite a lot about the subject itself, because during those heady pre-Hitler days Berlin was a hive of cultural, intellectual, and artistic activity, and one of the regular events in our home were the evenings when my father held seminars about psychotherapy and psychoanalysis for large numbers of interested people. It was a regular event, and I recall my mother spending hours beforehand baking mountains of her special goodies to delight the twenty to thirty members of the seminar who were served with coffee and cakes after they had received the other kind of feeding from my father. She attended all the talks and seminars herself, and participated in the animated discussions which followed them.

I worked in a pathology laboratory throughout my university course, but the pay was so low that I could not have existed on it had I not been able to live with my mother. She was delighted with my choice of becoming a therapist after the various aberrations of farm worker, kibbutznik, domestic help (which was my first job on arrival in England), and laboratory technician.

It is a great sadness to me that neither of my parents was alive when I finally achieved my goal and began to do the work I was determined to do, and which has never disappointed me. The disappointment lies only in the fact that I was never able to say thank you to those who made it possible.

Fantasies, myths and ideals associated with becoming a therapist

It seems to me now that for a long period during my childhood and adolescence all my reading consisted of Greek and Nordic mythology. I was a fanatical and voracious reader and the heroes of these myths were extraordinarily real to me – they formed part of my life. The myth of Oedipus was certainly one which made an enormous impact on me, but whether my understanding of it had any bearing on my subsequent choice of profession is doubtful.

The other historical figures which became very important to me were Ben-Hur and Jehuda Maccabeus. I came across Ben-Hur in the first film I ever saw, although I had read the story before and had been much impressed with him, but it was the defeat of his Roman rivals in the famous and spectacular chariot race which made such an impact on me.

Jehuda Maccabeus was the leader of a small band of zealots who defied the mighty Roman army for three years at Massada and when defeat became inevitable he chose suicide for all of them rather than allow them to fall into the hands of the Romans to become slaves.

I think these two Jewish heroes were so important to me because they contradicted all the unpleasant stereotypes of the ghetto-Jew who, according to the anti-Jewish propaganda which was beginning to make its way even into our relatively protected lives, were the very opposite to my two hero-figures. The propaganda depicted the Jew as feeble, cowardly, incapable of fighting or winning. I suppose this stereotype must have been all around us, even though none of the Jewish people I knew resembled it. My parents showed a great deal of courage even when it became dangerous to do so, and never discouraged my own uncompromising and defiant attitude at school when I refused to conform to the Nazi edicts and rules.

Nevertheless, I was very frightened, and believe that the need to defeat that part of me which fitted the stereotype of the cowardly Jew became a driving force in my life, although I did not recognize it as such until relatively recently.

My model of a therapist was, of course, largely based on my father. He had his own, original notions and concepts and followed no party-line. His book, published after his death, which describes his ideas and practice with many clinical illustrations initiated a totally new approach to therapy from that practised at the time. He was a pioneer and an educator. Unfortunately, he did not have enough time to develop and spread his ideas. Given a little more time, it is likely that there would have been an Alexander Herzberg school of psychotherapy. I have subsequently met a number of therapists who were much influenced by his teaching.

I do not myself use the model of therapy my father pioneered. I had to find my own way of working, plough my own furrow – as it were – and discover my own style. But there can be no doubt that his was the most important influence in my ultimate decision to become a therapist.

Some of the other reasons for my choice which I have already alluded to were the need to understand why things were happening to me the way they did. I think that my 'why' questions continued well beyond the time when children are normally driving parents to distraction with them.

Experiences which influenced my decision

I had had a number of traumatic experiences as a child at school in Nazi Germany, later as a civilian in Palestine, then in the British army and eventually in my personal relationships. It was very important for me to try to understand why people behaved as they did; why my former best friends turned into bitter enemies because they were told to hate Jews; why apparently civilized human beings turned into Nazi hordes. I had an experience of this myself at school when a teacher tried to force me to give the Hitler salute. When I refused he came towards me, looking very menacing, and then turned to the class saying: 'What shall we do with a pupil who disobeys her teacher?'

It was as if in an instant the girls I knew as Marta, Brigitte, Dora, Ilse, etc. had turned into a howling mob out to tear me to pieces. They did not, of course, do so, but it was very frightening. It did not feel good to be a Jew at that time. It was hard not to believe that there was something nasty and inferior about us. I also needed to understand what was happening to me personally.

There was a very shameful experience in which I denied my sister. She tried to join the sports club I belonged to and turned up at one of the classes to see whether she liked it. One of my fellow members turned to me and said sneeringly: 'Doesn't this girl look Jewish?' I made a non-committal response, but did not let on that she was my sister. She never came again and I was asked to leave two or three weeks later when I was told that Jews were no longer welcome. I was bitterly ashamed of myself, for it forced me to acknowledge the cowardly self I had tried to deny and purge.

I can actually remember the exact moment when that bad feeling about being Jewish changed. It was like a sudden revelation. I was just walking along the street when it came to me that I did not have to buy all this stuff about Jewish inferiority which teachers, fellow pupils, and everything around us seemed to be proclaiming. I would go to Palestine and be proud to be a Jew. It was then as if a terrible, dark cloud which had threatened to engulf me was lifted, and I felt free and somehow invulnerable. The latter was, of course, a delusion as far as the external world was concerned, but something had changed internally. It was as if a transformation had taken place. I was 14 years old at the time, but it was perhaps the most important turning point in my life. It meant I could be myself and did not have to be ashamed of being me.

It was the beginning of a search for an identity and a true self which continued through my analysis and my work as a therapist. The search for identity is, of course, a never-ending process, and many other factors contributed to making me into the person I am now, but the powerful wish to be myself and not to be coerced into becoming what I was not began at that moment. This also played an important part in the wish to enable others to discover their identities and true selves.

What did I imagine it would be like being a therapist?

When I set out on the long road of training to be a therapist I had very little idea what it would be like. I just knew that it was what I wanted to do. Understanding myself and others was probably at that time one of the most important ingredients. It was not a frightening prospect, because I had too little knowledge of what it involved. I did not think of it as uplifting, because although I knew that my father had been able to help many people overcome difficulties they had struggled with for years, it did not really occur to me that I might be able to do anything like that.

If I had wondered whether I had the personal qualities which would make me into a good therapist I would probably never have started. I knew my father was regarded as a very good and successful therapist, and I wanted to be like him, but I did not stop to think at that point whether I had the qualities which would enable me to do so. It was a very long, slow, and often very painful task to develop the characteristics which I believe to be important for a good therapist.

Doubts, dilemmas and obstacles

Perhaps I knew too little about the task I was undertaking to have many doubts, but the dilemmas and obstacles were formidable. I qualified as a psychologist in 1952 from London University, then trained at the Child Guidance Training Centre in London, and started my first job as a child psychologist in the south-west of England, in Devon, two years later.

When I was interviewed for this post, some members of the panel seemed to be a bit uncertain as to what the job entailed. One of the burly, all-male panel stands out in my mind. I don't know what his professional discipline was, but he looked hard at my five foot stature and said rather sternly: 'Do you think you are strong enough for this job?' It only dawned on me after some embarrassed exchanges among the panel that he thought I was applying for a job as a physiotherapist!

Psychology was still a fairly young profession at that time, and my employers were not too sure what my training qualified me for. It turned out that I was expected to do all the therapy in the three clinics we covered, since the psychiatrist only did the diagnostic interviews.

It was both my good and bad fortune that I knew so little when I started. It was hard on my young patients that I had so little experience, but it meant that I had to let them teach me, and they did. It was a marvellous opportunity for me, but my formal therapy training did not begin until two and a half years later, when I returned to London and got a job at one of the teaching hospitals. Here things were much more difficult, because in the hospital setting there was a much clearer division between what was regarded as the psychologist's job, which was to carry out tests, and psychotherapy which was done by psychiatrists. It was 1957, and there were no psychologists working as therapists with adult patients in the Health Service. I had to prepare myself for a long, hard struggle. Perhaps it is quite difficult to realize now, only three decades later, how much attitudes have changed during this relatively short period. It was obvious to me that every part of my training would have to be in my own time, and at my own expense, and that it might be best not even to mention it to my colleagues.

How did I become a therapist?

There was not a great deal of choice of training in 1957. I had not had any contact with Jungian analysis, except via the Guild of Pastoral Psychology. My first analyst had been a Freudian, and the Tavistock Clinic seemed to offer the only training in adult psychotherapy then available.

I had tried a year at the Anna Freud Clinic, which was training child psychotherapists, but even if I had been willing to go through the four-year course as a stage in training later for work with adults, I began to feel quite soon that I could never be the kind of disciple trainees and staff were expected to be. There were some fascinating seminars and lectures, but trainees were not expected to express opinions, let alone question any part of the dogma and beliefs. This at least was my perception, which may be quite unjust, but it was very evident after my first year that I would never survive another three in this atmosphere. It was, no doubt, a failure on my part, but I had never been able to accept authority unquestioningly. So I had to leave – to our mutual relief.

Even during my time at the Tavistock I felt that I occasionally committed acts of sacrilege by not totally accepting 'sacred religious doctrine'. It sometimes reminded me of the time at school when I plagued the religious teacher with awkward questions about religious dogma, whether Jewish or Christian. The teacher tended to get angry and defensive, but I don't think I was just being awkward. I was struggling hard to reconcile my father's atheism and rationalism with my own search for something that went beyond science. I wanted the teacher to convince me that it was all right to have faith.

My teachers at the Tavistock tolerated my scepticism, but I daresay that I was something of an irritant, because I still had very little experience and needed to learn a lot more about the doctrines before I was entitled to make judgements. In spite of this tendency I greatly enjoyed the varied and different aspects of the training process – the seminars, the supervision, the group observation and the meeting with other trainees, mostly psychiatrists working in very different settings from my own rather privileged teaching hospital department. It was also exciting to meet and listen to many of the eminent and interesting people in the field whose writings I had come across, and whom I was now actually seeing in person.

Some made a profound impact and had a lasting influence on me. There was Pierre Turquet who was one of my supervisors. I admired his intellect, his deep knowledge of psychoanalytic theory and practice and I was in awe of him. He was a stern, tough, and confronting task master who did not let his trainees get away with much. I often felt very inadequate and stupid in his presence.

There was Bob Gosling who taught us about groups which we observed behind a one-way screen. He seemed to me a bit like a Greek God on Mount Olympus, and his interventions sounded like oracles, but when he met us after the group was over to talk about it the gulf which seemed to be present between him and his patients was far less evident. His understanding and perception of the group processes were brilliant, and again I wondered whether I could ever gain such insights.

Two of the other teachers who stand out in my mind are Hyatt Williams who talked about the psychology of murderers, and Ronnie Laing who was to me the most intriguing of all our teachers, so much so that I later joined the clinic of which he was then director in order to attend the weekly staff meeting with him.

One of the non-Tavistock people who made an impression on me at that time was Joshua Bierer, a highly unorthodox innovator whose revolutionary ideas transformed some of the care of psychiatric patients in England. Unfortunately, it was very difficult for anybody to work with him for any length of time, because he was really a one-man team. He had remarkable drive, vision, and initiative and enormous confidence in himself. He did also inspire great loyalty and devotion in some of his workers, but sooner or later there was usually a rift.

Other people affected me more because of who they were rather than what school or orientation they belonged to. Vera van der Heydt was a devout Catholic as well as a devoted Jungian analyst. Yet there was an independence of spirit and personality which illuminated everything she did. I greatly admired her acceptance of Jung's ideas without any loss of her own autonomy.

I don't think I ever managed to have a guru figure myself. There were people I admired, but I had to work out my own approach, and my most important teachers were always my patients and, later, my students.

It is possible that I underestimate the effect of my formal training, but I felt that the theory meant little until I actually began to see patients myself. I then recognized that I had absorbed quite a bit which had become part of my equipment. Supervision was an important monitoring of strengths, weaknesses and blind spots.

Although there were the initial difficulties about being a psychologist who wanted to do therapy, I was, in fact, remarkably fortunate in having colleagues who were willing to let me go ahead, once I had trained and shown some aptitude for doing therapy. The head of the department of psychological medicine and one of the other senior consultants encouraged me and began to refer patients to me.

In the early 1960s I joined the Institute of Group Analysis except that it was not yet called the Institute. I spent four years learning about groups in seminars, supervision and therapy or training groups, including one run by Michael Foulkes who was the founder of group analysis in Britain.

Did my training nourish or violate my ideal of becoming a therapist?

As mentioned earlier, the degree course in psychology, with the exception of J. C. Flugel's seminars, was no help at all. It taught me very little about whole human beings, but was preoccupied with being scientific. It was at the university that I encountered the first of many polarizations. The faculty was split between those who believed passionately in an experimental approach to the study of human behaviour, and those who were interested in studying human beings in their social context.

Later, I encountered splits among clinical psychologists between those who believed that tests could supply definite answers and diagnostic labels for personality variables, and others who believed that projective techniques held the key to the understanding of the personality.

During my therapy training I encountered splits between the behaviourists and psychotherapists, and between the various analytic groups. At times they resembled the warring factions of political parties or the reform movements of churches.

The belief in the one true dogma offended my ideas and ideals of therapy. It was too reminiscent of other kinds of fanaticism which I had come to distrust and even abhor. I did not want to be this kind of therapist.

In spite of these feelings I accept the need for a conceptual framework to help me understand people's so-called normal and abnormal behaviour, their passions, their sorrows, their achievements and failures.

I experienced the group analytic training as more flexible and more open to other ideas. No doubt there were group analysts with very definite or even rigid concepts of a right and wrong approach to group work, but the society as a whole retained some of the openness and flexibility of its founder, and this made me feel nourished rather than indoctrinated.

Informal training

There were a number of events and people outside my formal training which affected me profoundly. In the early 1960s a Hungarian group analyst, Paul Senft, joined the department. At that time therapy groups, especially in hospital departments, were still something of a novelty, regarded with suspicion, and seen very much as a second-best treatment method. Paul offered a place as an observer in one of his groups to a member of staff. No one else showed much enthusiasm, so I grabbed the opportunity. It was a strange experience. Paul initially expected me to be totally silent, but, not unnaturally, this evoked powerful paranoid feelings in the group. Members wanted to know whether they were just objects of study for me, so that I could write a book about them, or whether they were intended to be guinea-pigs in an experiment. I felt very uncomfortable in this observer role myself, and Paul agreed that perhaps I could make some comments from time to time, but there was a change in my role from then on, and when I took the group on my own on occasions when Paul was not available, I began to be seen more as a co-therapist than as an observer. It was a most valuable experience and taught me a good deal about group-processes and a particular way of conducting a group. It was also a method of teaching group therapy which I adopted myself a few years later, and which has remained the preferred teaching method in the department at University College Hospital.

My enthusiasm for working with groups was born at that time. I do not think of it as a way of seeing more people at the same time, or as second-best, but as a very effective and powerful kind of therapy. Two years after joining Paul's group I had the opportunity of taking a group myself. It was my first experience of working as a therapist in my own right.

Another event which taught me some important, if painful lessons was the first International Congress of Social Psychiatry. I read a short paper on some work I had been doing with a group of African students, and as a result received an invitation to the French Institute of African Studies. I felt so honoured that I tried hard to amplify and improve the paper I had given, and in the process made it far too long and theoretical, so that the time which should have been spent in dialogue and discussion all went on reading the paper, which was quite boring to an audience which knew a great deal more about the subject than I. I realized how easy it was to spoil a good thing by trying to make it perfect. It was only when the craving for perfection was modified that I became relaxed enough as a therapist to be of much help to my patients.

The Congress was nevertheless an important event for me, because I met therapists from all over the world and heard about many different and interesting new approaches. It was the beginning of the various encounter types of therapy, and whilst I did not see myself becoming an encounter-type therapist it was all very stimulating and exciting.

It was also from that time onwards that my psychiatric colleagues began to refer patients to me for individual psychotherapy. One of them, Professor Desmond Pond, had close contacts with members of the clergy and with theological colleges. He passed several of these on to me. I had never before even met a priest or nun, and all sorts of fantasies on my part had to be re-assessed. I found that this group of patients was often able to use and take further whatever I had to offer more quickly and readily than others, and I became very interested in working with them. These encounters opened up a whole new world for me in the pastoral care and counselling field.

When I became a therapist

I had made a beginning, but it took several more years before I actually thought of myself as a psychotherapist, or was seen as such by my colleagues. To them

I was still basically a psychologist doing some psychotherapy. The point at which this image changed was when I was asked to take a group of medical students on for supervision. University College Hospital had started this project in the early 1950s, and 25 per cent of all our students elected to take a patient on for psychotherapy under the guidance of a supervisor.

I became a supervisor around 1970, thirteen years after I joined the department, and you obviously could not supervise other people's therapy unless you were perceived as a therapist yourself. My formal training had finished a long time before that, but informal training and learning have never stopped. They continue in exchanges with colleagues, in reading and occasionally writing or giving a paper myself.

Changes in thinking and practice

The changes in my thinking and practice are mostly changes of degree and emphasis rather than of anything more fundamental. I believe very much in the importance of balance between firmness and flexibility, closeness and distance, intimacy and separateness. Patrick Casement (1985: 30), in his book *On Learning from the Patient*, talks of 'the need to be psychologically intimate with the patient and yet separate; separate yet still intimate.' I agree very much with this approach.

I also ask more searching questions of myself about the kind of interventions and the manner of intervening I can fall into, which I have questioned when supervising others. Hopefully I am more aware of my shortcomings, and therefore a little more able to correct them.

I became particularly interested in borderline and psychotic patients after having gained some confidence in my ability as a therapist. There were always quite a few of these patients on our waiting list, and they tended to remain there for long periods of time. It was also a challenge, and I could never resist challenges. There was, no doubt, also a measure of omnipotence in my wish to work with people who were often regarded as difficult or impossible to treat with psychotherapeutic methods as out-patients, but once I began to work with them, I found that I enjoyed doing so, and that they frequently benefited from something I provided. There were some I saw individually as well as in a group, and this combination often worked well, although it broke many rules of group work, created rivalries and affected transference relationships. I felt, nevertheless, that the advantages of working in this way outweighed the disadvantages, and I learned more from these patients than from any other source. It was necessary to be even more alert, attentive and sensitive to changes in mood than with other patients. Such changes could occur very rapidly and could become very destructive if not responded to appropriately.

I also learned a great deal from my mistakes. All therapists make mistakes, but some mistakes can be very costly. Two of my former patients committed suicide. One went into a very sudden, acute psychotic episode after having been discharged from hospital and jumped out of a fifth floor window. This was a deeply upsetting experience, and I naturally asked myself whether it could have been prevented. It was with the second patient, Nicholas, however, that I felt I had a great deal to blame myself for. I had not heard his appeals, his desperation, his desolation. Nick taught me to listen better with the 'third ear', the ear which has to be attuned to the symbolic expression of some of the deepest hurts and hidden warnings. Shortly before his death Nick talked about an incident in which he quarrelled with a friend who deliberately stamped on his guitar. the thing he cherished more than anything. The guitar was broken, damaged beyond repair, but it seemed that something more than the guitar had been broken. His words could have been seen as a warning which I did not heed. I *now* take it to be so. His death occurred during my holidays, and I had made no provision for him to see someone else. It is too late for him, but he taught me much that I have never forgotten and will never forget, although it is now over twenty years since it happened.

What sustains me as a therapist

Most of the time I find what patients are telling me extraordinarily interesting, and it still feels an enormous privilege to be admitted into their secret worlds. On the occasions when I have been bored, an exploration of what was happening between us generally brought about a change in my feeling and yielded useful information about the patients' motives such as cutting off from painful feelings or withholding information, or because of something that had been touched off in myself which I wanted to cut off from.

The cultural, ethnic and social backgrounds my patients come from are often very different from my own, and I needed to learn a great deal about these varied cultures in order to appreciate the significance of attitudes and behaviour which may be the norm in their culture whilst they would be regarded as a sign of maladaptation in my own Western, middle-class, academic context.

It is not, of course, only the extreme differences in culture that are challenging. The culture and background of an English person who grew up in the East End of London during the war, of a member of the upper classes who only met his parents once a day until at the age of 8 he was sent off to prep school, a member of a religious community, or someone who survived a concentration camp are all so removed from my own experience that the capacity for entering into the patient's world – whatever his background – is absolutely vital.

I have also gained insights into many and varied occupations and the anxieties and problems associated with them such as rocks in the path of a train driver, assaults on taxi-drivers and probation officers, the tiny error in a calculation made by an architect, a mis-diagnosis by a general practitioner and many others. The therapist also learns that, whilst external environments and experiences differ so much from each other and each person's internal world is totally unique, basic human emotions are very similar. It is because of this that understanding is not so difficult after all.

It is, of course, very rewarding to see people change, grow and mature in the course of therapy, to see them acquire an improved self-image and different attitudes towards themselves and others and to notice changes in unhelpful patterns of behaviour. Perhaps the most exciting aspect of change to me is the patient's discovery of his or her creative potential.

But whilst some of these developments are gratifying from the therapist's point of view, it is not so much the arrival but the journey that both therapist and patient undertake which never loses its fascination for me. It is a very special and unique way of being with another person during their struggles, their doubts, their despair and their ups and downs.

What does it mean to me to be a therapist?

The most common feeling I have when I think about being a therapist is one of awe. Perhaps it is a little of the way parents might feel when they observe the unfolding of their young child's personality. This probably sounds rather grandiose, but the feeling has to be acknowledged. I appreciate it particularly, though, when a patient begins to find his or her autonomy, and gaining my approval or disapproval is no longer a priority.

Patients who nourish or violate my sense of being a therapist

As mentioned earlier, during my thirty years in the Health Service I was very happy to have a fair proportion of very disturbed patients, psychotic, borderline, suicidal, severely depressed people, many of whom had had several hospitalizations.

It, no doubt, fed my omnipotence to find that my kind of therapy could frequently bring about changes in these patients, but there was also a sense of joint achievement, when someone who had gone to the bottom of the heap as far as employment was concerned was enabled to obtain a post with high responsibility and became very successful at it. Or when someone else had been in and out of hospital for a period of ten years did not need any further hospitalization during the next decade after a therapy lasting three and a half years. Or when a patient who had suffered from delusions and hallucinations and had inflicted severe physical injury upon himself recovered his sense of reality sufficiently to go through a social work training (Certificate of Qualification in Social Work), qualify and become a successful social worker in a local authority. Another one who stands out in my mind was a severely obsessional post-graduate student who could not get on with her thesis. If there was one comma or full stop in the wrong place she had to re-write the whole page, so never got beyond page 1. In the course of therapy she was able to give up many of her disabling rituals and to start writing her thesis.

Talking of a few spectacular successes sounds too much like boasting to be acceptable, and though these successes are gratifying, I actually find that the really great moments are those in which there has been some really fundamental insight, incorporating past, present and future.

The patients I have found most difficult are the hysterical personalities whose need to control through symptoms or histrionic behaviour causes a tremendous sense of impotence and anger in me. The only way I have found it possible to work with this kind of patient is through insisting on extremely firm limits and boundaries and not allowing any kind of manipulation at all.

This is not the stance I take with other patients. It seems to me that occasionally it can be quite helpful to allow the patient to feel powerful, provided we are both aware of it. I know also that sometimes a breakthrough has occurred when I have allowed myself to feel vulnerable and to experience my own helplessness.

How far am I conducting my own therapy through my work with patients? If so is it legitimate?

In the sense that I continue to learn a good deal about myself through the work I do with my patients it is therapeutic for me. It means having to go on facing aspects of myself which I might prefer not to look at too closely. But this must not be confused with therapy for myself, because the interest of the patient has to be the first consideration. I am not entitled to burden the patient with my problems or my hang-ups. On the whole I follow where the patient needs or wants to go, not where I want to go for my own benefit. If I pursued a particular theme like, for example, a patient's sadistic fantasies because I wanted to discover or work something out about my own sadism rather than because it is important for the patient at this point, I would regard this as unacceptable. I am not suggesting that I have never been guilty of this, but it is something I would deplore and try to correct as soon as I became aware of it.

In so far as my behaviour and ways of relating to other people – as well as my sense of what matters in life – have undergone marked changes since I began to work with patients, doing therapy has certainly been therapeutic for me.

How far do relationships with colleagues and family sustain me as a therapist, and how far do they put a strain on my being a therapist?

Relationships with colleagues are of great importance in the sustaining of a sense of myself as a therapist, although this is not now quite as important as it was earlier on. I now feel that affirmation comes to me more through patients, supervisees and students. It is, nevertheless, good to have dialogue, discussion, feed-back and recognition from colleagues. Meetings with colleagues, formal and informal, are immensely valuable and necessary in order to continue to evaluate what I am doing in therapy, to keep me in touch with new developments and to force me to conceptualize what I am doing.

Writing or giving the occasional paper is another important way of communicating with colleagues and of clarifying for myself what I do.

Being a therapist put considerable strains on my marriage. My former husband often felt excluded from this important area of my life, which also took up so much of my time and emotional resources. He resented it. It was important to him to be married to a psychologist/psychotherapist for his own reasons, but he was very wary, lest he became the object of my therapeutic activities. It made me unsure of myself and self-conscious in my relationship with him.

I retired from the Health Service in the summer of 1984 and am now working privately, which is very different, but I cannot see myself giving up being a therapist unless I am forced to recognize that I am no longer any good.

Was the choice to become a therapist right for me?

If I had my time again I would undoubtedly make the same choice. There have been doubts, of course, not about being a therapist, but about the quality of my work. Yet although it may be immodest to say so I believe that on the whole I have not been a bad therapist. When working at the hospital I did follow-ups on all the patients I had seen over a period of ten or twelve years – just asking them six months after they finished therapy how they were. There was a high return of replies, about 80 per cent, and most of them felt they had gained something. The majority also recognized that the process which had begun during their therapy continued afterwards, and that they had discovered resources in themselves which helped them to deal more effectively with their life and its stresses and strains.

Implications for other therapists

I believe that what is most important in therapy is how we *are* with patients, and that this is more important than what we *do* or *say*. It is essential, therefore, that the therapist should go on working on himself. This is a process which continues throughout our professional lives and is never completed.

It seems to me that there is a great need for flexibility, for assessing thoroughly what any particular patient needs at a given point in time. I believe it to be dangerous and anti-therapeutic to have fixed ideas about the number of times per week or total length of time patients should be seen, about upper and lower age limits, social background, education and intelligence.

My own experience has taught me that it is not always better to see people more frequently, that there are some who cannot tolerate the intensity of two or three sessions per week and some who cannot even manage once per week. They can nevertheless gain considerable benefit from fortnightly or even less frequent appointments.

I have seen patients in their 50s and 60s who felt that they had been helped a good deal. Clearly the therapist's approach to people in the older age group has to differ from that for the younger one, and the goals may not be quite the same either. It is no doubt more difficult for older people to change attitudes and behaviour patterns which may have been in existence for a large number of years, and whatever change there may be in that respect is less likely to be as fundamental or to occur as quickly. The goal is more often a coming to terms with life as it has been, with dreams which remain unfulfilled and with pain which was never relieved, so that what remains of life can be lived more fully without too much resentment from the past which otherwise can poison it. A loss in the present often triggers previous losses which could not be mourned at the time. It often comes as a great relief to such people to have an opportunity to do their mourning even so many years later.

Above-average intelligence and higher education are often regarded as essential for people entering psychotherapy. In my experience these can be a hindrance as well as a help. For the sophisticated, intelligent, well-read person, information acquired from the literature – not always very well digested or understood – is often used in the service of resistance, whilst for those who have never read any psychoanalytic literature the way into the unconscious is beset with fewer obstacles, and the therapeutic work can proceed more rapidly. I generally tackle resistances very early on, frequently in the first session. It seems to have resulted in a much reduced drop-out rate.

Theory

Whilst I believe flexibility and responsiveness to individual needs to be of fundamental importance, I also recognize the necessity of having a theoretical framework, provided it is a framework and not a strait-jacket, 'a servant to the work of the therapist and not its master' (Casement 1985: 4). Freud (1927/1961) himself warned against the tendency to dogma in 'The future of an illusion', and attributes the creation of a store of ideas to 'Man's helplessness and his need to make his helplessness tolerable.'

Supervision

All of us need help in knowing our own unconscious, our strengths, weaknesses and blind-spots. I have found it very helpful and often essential to discuss some of my clinical work with one or two colleagues, especially when there appeared to be blocks to my understanding of what was happening between me and my patient, or when my countertransference reactions got in the way and the therapeutic process seemed to be stuck.

Transference

Like most therapists I recognize the importance of good transference interpretations, but I believe that such interpretations are sometimes forced on the patient when they are not helpful, and it is not always resistance on the part of the patient which makes him reject these. They can seem very text-bookish and stereotyped and make the patient feel less than a person, especially the ones about forthcoming breaks. Moreover, not everything the patient experiences is transference. It may in fact be a reality about us which has been accurately perceived, e.g. our tiredness, boredom, irritation, sadness and other emotions. One of the things that brings about change is the recognition of where the therapist is like the parent and how he or she differs.

Language

I have on several occasions had to write reports to other agencies, lawyers, courts, social work departments, and, of course, frequent reports to general practitioners. It has always paid dividends to use language free from clinical jargon, and to write in terminology which could be readily understood. People who are not therapists become frustrated and angry if they have to read through lengthy reports which are incomprehensible to the outsider.

Expressing feelings

There are times when it seems to me very important to express feelings experienced in the here and now, and that unless I do so I am neither genuine nor human. Some of the most dramatic breakthroughs have occurred when I have expressed anger. One patient who had been provoking me for weeks, sabotaging all my efforts to get through to her, almost shouted with relief when I finally said angrily that I did not see the sole purpose of therapy as triumphing over the therapist. 'At last,' she cried, 'I know you really do care about me, because you have been angry', and her hitherto hostile attitude changed considerably. I could not be experienced as real to her until I had shown I could be angry.

Humour is another way of sharing something with the patient which is different from interpreting. It can be extremely liberating and help to get things into perspective, provided it is experienced as laughing *with* the patient and *not at* him. It can also help to get the therapist off his pedestal. Expressing feelings and humour are no doubt controversial, but I have found them helpful. I have not infrequently deviated in other ways from the generally accepted way of working as a therapist and broken various rules, but not without knowing the rules.

Lastly, there is the recognition of the reciprocity of the process. It is never all one way. There is giving and receiving on both sides; it is a joint journey of discovery and exploration for patient and therapist. It can at times be frustrating, tiring, frightening, exasperating and pressurizing, but it is also exciting, always new and often rewarding.

What has writing this account revealed to me about my wish to be a therapist?

It was only when I came to write this chapter that I recognized how much some of my early experiences contributed to my choice of profession. I wanted to understand why people think and behave as they do. The study of human behaviour and personality, as revealed in the course of therapy and in the psychoanalytic literature, has helped me learn a good deal about individuals and groups and the interactions between them. At a personal level it has helped me to understand myself better. I have not always liked what I discovered, but have recognized how much my choice was determined by my early experiences in my parental home, at school and as a young child in Nazi Germany.

At that time Jewishness represented the despised, weak, unheroic, unattractive and unacceptable side of myself, which for a time was disowned and split off. Some of the unconscious motivation for choosing psychotherapy as a profession was the wish to reconcile and re-integrate this split-off self with the rest of me. The strong identification with my father created another split between the masculine and feminine in myself, but in my psychotherapy I have tried to bring masculine and feminine together and have tried to heal the split between the internal mother and father, and the thinking and feeling functions of both of them.

But greater self-knowledge was only one of my motives. It was equally important to understand the irrational and destructive behaviour of individuals in groups.

I have learned about the dangers of splitting, projecting, denial, scapegoating, labelling, stereotyping and other dangerous defences. Understanding helps, but it has not as yet resulted in any change of behaviour in the majority of mankind. The threat of war and even of annihilation is not diminished. In that sense I feel disillusioned.

References

Casement, P. (1985) *On Learning from the Patient*, London: Tavistock.
Freud, S. (1927/1961) 'The future of an illusion' in *The Standard Edition of the Complete Works of Sigmund Freud*, edited by James Strachey, 21: 3–56, London: The Hogarth Press.
Herzberg, A. (1945) *Active Psychotherapy*, London: Research Books.

Chapter four

The blessing and the curse of empathy

Brian Thorne

Why did I become a psychotherapist?

Whenever I think back to my childhood I find my eyes filling with tears. This is not because my early days were particularly unhappy. The tears are of nostalgia for a time of extraordinary intimacy and intensity. I grew up during the Second World War (I was 2½ years old when war broke out) and my earliest memories are of scenes played out against a background of anxiety and uncertainty. I remember vividly the horror of the first major air-raid on the city of Bristol in 1940 when my parents and I (I was an only child) were trapped for half the night in the house of my paternal grandmother, on the far side of the city many miles from our home. I recall the long walk back through shattered streets still ablaze and the arrival at the pile of masonry which, only hours before, had been the home of my mother's parents. I still remember my mother's scream and the comforting neighbour with the brandy bottle who assured her that my grandparents were safe and that their newly erected air-raid shelter had stood the vital test.

In such a world and at such a time there was no room for pretence or superficiality. We all lived with the possibility of sudden death. On another occasion, for example, my mother and I missed a bus in the city only to learn that minutes later the vehicle had been destroyed in a freak afternoon air-raid. At school, lessons were often interrupted by the chilling sound of the sirens announcing the German Luftwaffe and we would be herded into long and dank concrete shelters in the playground. It was in this environment that I learned from a very early age to live with the deepest human emotions of love and fear and to witness the extreme limits of human courage and vulnerability, of hope and despair.

The feelings of nostalgia are strongest when I recall my friends of those days. In an important way the fact that I had no brothers or sisters made me more available to others. I was constantly invited into other children's houses and I suppose I grew accustomed to adapting myself to different life-styles and to changing emotional patterns. Children whose fathers were away from home in the Services would often talk of their anxiety (sometimes tragically justified by events) and their mothers, too, would speak openly to me of their fears and loneliness. As I write now I realize how much I loved them all and how very loved I felt not only in my own home but in the whole neighbourhood. Looking back on it I think it would be fair to say that I grew up in a remarkably therapeutic community which was somehow learning to live creatively with the cruel vagaries of war.

I realized during my primary school days that I had an ability which seemed unusual and which was both a blessing and a curse. Today I would call it the capacity to empathize. At that time I simply experienced, with alarming frequency, the powerful sensation of knowing what it felt like to be in someone else's skin. In some ways this gave me exquisite satisfaction for it enabled me to come close to others (especially my own contemporaries) and to share a warmth of companionship which I know now was exceptional. Often, however, it would lead me into very painful situations where I felt helpless. The worst example of this was with a spinster teacher at my infants' school whom I knew to be desperately unhappy and who was ragged unmercifully by the other children. With sixty in a class there was little I could do to influence the environment and I would sit in misery as I watched this poor woman's gradual disintegration. She eventually put her head in the gas oven one summer's morning. I have never forgotten her and the occasion of her death was perhaps the first time I experienced a powerful resentment about my own nature. Then and often since I have raged against my own empathic ability and insightfulness. I have wanted to be preserved from the burden of my own understanding and have even felt moments of hatred for those who suffer and whose sufferings are so obvious to me but not apparently to others.

The spiritual event which undoubtedly determined the direction of my life was also in some ways the outcome of this empathic ability. I have described it at length elsewhere (Thorne 1987a) but, in essence, it was the almost unbearable experience of glimpsing the nature of the Passion and Crucifixion of Christ. This happened on Good Friday afternoon in 1946 and left me, after what seemed like hours of solitary weeping, exhausted and at peace. There is no doubt, I believe, that from that moment my journey towards becoming a psychotherapist was inevitable.

I was 28 before the idea took final shape. During the intervening years I had won a scholarship to a famous boys' public school (which provided yet another context of intensity and intimacy), served as a National Service Officer in Cyprus (where, again, sudden death was always a possibility), gone to Cambridge to read languages, trained to be a teacher in my own home city and taken my first post as a school-master in a public school on the south coast.

I am not, I believe, a natural linguist but it gives me great pleasure to speak German, French, and a smattering of other European languages. The decision to specialize in German (taken when I was 12) was clearly fired by my war-time experiences and my first trip abroad at the age of 16 was to Hamburg to stay with a German family where the father had died at the Russian front. Looking back on it, this, too, was a pivotal experience. Speaking a different language to my own enabled me to find parts of myself which had previously lain dormant and I drew on such a well of emotion that I wonder now how my new German friends coped with me. German and French literature, too, touched me deeply. In many ways the study of literature is a training in empathy and a profound challenge to the imagination. During my time both as a student and as a teacher I realize that I lived in a world which was densely populated by novelists and poets and by the fictitious characters of their creation. In such company it was impossible to feel parochial.

The same is true of my experience of the Church. Anglican by denomination and catholic in spirit, I have from an early age known something of the universality of the Church and of its existence outside time and space. I have talked with saints and heard angel choirs. In all this I was much encouraged by a series of remarkable priests whose influence on me was profound. Gerard Irvine, poet, writer, man of letters and the friend of writers and artists, befriended me when I was 10 years old and treated me as an equal. Stuart Tayler, former naval officer, skilled confessor and passionate lover of Italy, invited me to be his travelling companion when I was 17 and for the next twenty-five years opened up the treasures of European culture to me while showing me that the disciplined life and having fun are not incompatible. Hugh Montefiore, later Bishop of Birmingham, revealed to me while I was at Cambridge the fascination of theology and the beauty of intellectual and spiritual tolerance. Richard Eyre, now Dean of Exeter, allowed me to be his companion at the altar and in the daily offices of the Church as we both struggled to make sense of our unlikely presences in the daily turmoil of the life of a public school at a time of educational change. All these men, through their friendship and their generosity of spirit, enabled me to live in depth and to experience myself as intelligent, insightful and loving.

It was perhaps not surprising that my experience as a schoolmaster provided the final impetus for my pilgrimage towards the therapeutic profession. A boarding school is full of wounded souls, many of them suffering from feelings of rejection or suppressed rage. It was not long before I was working well into the night as a constant stream of adolescents came to my door to pour out their misery or to seek support in their psychological pain. In 1965 one such young man was taxing me beyond the limits of my competence and energy and although by now I had gained much in confidence through contact with local psychiatrists and through seminars at the Tavistock Institute, I knew I was out of my depth. It was about this time that I came to hear of George Lyward, the remarkable therapist who had established Finchden Manor in Tenterden, Kent, as a therapeutic refuge for badly disturbed young men, many of whom were products of public schools. I knew little of the nature of Lyward's work but was increasingly awed by what I heard of its effectiveness and power. One night, in desperation, I telephoned him and told him something of myself and of my predicament with my unhappy student who seemed by now on the verge of psychosis. Within forty-eight hours I was sitting in Lyward's study at Finchden and my life's work for the next twenty years was determined.

George Lyward was a genius and this is not the place to attempt a description of what he achieved or of the methods he employed. For me his importance lies in the way he related to me that day and in the following years until his death in 1973. Within minutes, it seemed, I felt recognized, valued, and seen through. This last aspect of the encounter was both disturbing and liberating. I felt totally exposed and yet, because there was no point in pretending, I was able to relax into being myself. This sense of my own authenticity was crucial for what followed because otherwise it was unlikely that I could have taken Lyward seriously. I should simply have assumed that his judgement was based on his imperfect knowledge of me or on my own successful play-acting. In the event, Lyward informed me that I was a therapist already and that clearly only I could see my client through the next part of his journey. He then said many helpful things about adolescence, allowed me to stay while he talked at length with several of his own young residents, served delicious Lapsang tea in beautiful china cups and asked me to come again when I wanted to do so.

After that meeting with Lyward I knew that my days as a teacher were numbered. There were more visits to Finchden, a deepening of many of the relationships I had with both boys and colleagues in the school, the falling in love with the woman who is still my wife and, finally, acceptance at one of the first counsellor training courses to be established in a university in Britain. In the autumn of 1967 I entered full-time study at the Guidance Unit of Reading University and began my training as a client-centred counsellor.

I have no doubt that at that stage I had many fantasies about the work of a therapist. In the first place, I did not envisage myself ever leaving the education scene. I suppose I thought of the therapist as a kind of teacher/priest. Certainly my image was of a somewhat patriarchal figure who would have wisdom to impart as a result of his training and experience. Second, I was fascinated by the mystery surrounding therapeutic encounters and I believe I was excited by the prospect of sharing many secrets and exercising a subtle power on the inner lives of others. I do not think I underestimated the hard work which would be involved. George Lyward maintained that he had been tired for most of his life and the depth of his dedication to the young men at Finchden left me in no doubt that the life of a therapist was a tough and demanding one. There were times when I suspected that I could not summon up such commitment and, having only recently married, I was also worried about the effect on my wife of this life of intimate relationships upon which I was now embarking. I feared that I might pay a high price for such 'promiscuity' and that my wife might pay an even higher one.

Some of my friends at that time made it clear to me that they were greatly alarmed at my apparent foolhardiness in subjecting a recent marriage to such a premature trial. There were those, too, who were opposed to my plans for a quite different reason. One of my own sixth form pupils voiced clearly what others only hinted at. 'You're being a traitor to your vocation. You're a born teacher: how can you go off to become some kind of glorified social worker?' For me, this was without question the greatest dilemma. I loved teaching and the world of the intellect. What is more I knew I was a good teacher and could look forward to a successful career in education. There were many times when it seemed totally absurd to be leaving something I loved so much. So acute was the dilemma that I hedged my bets. I asked for – and was granted – leave of absence from my school for a year. If things did not work out I could return and resume teaching German and French as if my aberration had never occurred. When I eventually left for Reading University in the autumn of 1967 there was no marked sense of excitement or pleasure. In many ways I was going because it seemed I had to go. For financial reasons (I was once more on a student grant) my wife remained behind in our flat and continued to work in the school. I remember experiencing almost intolerable conflict as I waved good-bye. It seemed that I was leaving behind all that I valued most and that I was doing so because of some inner drive which in my heart I still could not fully trust. This sense of almost being pulled screaming towards the meaning of my life comes back and haunts me still today. When I am exhausted or am caught in an impossibly demanding therapeutic relationship, I can literally scream or shout with resentment and anger. At such times I have little sense of having chosen my life, and come within an ace of rejecting a God whose love seems to have trapped me into a moral compulsion which fills me with loathing.

How did I become a psychotherapist?

As a student at Cambridge I had stumbled on the work of Carl Jung as a result of studying the novels of Hermann Hesse for the second part of the Modern Languages Tripos. I was fascinated by Jung's writing and the wide sweep of his conceptual map delighted me. His essentially hopeful view of the human personality came as a refreshing antidote to what I already knew of the Freudian perception of reality and I was particularly enthralled by the Jungian notion of individuation and of the encounter with the Self. It was also a relief to me to discover so eminent a therapist who clearly placed high emphasis on the spiritual dimension in human nature.

One of my most vivid memories of Cambridge is of a glorious summer afternoon in 1961 after I had finished my final examinations and was luxuriating in a period of well-earned idleness. I recall lying on the grassy bank beside the river Cam caught up in the compelling urgency and fascination of Jung's *The Undiscovered Self* and breaking off only to attend evensong at King's College Chapel, sung with the exquisite perfection which can only be attained by a choir of rare distinction. The memory for me is of integration. I can still dimly recall the sense of physical well-being and the delicious heat of the summer sun accompanied by the gentle sound of flowing water. Jung's book spoke of dark forces and the terror of possible annihilation while insisting on the wonder of the human psyche and its potential for transformation. The music of King's spoke of a transcendence and a glory which took the breath away. And, then, at the end of the day there were my friends with whom to drink and talk far into the night. This was heaven.

Reading University Guidance Unit had none of the romantic and powerfully evocative atmosphere of Cambridge in mid-summer and looking back on it, I believe I began my formal training determined not to be swept into what I suspected could become a psychological ghetto. I remember vowing to myself that I would adopt a critical stance to everything I was taught and that nothing would prevent me from continuing to read novels and poetry or from dabbling in the latest theological issues. In short, I was keen to integrate my training into my life and to avoid being taken over by it. In the event, two significant events occurred in the first months which ensured that no such take-over could happen: my mother died after being in poor health for some time and one of the sixth-form pupils, with whom I had been much involved in the school, committed suicide by hurling himself from the school tower. In the light of such powerful events it was unlikely that the therapist-in-training would be taken over by new learnings obtained in the lecture room or even in personal supervision sessions. I was too preoccupied incorporating into my life the impact of two such momentous occurrences. I also became aware at this time of the stabilizing influence of my theological understandings and of the power of the rituals and offices of the Church to sustain me. I found myself, too, drawn back repeatedly to Jung's writings while I attempted to struggle with dark feelings of despair and impotent rage as my grief came to the surface and demanded attention. For me at this time Jung was a never-failing repository of hope primarily because he seemed never to evade or deny the negative and yet did not succumb to the dark.

During my first term at Reading, a second Carl edged quietly into my life almost without my being aware that he had slipped in. I shall never know if he would have found such easy access if Christ and Jung had not preceded him into the inner sanctuary of my being. As it was, once I acknowledged his presence, I realized that I had somehow discovered the ideal companion for this phase of my life on which I was now irretrievably embarked. I had, of course, seen Carl Rogers' name on the book-lists which had been sent me before I went to Reading and I had probably read that Bruce Shertzer, my principal trainer from Purdue University in Indiana, was a client-centred practitioner, much influenced by Rogers. It was only gradually, however, that it fully dawned on me that I was being trained as a client-centred therapist and that Carl Rogers was to be the principal source of learning for my new professional identity. By the time I had fully grasped this fact I knew that it was a situation with which I felt wholly content. As I read Rogers' books with increasing enthusiasm I realized that I was not being asked to take on board a whole new perception of reality or a complex theory of human personality. I was not even being required to change my basic way of being with those who sought my help. Instead, I found in Rogers someone who seemed to esteem the validity of my own experience and who gave names to attitudes and activities which I had falteringly attempted to embody for many years. And so it was that Carl Rogers became for me, not the new guru or source of all wisdom for the aspiring therapist, but a gentle companion who spoke of unconditional positive regard, empathy and genuineness and thus gave shape to what, for me, had previously been an almost instinctive and somewhat incoherent response to others in need.

I have spoken above of my early recognition of my capacity to empathize. When I went to Reading I had been a naturally empathic person for as long as I could remember. What was surprising was to discover that this was by no means the case for many of my fellow-trainees. Even more important was the discovery that most people do not expect to be understood and that it is therefore important to let them know when you are actually empathizing accurately. I realized that although I had been understanding others for years I had not always had the wit to let them know that this was the case: the empathic response had been left incomplete because unexpressed. Rogers' insistence on the quality of unconditional positive regard or non-possessive warmth showed me that, in this respect too, I had always attempted to cultivate just such an attitude towards others. In my grieving, however, I quickly came up against many guilt feelings (especially about the young man who had committed suicide) and realized with the help both of Rogers' writings and of Bruce Shertzer's gentle supervision that I often fell dismally short when it came to offering myself such regard and acceptance. There could hardly have been a more ideal moment for remedying this deficiency and the working-through of my grief was greatly aided by the movement towards self-acceptance which took place in the months immediately after the two deaths.

In Christian terms it would be possible to describe what happened as my growing ability to internalize God's love and forgiveness whereas previously I had been largely dependent on the sacrament of penance in order to feel acceptable and valuable in my own eyes. It is perhaps a tribute, however, to the basic healthiness of my theology that the movement towards self-accept-ance proceeded with commendable speed once Carl Rogers' influence had permeated my thinking and feeling. Often since I have discovered that, for other Christians reared in a more evangelical or judgemental tradition, the encounter with Rogers' work has meant an upheaval of major proportions which not infrequently results either in a rejection of Rogers or of Christianity. It is significant that for me my training as a client-centred practitioner simply deepened and extended my Christian understanding. Carl Jung had shown me that it was wholly reasonable to believe in God and to acknowledge the spiritual dimension in human beings. Carl Rogers showed me what it might mean to take the second great commandment seriously and to attempt to love my neighbour as myself.

Rogers' third core condition for therapeutic movement, genuineness or congruence, also resonated with my previous belief structure and with my own way of being. I had long since valued my uniqueness and had revelled in my own individualism. I was sceptical of experts and had learned to trust my own thoughts and perceptions. Furthermore, I had never seen much point in pretending to be someone I was not. This is not to say that I had always found it easy to resist group pressures or to rise above conventional norms. Often I was as frightened and inhibited as anyone else, but it was clear to me that I did not wish to be so. Rogers' insistence therefore on the importance of the therapist's own thoughts and feelings and on his willingness when appropriate to express these was both challenging and confirming of what I truly wished to do and to be for my clients. Once again, Rogers was, in a sense, telling me nothing new. He was giving me the courage and the clarity to develop my own way of being in the knowledge that to do so would be to the benefit of my future clients.

The longer my formal training went on the more clearly I recognized that I was not learning to become a patriarchal figure with wisdom to impart. What is more it was becoming increasingly evident to me that I no longer wished to be such a figure – if, indeed, I had ever done so. Weighty theories about personality development and complex maps of the unconscious have their fascination, but they tend to make those who have studied them feel important and erudite. In the behavioural tradition, too, the acquisition of techniques and the development of methodologies for changing overt behaviour can give the therapist a sense of power and competence which, for me, I feel, would not have been healthy. I knew only too well that I was a powerful person and anything which could have added to my sense of power might well have been to the detriment of my growth as a therapist. I was glad to be challenged by the simple but totally demanding task of becoming more empathic, more accepting and more in touch with myself.

Bruce Shertzer offered a compelling model of the client-centred practitioner. He lectured conscientiously and with clarity but it was in his one-to-one relationships and in small groups that he embodied most strikingly the qualities which characterized the client-centred therapist. He listened; he valued those with whom he spoke and made them feel uniquely recognized; he went to infinite pains to make sure he understood and he did not hesitate to offer his own thoughts and feelings when he believed these would be helpful. In his presence it was possible to relax into learning and to feel not pressure, but the space in which to feel and to think. In personal development groups he provided security and absolute attentiveness but never took anything away from trainees by dominating the group or intruding with inappropriate exercises or information. None of this is to deny the value of the more formal opportunities which we were afforded to develop our counselling skills and attitudes through intensive role play and other experiential workshops. Nor, again, would I wish to undervalue the hours spent in the library and the challenge of writing essays to convey my understanding of therapeutic process and developmental psychology. In the last analysis, however, I know that the deepest learning came from my contact with a therapist who embodied the value system which he sought to impart in the lecture theatre and the seminar room.

My fellow students were also of crucial significance to me. They allowed me to meet them as persons and together we shared our strengths and weaknesses. Some of them became important friends during this period and showed me great kindness and understanding, for example, when my mother died. Much of the training took place in small groups and without this level of openness and responsiveness it is difficult to imagine what would have happened. As it was, such times were often deeply involving and certainly the hours spent with fellow trainees in pubs and student rooms after the formal training sessions were a rich source of further learning and stimulus. I benefited enormously, I now realize, from being a member of a course where almost all the participants were resident in the same university town and were therefore available to each other almost twenty-four hours a day.

The sense of openness and responsiveness within the training group as a whole was particularly important when it came to the counselling practicum. We were strongly encouraged to make tape-recordings of our sessions with our clients and these were a primary resource in discussions with our personal supervisors. Of equal importance, however, was the opportunity to present a taped interaction to a whole group of fellow trainees and to receive feedback from them. This discipline was, for me, an invaluable source of learning and its effectiveness would have been much reduced if there had not been a willingness to reveal weaknesses and inadequacies on the part of all the members of the training group.

It says much for the flexibility of the course that in my final term I was permitted to spend an intensive fortnight at Finchden Manor. For me this provided the ideal opportunity for reflection and for consolidating my learning in an environment where there was no possibility of pretence or self-deception. George Lyward, his staff and the boys of Finchden were my real examiners and it was fitting that the man who had first expressed his confidence in me as a therapist was able at this stage to mark my progress and also gently to tease me if it seemed to him that I was in danger of losing myself in the role. Looking back on the whole training experience I am aware that without it I could not have become a therapist and yet at the same time I knew that the academic study, the formal training sessions, the increasing knowledge of therapeutic process and human development would all have been in vain if it had not been for the quality of the people who were my trainers and fellow students and for the depth of relationship which was offered to me. I suspect, too, that my mother's death, the suicide of my sixth-form pupil and the challenges of the early days of married life, all contributed in a major fashion to my understanding of myself and to my ability to assist those very first 'official' clients who were trusting enough to put themselves in the hands of a somewhat callow apprentice.

When did I become a psychotherapist?

It is seldom in my professional career that I have referred to myself as a psychotherapist. In the person-centred tradition, the word has about it a certain mystique which is alien to an approach which strives to establish an egalitarian relationship with clients and to eschew the role of the expert. Most of the time, then, I have been content to call myself a counsellor but for me this word implies a professional practitioner with substantial training and experience who enjoys a high level of self-knowledge which he or she brings to therapeutic relationships. When did I become such a person and experience the reality of a confident professional identity? Certainly it was not on the day that I received my diploma from the University of Reading, important as that day was. The movement towards such an identity was more complex and concerned with profounder issues than that of receiving legitimization from an academic institution.

In the eyes of many of my former colleagues and certainly as far as my immediate family was concerned I became a counsellor when I completed my formal training and obtained my first post in a counselling service. For some of the pupils at the school where I had taught I suspect that I was a therapist long before I embarked on formal training. For me, however, the transition from schoolteacher to counsellor was a lengthy one. The first day I entered my counsellor's consulting room I felt fraudulent and sad. I longed to be back in the classroom with a syllabus to teach and with the stimulus of a responsive and appreciative group. I felt almost trapped by the one-to-one relationship and frightened by the unpredictability of what the client might bring. I felt hopelessly ill-equipped and what a few weeks previously had passed for a sound and creative training experience now seemed in retrospect to be inadequate and superficial. My new colleagues were considerate and helpful but their very competence added to my sense of ineptitude.

The uncomfortableness with my new professional identity persisted for some weeks during which time I never ceased to be amazed by the way in which clients seemed to be able to trust me and to behave towards me as if I were a *real* therapist. Much of the time, however, I felt as if I were taking part in a dramatic enactment and that soon the curtain would come down and I should be able to return to my familiar environment and resume my teaching of French literature. I believe now that I was grieving for my past identity and that throughout these opening weeks I was mildly depressed. I remember, too, that I was physically ill for a week or so (something that had not happened for years) and that during this illness I seriously wondered if I should resign before I was irrevocably trapped in what appeared to be a somewhat elaborate charade.

Shortly after this illness two clients appeared who rapidly jerked me out of my transition state. Both were young women and they could not have been more dissimilar in their response to me. The first treated me with cold disdain and as good as challenged me to sort out her problems in half-an-hour. In her presence I felt a rising anger which, after fifteen minutes, I could no longer contain. I shouted at her to get out of my room and she left with an arrogant toss of her head while I collapsed on a colleague in the next room, feeling that my counselling career was possibly already at an end. The same afternoon, however, another girl presented herself and revealed within minutes an inner desolation of such intensity that I found myself responding at a level which I had not previously experienced. It was as if my own fear – and ignorance of the young female psyche – evaporated in the presence of her desperation. I was awed, too, by her trust in me and by her preparedness to reveal her total vulnerability. For the first time I experienced what I have come to recognize as an overwhelming surge of loving commitment. What is more, her weakness put me in touch with my own strength. For the first time I felt authentic in my therapeutic role and knew that I could be a faithful companion to my client no matter how dark her world and unpredictable her journey.

These two young women in their different ways forced me to own my new identity. The first revealed to me my inadequacy in the face of her contempt but at the same time showed me that I cared deeply about being a therapist, that I could not bear her scorn. The second compelled me to be real and not to deny the extent of my resources as a person and as a professional. She affirmed me in a way which no amount of praise or encouragement from colleagues or success with less demanding clients could have done. She challenged me to the depth of my being and I found myself not only responding to the challenge but doing so immediately and confidently. In the event, our relationship was to take us into areas of fear and confusion which threatened her sanity and constantly made me question my own competence. But her commitment to me and mine to her never wavered. She showed me that I had the will and the courage to stay with a process come what may and it was this assurance above all others that I needed. When, several months later, she began to smile and to discern a future for herself I knew that my apprenticeship was over. I was a therapist whether I liked it or not and much of the time now I found myself rather liking it.

What sustains me as a psychotherapist?

I have never attempted to deny to myself or to others the arduous nature of a therapist's work. The intense concentration required in therapeutic relationships, the anxiety generated by close involvement with those who are often highly self-destructive, the relentless pressure of a seemingly endless stream of clients – all these can induce exhaustion and a sense of powerlessness in the face of implacable forces. What is more, there is often the experience of battling against formidable odds because of family or societal pressures which constantly threaten to undermine the client's progress in therapy or seem to reduce the therapeutic relationship to little more than an ineffective palliative administered once or twice a week. It is gruelling and demanding work and the therapist who denies this is mendacious, deluded or incompetent.

There are certain obvious factors which have contributed to my honourable survival for twenty years in the profession. In the first place, I have never had the misfortune to work on my own. Both in educational institutions and in private practice I have always been a member of a team and have enjoyed the immediate support and stimulus of other therapists working alongside me. Second, I have always had easy and ready access to medical and psychiatric resources and this has relieved me of the intolerable burden of coping unsupported with clients who are on the verge of psychosis or seem to have lost the capacity to hold their lives together in the practical world of day-to-day existence. Third, I have a regular and valued supervision relationship where I can talk through those aspects of my work (or of my own life) which are proving particularly difficult or stressful. Fourth, I have a wife and family who are astonishingly supportive of my curious mode of earning a living and even seem to take some pride and interest in my work.

Clearly this network of human support forms the context of much of my professional life but it is not in itself sufficient to explain why I continue to feel not simply sustained but positively nourished by my work as a therapist. The deeper reasons for this happy state of affairs lie in the nature of the relationships I form with my clients. It is my conviction, as I have argued earlier, that the work of the therapist is not essentially concerned with dispensing wisdom or expertise or even with the deploying of skills. It is more to do with embodying values consistently no matter how great the client's confusion, resistance or even hostility. For me this means not only that I attempt to demonstrate unambiguously the unique value which I place on an individual life but also my conviction that in the last analysis it is love with understanding which heals. In a sense, therefore, my work as a therapist, although it is hard, demanding and exhausting is easy because it gives me the permission and the constant obligation to be the person I truly wish to be. Obviously, I do not always succeed in embodying such values or in being this person, but the very fact that I construe my work in this way means that many of the relationships which I form in the process of being a therapist are a source of the profoundest satisfaction. In the first place, I am enabled to love not in some wishy-washy generalized way, but in a focused manner which is devoid of possessiveness and refuses to be easily side-tracked. What is more, I am challenged to put whatever intellectual abilities I possess at the service of my loving. In short, every therapeutic relationship offers me the possibility of living in as integrated a way as possible. Second, I am not infrequently on the receiving end of my client's loving. It is, I believe, one of the therapist's rare privileges to be loved by those who in the past have often experienced their loving as destructive or damaging. I say a privilege because for such a person to discover that their loving can be creative and positive is often to unleash a flood of energy which can irradiate the therapist and become a source of renewal and refreshment for him. There is all the difference in the world between this kind of client loving which is life-enhancing, and the desperate dependency which is often the mark of the client who has not yet been able to receive the therapist's understanding and acceptance. What is more, the client's discovery that he or she can enter deeply into a relationship without being destructive not only makes it possible for the therapist to receive love but also provides him with the surest evidence of his client's development.

One of the chief advantages of working with a predominantly youthful clientele (as I do in my university setting) is the rapidity with which such development often takes place. I know that I possess qualities of patience and perseverance which enable me to commit myself to clients for years if necessary, but I am equally aware that I would soon be worn down if *all* my clients needed such long-term attention. My brief counselling encounters, lasting perhaps two or three months, do much to remind me of the remarkable capacity of many human beings to discover their own resources and strengths once they have been offered a modicum of acceptance and understanding. I believe that my long-term clients owe much to these others who continually delight me by their ability to move forward rapidly and confidently and who therefore provide me with constant proof that therapy 'works'.

With those whose journey is more arduous and complex it is not always so easy to hang on to my faith in the process and it is in these cases that my religious faith becomes of such cardinal importance. With the short-term client it is comparatively easy to imagine that I have been the chief facilitator of the client's growth and progress. With those who are more damaged, however, the experience is often one of frustration, stuckness and even of powerlessness. It is in such relationships that it becomes so blindingly obvious that I am not a powerful magician who can work miracles by offering acceptance, genuineness and empathy. I am learning increasingly to accept my stuckness and powerlessness so that I can get somewhere near the humility which is necessary if I am to become a channel for a power greater than my own. If I can let go of anxiety and simply relax, I experience what I can only describe as a new resource which becomes available to my client and to me. To non-religious readers this may sound strange, but to those familiar with the disciplines of prayer and worship, it will not be difficult to see the process as akin to that of resting in the presence of God. Such a resting is in no sense a giving up. It is rather a willingness to be open to forces greater than oneself and a readiness to co-operate with them. In Christian terms, it is best expressed as being open to the Holy Spirit or being a willing participant in the operation of grace. Interestingly enough, my experience of opening myself in this way does not seem to be dependent on the spiritual or religious understanding of my client. On the other hand, where the client is a fellow Christian and the process can be acknowledged and openly shared, the developments can be all the more surprising and dramatic (Thorne, 1987b).

It will now be clear that for me the practice of psychotherapy is serving my own needs and desires in fundamental ways. It allows me to love and to be loved and encourages me to develop my relationship with God by continually opening myself to His presence. Emotionally and spiritually I am nourished and challenged every day. As I grow older I discover that I yearn for more solitude although sometimes it feels like a kind of greediness to have more of God and less of His creatures! If I can learn to trust this feeling then it seems likely that my activities as a therapist may diminish in the years ahead and I can well imagine that by retirement age the day-to-day conduct of my life may be looking very different. Perhaps, too, I will have learned to do without the prestige, the respect, and the reasonably generous salary which my work as a therapist has brought me and which have done much to bolster my failing ego when the pressures have seemed too overwhelming.

I cannot conclude this section without referring once more to that part of me which profoundly hates being a therapist at all. There are times when I long to be blissfully unaware, shallow, and pleasure seeking. I could easily succumb at such moments to an almost anarchic urge to lose myself in wine, women, and self-indulgence. I am heartily sick of the sufferings of others and of the God who tells me to recognize Him in them. It is then that my long-suffering family comes to my rescue. They allow me to rage, usually unjustifiably, at them and not to feel too guilty afterwards and they even listen to my complex anecdotes (often drawn from Army life) which always reduce me, if not them, to uncontrollable mirth and a state of imminent apoplexy. Without such an arena where I can froth with rage and dissolve in laughter I do not know what would have become of me.

Implications for other therapists

I am doubtful about the usefulness of my experience to other therapists because I am aware of its idiosyncratic nature. Writing about myself in this way has revealed to me that, viewed from the outside, my life may appear to have about it a pattern which would be the delight of many a career planner. My essentially empathic personality, fed by war-time experiences and buttressed by reasonable intelligence, might naturally be expected to find expression first in teaching and then in the therapeutic field. As an only child, too, it is perhaps not surprising that I have sought intimacy beyond the family and have ensured that I always have someone to love and from whom I can, in return, receive affection and esteem. All this in a sense is true, but it does not reach the heart of the matter.

When I first decided to become a teacher (on a summer's day in an Italian cathedral) and when later I decided to seek therapist training, I do not recall anything approaching an 'Eureka' experience. On the contrary, there was a sense of inevitability mingled with something akin to dread. I knew I had little choice if I was to obey the voice within me. In short, my work as a therapist has in a sense been an act of obedience. I suppose this realization may in itself be of value to others insofar as it suggests that the overt desire or ambition to be a therapist may be a somewhat treacherous motivation. Certainly over the years I have found myself being less than enthusiastic about the aspirations of some who have voiced their intention to me of becoming therapists. It has seemed that in some cases there has been a highly romantic and unrealistic view of the therapist's life whereas in others there has been a scarcely concealed lust for power.

To those who have made it into the profession I would warn against neglect of self. I know how often I have been near the edge of self-sacrificial stupidity and have been pulled back at the eleventh hour by the kindly or stern warnings of colleagues, friends or spouse. I realize furthermore how vital such people are to me in the preservation of my own well-being. Heaven preserve me from the life of solitary private practice where the need to earn money means the rapid disappearance of a social life and the end of friendships and family relationships.

Perhaps the chief insight for me from this autobiographical reminiscence has been the way in which I have somehow incorporated therapy into the overall understanding and conduct of my life. The important people for me in the therapeutic world, Lyward, Shertzer, Rogers, have impressed me primarily as human beings rather than as theoreticians or therapists. Their therapy was an extension of their personalities or an expression of the values which permeated their lives. I have met therapists who seem somehow to have stuck their therapeutic ideas and practice on to a personality which then lives in great discomfort with such an accretion. Strangely enough such people seem to talk endlessly about therapy and leave me with grave doubts about their effectiveness. I have recorded how, during my period of formal training, I consciously refused to be sucked into a psychological 'Weltanschauung' and stubbornly held on to my literary and theological slants on reality. It is, I believe, dangerous when a psychological understanding of life and a therapeutic approach based on it begin to take the place of religion or of a fervently held philosophical or political credo. The therapist who falls into this trap is in serious trouble when clients fail to behave appropriately or reject what is on offer for he is likely to feel undermined and to have his whole identity threatened. This is even more painful if his identity is in any case a somewhat makeshift affair where therapeutic ideas and practice are an accretion rather than an extension of his personality.

Brian Thorne

Finally, I doubt if a therapist who is incapable of loving or of allowing himself to be loved can do much good. Therapeutic technicians may perform an effective service for robots or computers but they threaten to finish off human beings who already have little sense enough of belonging to the species. I could not know as I grew up in the dark days of the 1940s that I was receiving an ideal education for someone who was later to accompany those who were struggling with life and death issues and had often run out of hope. The therapist for whom life has not thrown down the gauntlet and compelled love to declare itself may have to follow Jung's guidance and go in search of a deeper reality:

> The man who would learn the human mind will gain almost nothing from experimental psychology. Far better for him to put away his academic gown, to say goodbye to his study, and to wander with human heart through the world. (Jung 1953: 71)

References

Jung, C. G. (1953) *Psychological Reflections* (an anthology of writings, edited by J. Jacobi), London: Routledge and Kegan Paul.
Thorne, B. J. (1987a) 'A Good Friday encounter: escaping from guilt in the Christian tradition', *Self and Society* 15(1): 4–11.
Thorne, B. J. (1987b) 'Beyond the core conditions', in W. Dryden (ed.) *Key Cases in Psychotherapy*, London: Croom Helm.

Chapter five

Chance and choices in becoming a therapist

P. Paul Heppner

About two years ago I was talking with a biology professor over dinner; he was curious about what it meant to be a therapist. I described various aspects of the work, what was rewarding for me, what was frustrating, etc. During the conversation he finally remarked, 'I can't imagine dealing with all of that emotional intensity, it must be a tremendous weight on you.' I reflected a moment; 'Yes, sometimes it is . . . and sometimes that is what makes it so rewarding.' At that particular point in time I was feeling physically tired and emotionally drained. I wondered what work was like for this biology professor who was 'only' involved in teaching and research. How pleasantly simple his life seemed from afar. Why did I become a therapist? Maybe I chose the wrong career.

The designated purpose of this chapter is to examine my process of becoming a psychotherapist. Such a retrospective analysis is difficult to do with much certainty of the causal events. What follows are my best guesses. I will detail a number of factors, most notably: (a) values, skills, and anxieties acquired during my childhood; (b) chance events; (c) models of therapists; (d) broad-based training; (e) mentors, colleagues, and support systems; and (f) ongoing training and learning experience.

By way of introduction I am currently a counselling psychologist at the University of Missouri-Columbia, teaching in the psychology department and a senior staff psychologist at the university's counselling service. I have been in this position ten years since obtaining a doctoral degree in counselling psychology (1979). My teaching responsibilities are focused primarily in the graduate training programme of counselling psychologists, which is a programme accredited by the American Psychological Association. I regularly teach courses in research methods, counselling research, and an advanced counselling practicum. At Counselling Services, I regularly conduct individual therapy, supervise and provide training for doctoral level interns.

My observations are organized by the five major questions or sections suggested by the editors: Why did I become a psychotherapist? How did I become a psychotherapist? When did I become a psychotherapist? What sustains me as a psychotherapist? What are the implications for others? These questions serve as the section titles of the chapter, followed by a short phrase indicative of the major theme of my response.

Why did I become a psychotherapist? Some hypotheses

It is literally impossible to identify with a great deal of certainty what caused me to become a psychotherapist. Many times I believe that I could very well have pursued several other careers, and probably been successful and happy. I do believe that several aspects of my early personal development *predisposed* me to be well suited for being a therapist; I will discuss these personal developments below. I have also included some details pertaining to my background to establish an historical context in time, social class, and training era, all of which I believe have affected my particular process of becoming a psychotherapist thus far. I also believe that chance events played a substantial role in my career choices, and I will detail these as well.

I was born in the post Second World War 'Baby Boom' era (1951) and raised in a blue-collar, German-Catholic family in North Dakota (rural Midwestern United States). I was the first-born child, with one brother, ten years younger. My father was a second generation American of Russian descent; his grandparents emigrated from Prussia to southern Minnesota and settled into a predominantly Mennonite community. This group established a reputation in that region for their industrious and resourceful work-style; these are adjectives that now describe my father and myself as well. My mother was German, and the victim of childhood polio.

The adults in my nuclear and extended family maintained a living primarily by working with their hands, in occupations such as farming, carpentry, electrical work, welding, or operating small businesses such as restaurants and liquor stores. My guess is they viewed their work as menial and lower status, while college-educated people had 'better' work and lives. As a child, I learned the skills associated with wood-working, farming, and other manual-labour jobs; I now use these skills in avocational ways (e.g. gardening) as ways of relaxing.

Psychologically, I always felt loved and cared for in the family; I cannot recall that this love was ever explicitly stated, but primarily shown through their actions, preparations, sacrifices, family interactions, and occasionally through touch. During my childhood, our family moved from one community to another, six or seven times, with perhaps four years being the longest residence in any one place. A predominant feeling for me when I was growing up was of being an outsider, and being different in some way (e.g. Catholic in a predominantly Protestant area). As a child, I sometimes felt embarrassed by my first name, Puncky, because it was different. (Because of a deep sense of gratitude for what a delivery-room nurse did during the childbirth process, my mother named me after the nurse's son.) These feelings of differentness influenced me to feel inferior in some global way, and subsequently to be cautious with peers as well as to try harder to be liked and accepted.

Probably what affected me most during my early childhood and adolescence was not the early work experiences, but rather the values instilled by my parents. My father was a young man trying to find a niche in life as the Great Depression of 1929 swept the United States; his sixth grade education left him ill-prepared to gain employment and 'make a decent living'. Those desolate Depression experiences left lasting memories and anxieties about the unpredictability and unknowns of the future on my father.

As a child I was often told by my father, 'Don't be like me, get an education; they can't ever take that away from you.' As a result, my academic performance was important to my parents, and often my father would reinforce me with money, so much for each letter grade. I entered grade school around the time that the Russians launched Sputnik, which meant that I and other 'Baby Boomer' children benefited from massive innovations within American education. My family also emphasized other values, reflected in well-worn family phrases such as 'make something of yourself; go out and get a good job' (achievement orientation), 'if you're going to do something, do it right' (compulsiveness), 'you have to treat people right, meet them half-way' (interpersonal sensitivity and fairness) and 'you've got to make up your own mind about this' (independence). In short, these values helped build a foundation that allowed me to obtain the necessary skills and experiences that later enabled me to pursue graduate training in counselling psychology.

During childhood and adolescence, my parents allowed me to pursue a wide range of sports (e.g. baseball, basketball, track, cross-country running, and hunting) and school activities (e.g. various clubs and science fairs). Sports, and particularly baseball, were my major interests in life. My boyhood hero was the switch-hitting, clean-cut, Mickey Mantle of the New York Yankees; my dream was to become a major league baseball player, for the Yankees of course. I had no thoughts at all about being a therapist, nor did I have any idea about the world of graduate education; the closest association I had to a therapist was probably the community priest. Most importantly, my parents encouraged and allowed me to be independent, making my own decisions and living with the consequences. Interpersonally, I remember always having friendships with a handful of close chums with whom I would do the typical boyhood activities (from pick-up baseball games to 'sampling' a neighbour's crab-apple tree).

Perhaps the most critical decision-making time in my choice of a career was during my undergraduate years. Prior to attending college, I had not thought much about a career, and entertained fantasies about being a pharmacist (chemist) or a high school teacher in mathematics or biology. I entered college in 1969 at the University of Minnesota-Morris (UMM), and soon became a participant in the ferment and rebellion on many college campuses associated with the Vietnam War and the Hippie generation. These experiences taught me to believe in the possibilities of change, and affirmed my liberal and humanitarian values as well as my general distrust of politicians and administrators. I started college with vague career goals associated with a major in mathematics. After one quarter of study (three months), the abstractness of numbers began to bore me and interpersonal relationships became more important to me. I enrolled in the course 'Introduction to Psychology', primarily because a friend had taken the course and had enjoyed it. I found myself pleasantly intrigued and stimulated; the following quarter I rather quickly changed my major to psychology based on minimal information. My parents did not really know what psychology was, and simply allowed me to follow my interests.

In reflecting on those undergraduate experiences, there were at least two significant events that turned me towards being a therapist. While I enjoyed learning the content of psychology, I had no idea how I might use such a major in a career. As a junior, I entered therapy with Dr Joseph Jesseph (a counselling psychologist at the university counselling centre) to discuss mostly intrapersonal difficulties. While the process of counselling was initially anxiety-provoking, I was also excited by learning more about myself and how I interacted with people. But most importantly, I came to admire Dr Jesseph. He appeared to be a rational, scholarly man who seemed kind, supportive, accepting, self-aware, comfortable, and enjoying the challenges of his work with people. While my father had some similar characteristics to Dr Jesseph (e.g. rational, kind, supportive), Dr Jesseph differed in some important ways, namely being more facile with his internal processes. I remember at the time perceiving Dr Jesseph as 'having it all together', and clearly idealized him as a role-model. I liked him, and felt he not only accepted me but respected me. In short, he was a man who presented an appealing male role-model for my personal life.

During this time I was well on my way to majoring in psychology (and almost sociology too), but I had no career plans whatsoever. This did not concern me much because such career indecision was not unusual during the early 1970s, as the emphasis was on learning *per se* (in the liberal arts tradition). During the course of counselling I became much more aware of and drawn to the work of a therapist. First, at that time it seemed to fit my global values of 'helping other people'. I am uncertain how this value developed in me; perhaps it was an outgrowth of my early Catholic training combined with the 1960s liberalism and emphasis on human growth. Second, counselling was an area that appealed to my curiosity about people at that time, and 'what made them tick' psychologically. I am certain that my curiosity about people in general was influenced by my interest in learning more about my own psychological dynamics.

The second major event was a sequel to the first. Having had a productive counselling experience, I enrolled in an introductory counselling course, with the goal of learning more about this area of psychology. The course was taught by Dr Jesseph, and structured in a Rogerian self-directed mode of learning. In essence, a new world began to open up for me – unconditional positive regard, reflection, helping skills, self-awareness, and peak experiences. I read Carl Rogers' book, *On Becoming a Person*, which had a profound impact on me. In an over-simplified way, it became much clearer to me that I wanted to be a therapist and to facilitate others' growth. Subsequently, I volunteered for human relations training and worked as a para-professional in the counselling centre in a student-run office, called 'Third Ear'. I found this para-professional experience of helping other students to be extremely rewarding, I think, because I liked the disclosure and intimacy as well as the challenge of providing the Rogerian conditions and helping others. After about a year of such volunteer experience, I yearned to learn more about this world of psychological dynamics and counselling.

I imagined in a general way that if I were a therapist, I would be like Dr Jesseph, and therapy would be an uplifting experience, emotional, intimate, and psychologically intense. I felt a sense of importance with this type of work and career. I did not perceive the work as being emotionally draining or taxing, nor could I imagine being bored or frightened by the work. In retrospect, I had almost no idea of what skills might be required to be effective with different clients, nor how long it might take to acquire those skills. I did not see any role for research in this career, nor was that attractive to me; I just wanted to work with and 'help people'! Within this bliss and idealization, my major doubts centred around whether I would get accepted into graduate school to be trained, and if accepted, whether I could perform adequately in the academic coursework. My fantasy was not only to obtain a doctorate, but most importantly to increase my awareness of myself and others, 'grow psychologically', and become almost totally congruent (in a Rogerian sense). In short, I had a very unrealistic picture of the counselling profession.

To conclude briefly, I was initially attracted to being a psychotherapist because of some chance events, like Dr Jesseph being a therapist at UMM during my time there. My selection of psychology as a major was made on minimal information, based mostly on curiosity and intrigue, and left me searching for a meaningful way to use psychology. I inherited and/or learned some personality characteristics that favourably predisposed me towards being a psychotherapist and professor, such as being resourceful, curious about people, introverted, and attentive to detail (compulsive). A number of seeds were planted in my familial and social background, which also allowed me to acquire the necessary academic skills, develop the confidence to act on my environment and achieve, appreciate individual differences, being different, and wanting to 'help others'. Attending UMM during the late 1960s and early 1970s provided a learning atmosphere that emphasized personal development and social responsibility. Most likely, I could have easily ended up pursuing several other careers within psychology, biology, or even wildlife management

(I enjoyed the outdoors, hunting, and learning about animal behaviour); other occupations were especially feasible had I entered college ten years later when the learning environment on college campuses was different to that of the 1970s.

How did I become a psychotherapist? Graduate training and life experiences

In the United States the most common way to become a therapist is to obtain formal, graduate level training. Thus, my first goal was to be admitted into a graduate programme; I harboured serious doubts that I would be admitted, and worried about not being admitted. Based on my positive counselling experiences as an undergraduate, I wanted to study in an environment that was humanistic, and particularly Rogerian. I decided (in retrospect, again on very little information) to pursue counselling psychology rather than clinical psychology because counselling psychology seemed more developmentally focused and less oriented around a medical disease model. I collected information about various graduate programmes in counselling psychology, and identified about ten programmes that looked like they would be educationally stimulating and offer opportunities for personal growth. I did not worry about the financial costs of the education, in part because I had always received educational grants, scholarships, and loans from the university, supplemented by working summers and various part-time jobs.

During the application process, another chance event occurred. One of my housemates invited me on a week-end trip to a camp in northern Minnesota. There I met a humanistically-oriented doctoral student at the University of Nebraska-Lincoln. I talked with him briefly, he strongly endorsed the Nebraska programme, so I quickly applied to that programme as well. As it turned out, I had relatively low GRE (Graduate Record Examination) scores; the only programme that accepted me for graduate work was Nebraska. Given my general humanistic impression of Nebraska, I decided to attend graduate school there. Of course, I was extremely surprised when I began graduate work to learn that the counselling programme at Nebraska had a strong behavioural orientation.

Despite my surprise at the theoretical orientation, my training at Nebraska was very good. (I will use training in a broad sense to include required and optional coursework, teaching and research assistantships, working with members of the faculty on a broad range of projects such as committees, co-teaching, research, and interactions with my peers.) In fact, after obtaining a master's degree in counselling, I re-applied to several counselling programmes for doctoral training; although I then received very attractive offers from several programmes (e.g. Minnesota), I decided to continue my graduate training at Nebraska and work with a faculty member, Dr David Dixon, who turned out to be a valuable mentor.

In essence, the formal coursework (about thirty courses) laid the foundation of my becoming a counselling psychologist. For example, the traditional learning courses helped me understand how clients might acquire new behaviours, while the developmental courses provided a framework for understanding critical developmental processes in general, and specifically clients' development with various family environments. I learned to think like a psychologist as well as a scientist. The behavioural and especially the cognitive-behavioural orientations became extremely useful theoretical models for me, which helped me to understand a wide range of human behaviour, even the impact of the Rogerian conditions in counselling. In short, the coursework in counselling (and psychology in general) opened a whole range of theoretical orientations, techniques, and ways of processing information about the counselling interchange between the client and counsellor (as well as understanding myself).

For me, the coursework was preparatory, like a basement foundation. The actual applied experiences of working with clients and receiving supervision added a substantial amount of information about clients in terms of knowledge of personality dynamics, assessment methods, intervention strategies, the therapeutic relationship, the counselling process, and evaluating counselling outcomes. In retrospect, it was not only having the applied experiences and supervision that was beneficial, but the broad diversity of applied experiences, such as working at three different university counselling centres, an adolescent training unit, an elementary school, a child care centre, a penal complex, Planned Parenthood, and a Veterans' Administration Hospital. These experiences provided a broad experiential knowledge base which helped me to understand the psychological aspects of behaviour at a deeper and more sophisticated level.

Essential components in becoming a therapist have been my experiences as a client and my own developmental experience as a human being. I sought individual counselling twice during graduate school, initially to discuss problems in adapting to graduate school (e.g. performance anxiety) and later with intrapersonal concerns about not feeling congruent. During graduate school I also acquired a wide range of information about psychological constructs and processes (e.g. performance standards, irrational beliefs, covert conditioning). In retrospect, this knowledge seemed then to enhance my awareness of my own internal cognitive and affective processes. Consequently, by observing and monitoring my own internal processes, I enhanced my understanding of human psychological dynamics. In addition, I learned a great deal about the therapeutic process by being a client or participant in various self-help groups (e.g. men's groups, human sexuality workshops, a therapy group), again closely examining my reactions and processes. My own therapeutic experiences not only taught me new ways of resolving internal conflict, but also made me more sensitive to the client role and issues pertaining to help-seeking.

Being a graduate student at a major university also opened up many new arenas for me personally and socially. I was initially quite shy as a student and would sort of 'tiptoe' through the halls. I initially believed that only extraordinary people went to graduate school, perhaps a reflection of my working-class social background. I was amazed and impressed that one of my peers had attended school in Peru, but later quite chagrined to learn he meant the small town of Peru, Nebraska! In short, my range of social experiences greatly expanded, which stimulated both my social and personal development.

I also married Mary Jean Soehren as I began graduate school, which over time not only taught me a great deal about human relationships, intimacy, and trust, but also provided an essential source of emotional and psychological support. Her support is different from familial support because she is more knowledgeable about the academic and therapy contexts, and thus she can be more empathetic, facilitative, and nurturing across different situations. In retrospect, this single but complex relationship has not only provided me with my best friend with whom to share life, but also stability and security to withstand the rigours of graduate school (and beyond).

Also during this time I examined a number of identity issues such as my own sexuality, a host of gender issues pertaining to masculinity/femininity, and my role as a helping professional. My mother died from breast cancer during my fourth year in graduate school, which introduced me to new life experiences, such as the grieving process and changing family dynamics when one parent dies. Only later did I realize that this first-hand knowledge would be very useful to me as a therapist understanding clients with aborted grief reactions. In short, examination of my personal experiences and development not only increased my understanding of various psychological issues (e.g. grief, performance-anxiety, male issues), but also I became more accepting of myself and stronger psychologically. In retrospect, this self-acceptance has been important in allowing me to maintain the Rogerian therapeutic conditions.

Finally, an important part of my learning to be a therapist came from the faculty at the University of Nebraska and Colorado State University (where I performed a ten-month internship to complete my doctoral training). Members of the faculty such as Drs David Dixon, Jack Corazzini, James Pinkney, Janet Krause, and others all provided supervision and modelled various aspects of being a therapist, such as accepting and responding to one's own personal reactions to clients, crisis management, handling ethical dilemmas, and believing in the therapeutic process. While supervision from these people increased my knowledge of therapy, their modelling provided very important information about how to manage the personal elements of being a therapist. In addition, they were intrigued by research and involved in professional organizations within the field of counselling psychology, and actively introduced me to and provided training in these new arenas. I began to recognize that being a skilled and knowledgeable therapist could involve much more than simply counselling clients. Annual conventions of the professional organizations could not only provide new information about various aspects of counselling, but also about larger professional issues affecting the field (e.g. licensure, accreditation of training programmes). Research provided another means of exploring and learning about specific aspects of therapy or training; actively examining the research literature revealed a wealth of new information.

Overall, the training in graduate school provided me with a solid knowledge base about research, psychology, and counselling psychology in particular. I actually enjoyed the life of a graduate student and learning about various aspects of counselling psychology; as a result I spent more time than was typical (six years) as a graduate student in an attempt to acquire more knowledge and skills. In retrospect, I have often thought that this 'extra training' has been worthwhile and a clear benefit to my career.

I did not feel that my graduate training contradicted any of my initial ideals about what a therapist is or does. Rather the training helped me to examine the oftentimes ambiguous or even mystical aspects of counselling with greater precision. The training offered me theoretical models to understand the therapeutic process, and simultaneously challenged me to be more specific in thinking and talking about therapy. In many ways, the training nourished my curiosity about the psychological processes of people, and stimulated me to learn more. While all of this sounds positive, I do not want to imply that my training was not also laced with the typical graduate student disappointments, anxieties, and conflicts (e.g. disappointment with course content, performance anxiety, peer competition). I can remember only one time in which I felt deeply insulted; one day in class a professor *read* to us, word for word, out of the assigned course text book for at least thirty minutes.

Probably what I did not receive from graduate school was an understanding of the developmental processes after adolescence. Conversely, plays, movies, novels, as well as my own and friends' life experiences, have greatly increased my understanding and appreciation of life's many experiences, trials, and tribulations. In particular, discussions with my friends have provided me with instances where I was able to peek through new 'windows' to learn more about life's experiences. These experiences have provided me with more depth and sensitivity in understanding the human experience and human development.

When did I become a psychotherapist? Completing the degree and still evolving

A major turning point for me was the ten-month internship at the university counselling centre at Colorado State University, which occurred during the last year of my formal doctoral training. Prior to this point, I felt an increasing amount of confidence in my abilities as a counsellor, but there was a void; something was missing. I had consistently received positive feedback about my counselling skills from supervisors, faculty members, friends, and clients. Although on a surface level, I believed in my capabilities as a therapist, at a deeper level I harboured some doubts. When I was really honest with myself, I would become aware of an ambiguous fear of being incompetent. I was afraid that the next supervisor would really scrutinize and find me out, that somehow I was hollow. I feared that I really did not know as much as I needed to, or should know. Maybe I had not read enough of the 'right books' yet, or maybe my supervisors had been too lax with me. In a way, I feared I was a 'fraud' (i.e. the impostor syndrome). Oddly enough, when I compared myself with faculty members and supervisors, I was not aware of feeling inadequate with these comparisons, but rather attracted to the new learning opportunities afforded me from these experts.

In essence, during the internship I began to feel that I was a therapist, and more confident in my therapeutic capabilities. Several events seemed to contribute to this change. First, I worked with a broad range of university clients, some of whom had long-standing personality disorders. That year I witnessed several clients changing in significant ways during the course of therapy. It seemed that, with more and more therapeutic experience, I became more facile in assessment and therapeutic interventions. Second, supervisors (Jack Corazzini and M. Kathryn Hamilton) facilitated my understanding of a psychodynamic orientation at a deeper level. In essence, I developed a more comprehensive theoretical orientation, integrating the psychodynamic thinking into the behavioural and cognitive-behavioural orientation, and keeping the Rogerian conditions as essential in developing the therapeutic relationship.

The initial attempts of integrating the psychodynamic thinking into my existing frameworks were stressful and anxiety producing; my inability to understand and conceptualize within a psychodynamic framework threatened my feelings of competence during supervision. Additional reading and many talks with my supervisors, however, helped to erase some of my doubts. A third event was the increased socializing with members of the faculty; these people seemed genuinely interested in me and shared their personal world with me. Although again I often felt awkward socially, I began to feel more like I was one of them, as if I actually belonged in this social group, and more importantly, in this profession. Lastly, in May of that academic year I was granted the doctoral degree; I was technically finished with my formal training which also implied I was supposed to be a therapist now. All of these events (and perhaps others) contributed to a feeling of 'now I am a therapist', I can rather consistently facilitate client change, and I have some theories to help explain the therapy process that seem plausible and useful to me. I felt that the kid named Puncky from the hills of North Dakota had made it.

At the completion of my internship, I accepted a joint position at the University of Missouri. Ten years later, I am in the same position. I consider myself more a therapist now than in 1979 when I obtained the doctoral degree. First, I have a much larger base of therapy experiences. I have more effective assessment skills, and more assessment tools which I use. I am more sensitive to individual differences, and now take those differences into consideration when developing intervention strategies. I have more knowledge of various therapeutic processes (e.g. affective restructuring versus cognitive restructuring) and obstacles (e.g. client psychological defences, energy, and limits). I have more intervention strategies and skills as well as more theoretical knowledge to understand how clients regulate their cognitions, affect, and behaviour, consciously and unconsciously. My research and writing is becoming closer to the therapeutic process, especially as I conceptualize counselling from an information processing perspective. My research activities have been a major stimulus for me, providing new insights into clients' problem-solving processes, pushing me towards greater specificity, and challenging me not only to understand but also to measure the therapeutic process.

Being in the role of teaching, supervising, and advising graduate students in counselling psychology has also been a critical developmental process for me as a therapist. Graduate students are typically bright, energetic, and challenging; these people have been a major stimulus to acquire more knowledge and understand the therapeutic process with greater clarity and depth. I have also learned a great deal from students, their questions, and from observing their development. Supervising doctoral interns has been a particularly rich source of information about the therapy process and about developmental processes in becoming a therapist. Finally, adviser relationships with doctoral students have provided unique opportunities for collaboration and mutual support in a broad range of learning experiences. In short, being an educator has not only stimulated new learning about the therapy process, but also facilitated the development of my identity as a therapist.

As a human being, I also now have a broader set of life experiences and a wider perspective of life. For example, I have had more glimpses at both the uplifting and depressing sides of life. After having lived in two other countries, I have a deeper sensitivity to cross-cultural issues and individual differences in general and within counselling in particular. My personal experiences have heightened my awareness of bodily changes typical in one's thirties (e.g. weight gain, loss of muscle tone, less physical energy). I am also more aware of the interrelationship between physical health problems and psychological processes, and more fully understand the ramifications of chronic illness. Having been married now for fourteen years has taught me a great deal about some of the evolutions in long-term relationships (e.g. progressively deeper levels of intimacy, evolving systems to manage home-related tasks, balancing relationships outside our primary relationship). On a broader level, human relationships in general have taken on added dimensions of comfort and pain, honesty and deceit. I believe these and other experiences have allowed me to be simultaneously more cautious in trusting as well as more accepting of clients. Finally, the name Puncky seems to fit me much better, and I enjoy it like a well-worn boot.

In terms of the therapeutic alliance with clients, I believe I develop strong working relationships. I have even more of an attitude of approaching each client in terms of learning from them, either about life or about the complex psychological processes of human beings. I think this attitude is a function of a deeper understanding of psychological dynamics, increased recognition of how much I learn from my clients about psychology, and both a greater awareness and a deeper acceptance of my own psychological processes. I seem to have less of a desire to be a therapist for some clients, in general, and sometimes it takes more energy to be 'present' with some clients. Perhaps the novelty effect of therapy has simply worn off, or maybe it is not as critically important for me to help yet another client. Conversely, sometimes I have been struck with my ability to empathize with a particular client which surprises not only the client but me as well. Specifically, I have found that when I concentrate I can process and integrate very tiny pieces of information in meaningful ways, a facial muscle movement here, a voice tone there, or certain eye contact. I believe the enhanced empathy can be explained by my increased ability and facility in processing information about the clients (and the counselling process), which also allows me more time to concentrate on the relevant events. Sometimes the emotional contact with clients takes a greater toll on me than before, and I have found that I have to protect myself from being emotionally drained.

All of this is to say that ten years since I labelled myself a 'therapist', I have acquired more knowledge, skill, and appreciations as a therapist. I see myself continuing to evolve and learn as a therapist; there is not an end to the learning in sight. In retrospect, obtaining the doctoral degree was like obtaining a licence to learn more about therapy through practice. In 1979 I could not have imagined all of what I would learn about therapy in the years that were to come.

What sustains me as a therapist? The therapeutic alliance, curiosity, limits, and relationships

Probably what sustains me most immediately as a psychotherapist is being a part of a functional therapeutic alliance with a client, and helping that person live a more adaptive life. I find it rewarding to 'join forces' with another person, to become a team in a way, and to be a part of another's genuine struggle to have a better life for themselves. When therapy is successful, I rejoice because 'we made it'. I feel proud of our mutual accomplishment, and gratitude in our progress. Conversely, when therapy does not work, I generally feel sad and incomplete; my first reaction is to wonder if it was me or the client, although later it actually turns into a shared responsibility. Perhaps I protect myself with my philosophical beliefs about counselling, such as if (a) the conditions (and counsellor) are facilitative, *and* (b) the client wants to change, we usually will be successful.

I typically find the process of therapy both meaningful and stimulating. I find it particularly gratifying to learn about another person's life experiences, and to develop a collaborative working alliance with that person. I appreciate the opportunity and challenge to be genuine and congruent (in a Rogerian way) with another person, and to experience the emotional intimacy that often develops. I feel very stimulated by the critical moments when the client changes in some important way, such as (a) dropping a psychological defence and being honest, vulnerable, (b) allowing him or herself to clearly understand an issue for the first time, or (c) marvelling at the accomplishment of changing some part of his or her life. In short, I enjoy the 'dance' of therapy, and all that is entailed when two people collaborate in bringing about change.

As a psychologist, I am curious about the psychological processes of human beings. I enjoy learning more about these psychological processes from clients. The observations and hypotheses that I make about psychological dynamics, how people process information, and how my clients then cope with their problems not only intrigue me, but stimulate me to investigate these processes empirically.

As a person, I find satisfaction in 'giving' to my clients, giving in terms of information, emotional support, and positive psychological outcomes. In a way, this seems like a feeling of generativity in an Ericksonian way. I do not have any expectations of receiving anything material in return. Rather the pleasure is in helping others along in life, with the hope that they will be able to adapt and find life more rewarding, productive, and meaningful. I am always delighted to learn of previous clients being successful in some part of their life.

The type of clients that I find to be most rewarding or nourishing for me is quite broad. Of course, the YAVIS (young, attractive, verbal, intelligent, and socially skilled) clients are typically rewarding, because these clients are usually most successful in therapy, as research has indicated. In general, I tend to be the most stimulated by clients who are able to be more honest and genuine with themselves, and subsequently with me. I enjoy working with males as well as females, although I am particularly engaged when working with male clients who are examining the traditional male sex role and societal norms. Such male clients are rewarding because of my own journeys within the male role, and because of the pain I see in men caught in societal norms that restrict them. I am drawn to some clients with more severe personality disorders, such as a person with a schizoid personality.

Growing out of my personal experience and work with Corazzini, I now have considerable therapeutic experience working with clients who have been unable to complete the grieving of a significant other's death. I find these therapeutic encounters a rewarding challenge. Conversely, I experience destructive marital relationships that are hostile and out of control to be particularly depressing. Clients who are victims of violence typically tax me, physically, emotionally, and psychologically. I experience more tension with suicidal clients. I experience the most difficulty in fully accepting a person with a passive, dependent style, or a person who whines about how unfair life is to them. I feel most guarded, and the least fully accepting and therapeutic with clients who seem to be manipulating me, particularly clients with borderline personalities. In short, clients with whom I can develop a working alliance generally are most rewarding or nourishing for me as a therapist. Conversely, those clients who tax me more involve elements of destructiveness and loss of control (especially physical); in addition, those who are able to sabotage the working alliance successfully tend to be less rewarding.

I have learned from my experiences as a therapist that I cannot work with very many clients at any one time. In many ways I have an introspective style and am an introvert; other people tend to tire me rather than rejuvenate me. Thus, at this point I have found it necessary to set rather strict limits on the number of people I am emotionally and psychologically engaged with in my life, which includes clients, supervisees, advisees, students, colleagues, friends, and significant others. In addition, I have found that other professional activities are absolutely essential to my well-being, such as research, teaching, and supervision. These activities allow diversity in my work, and provide a different kind of stimulation and challenge to keep me wondering, hypothesizing, and inquiring about the psychological nature of human beings.

My colleagues in Missouri and elsewhere have been very helpful to me as a therapist. First of all, they have provided me with role models for being a therapist and have established high standards of moral, ethical, and professional behaviour. They have also been invaluable in helping to normalize the emotional and psychological aspects of being a therapist. Consultation with colleagues has also been informative in clarifying the therapeutic process, or a particular client's personality dynamics. General discussions with my cohorts have also added greatly to my knowledge about psychology and the therapeutic process. Others have been willing jointly to examine, normalize, and clarify our developmental experiences over time. Finally, my friends have helped to ease tension and frustration through their emotional support, self-disclosure, and commiseration.

Colleagues typically have not put a direct strain on my work as a therapist, although conflict in departmental politics often leaves me with less energy to be a therapist. In a way, colleagues at Missouri and nationwide have provided me with models of 'how to be' or 'how not to be'. In short, other professionals have been very important models in my identity formation as a therapist, and as a person with various leisure interests.

Probably the most pervasive and powerful variable in sustaining me as a therapist, academician, and person has been my long-term relationship with my wife, Mary. She has been a constant source of emotional and psychological support, helping me to understand myself and other people in my life. Her encouragement has been essential in my development as a therapist and person, and highly influential in my own sense of efficacy as a therapist and person.

Mary has greatly facilitated my ability to cope with personal and professional demands and thus helped me to solve many life problems and decisions. Socially, she has enriched my life and helped me to have a personal life apart from the professional work with clients. She has been a source of intellectual stimulation and a partner in exploring new horizons in life (e.g. travelling, living abroad, cooking). This relationship is now so intertwined with almost every aspect of my life that it provides a central core of my being; without the constancy and security of this base I would be far less effective and satisfied in many arenas of my life, including my work as a therapist.

If I were to go back in time and re-examine my choice to become a therapist, I would probably make a similar decision to become a part-time therapist in an academic setting. Such a setting allows me a diverse set of stimulating activities to explore, freedom and time to explore my unique interests, and flexibility to develop a rewarding lifestyle. Frankly, I have not been able to identify another occupation that would suit me better. Such a position also allows me to arrange an optimal client load, something that probably would be less feasible in a private practice or mental health setting. The lingering doubts I have pertain to fears of getting 'burned out', or being unable to withstand the emotional drain from clients.

In conclusion, I believe I am sustained as a therapist by the challenge involved in developing a therapeutic alliance with a client, as well as by the complexity involved in the change process in therapy. I find it rewarding to become a part of a client's struggle to have a better life, to have been 'there', and been helpful in some way. Each client provides another experience or 'window' for viewing the world and myself, which provides additional information to me as a psychologist who is intrigued and intellectually stimulated by the psychological processes of human beings.

What are the implications for others? Themes, conclusions, and implications

As I have reflected on my experience in becoming a therapist, I have emphasized several events in my experiences, such as early childhood background, training experiences, applied experience, my research experience, and being an educator. It is difficult to ascertain, however, how much my experience will generalize to other people as many of my experiences may be idiosyncratic to me. In addition, I would like to make a few other observations about my process of becoming a therapist.

I like to believe I have some amount of control over events in my life. Yet, I must acknowledge that chance events have had a significant impact on my life. It was a chance event that a person such as Dr Jesseph happened to be director of the Counselling Centre at UMM, and made available opportunities for me initially to consider counselling psychology as a career. In retrospect, if I had not had contact with Dr Jesseph, I cannot imagine even contemplating being a therapist now. Likewise, if I had not met the humanistically-oriented graduate student from Nebraska, I would never have applied to the Nebraska programme, which also means I would not have been admitted into a counsellor education programme at that time – and most likely would not have re-applied for some time, if ever. If Dr Dixon had not been a faculty member at Nebraska, I would have probably entered the doctoral programme at Minnesota instead of staying at Nebraska. In short, it seems that chance events have played a significant role in my life. This is a rather humbling observation.

Part of me would also like to believe that I achieved this goal of becoming a therapist on my own, independently. But I know this is not true. I know that the helpful support of other people has been critical, beginning with my parents, including my therapists, mentors, faculty members and now my colleagues, students, and many others. The most influential person of all has been my spouse. In essence, I am struck with the role of my support system in my development as a therapist, as a buffer to stress. I believe that social support from others has been very influential in my professional life in general. Having a good social support system as a therapist has also allowed me to establish a professional, therapeutic working relationship psychologically with clients without letting my social needs become a dysfunctional part of the therapy relationship. In short, social support seems to have been an important factor in my development. If this generalizes to other therapists, then perhaps educators and therapists in the field may need to pay more attention to social support. Perhaps as therapist educators, we need to help trainees not only understand the role of social support in a professional life, but also facilitate the development of trainees' interpersonal and social skills in general and particularly within a professional context.

I entered graduate school with the single goal of becoming a therapist. Now I am a therapist, educator, and researcher. It is difficult to predict one's future interests. In many ways, it is also difficult to predict what knowledge and skills will be needed in one's future, especially with the many technological and societal changes we are currently experiencing. I would encourage students to obtain a very broad array of therapy experiences and skills, even if that means spending another year or two in graduate school. The risk of a potential employer questioning an extra year in school is relatively small, especially in comparison to particular skills or experiences that happen to match a position very well.

As I reflect on my formal academic training, I would encourage students to be creative with their learning programme and to conceptualize their graduate education beyond the basic requirements of the American Psychological Association or specified courses, especially in terms of skills they want to acquire. Too much time is wasted in the graduate training of therapists in the US. After identifying the skills a student wants to learn, I would suggest that students then explore a wide range of alternatives for acquiring these skills, such as auditing certain classes for particular lectures or weeks, individualized directed studies, part-time employment, or special apprenticeship projects with faculty members. In short, I would encourage students to become more active in developing their programme of study by conceptualizing their training in terms of skills/goals rather than 'required courses'. Parenthetically, I was recently impressed with the initiative and independent learning-style of some English students learning to be therapists; my impression was that in that country there is more of a tutorial learning-style which results in more student involvement in learning.

In reflecting on my development as a therapist, I am struck with the number of skills I learned in both my undergraduate and graduate education. Moreover, I am struck with the amount of knowledge and skills I have obtained since I was awarded the doctoral degree. Learning does not stop with the degree, rather continued learning is essential. It seems that the range of skills and depth of a knowledgeable therapist takes an incredible amount of time and practice. It actually astounds me now looking back on what I did not know earlier.

It has become increasingly clear to me that as a therapist it is critical that I pursue other interests and am able to separate myself physically and psychologically from that role for extended times (e.g. vacations, sabbaticals). Within the last five years or so I have had a growing concern for the physical and psychological well-being of therapists in general, and their values as helping professionals. Being a therapist is a demanding activity for many people, and necessitates not only concentration and energy, but also the ability to use appropriately the power inherent in a therapeutic relationship. Beyond the basic ethical responsibilities of a therapist, I believe therapists have a personal responsibility to maintain themselves physically and psychologically in a manner that is conducive to being a therapeutic agent.

My final comment pertains to the continued nourishment of therapists. Carl Rogers once noted that some academic psychologists made career moves which led them out of psychology, perhaps because they were not involved in activities that truly interested them in the first place. I believe Rogers' observation is also accurate for therapists. Something needs to be inherently interesting or stimulating about being a therapist in order to nourish the professional helper. I believe for me it is the chance to learn about and understand the psychological complexities of human behaviour, and to develop a professional working alliance with another person to facilitate his or her development. I do not know if these things will always be inherently stimulating to me in the years to come, nor for how long I will continue to be a therapist. I hope that whatever the future holds I will be able to have the flexibility and courage to pursue what is intriguing and meaningful to me. Perhaps some day I will become a biology professor, although right now that alternative feels like I would miss much which fascinates me.

Author's note

In addition to the book editors, I would like to express gratitude to the following people who made very insightful and stimulating comments, queries, and interpretations on earlier drafts of this chapter: Stephen W. Cook, Mary J. Heppner, W. Calvin Johnson, Carolyn (Ball) Jones, Pamela A. Mauch, and James M. O'Neil.

Chapter six

Living vs. survival: a psychotherapist's journey

Marcia Karp

Why did I become a psychotherapist?

> The human mind is the most complex and delicately balanced of all created things. Wisdom cannot foresee all the consequences of its sickness.

This statement was made at a memorial service after the massacre of many innocent people at Hungerford in Britain. It speaks about the intricacy and unexpectedness of human behaviour.

There are many reasons why I choose to listen to people talk about their lives. Four formative reasons are: (1) the adoration and protection of two brothers; (2) the rabbi's declaration, 'Your daughter is an intellectual'; (3) a childhood speech defect which gave a taste of therapy; (4) a high school choice.

The adoration and protection of two brothers

He twiddled his hair, looked skywards and declared, 'I think I'll become a psychologist.' My brother Bob was witty, sensitive and could talk to anyone. I liked the satisfaction in his face when he made a connection with people. He was nine years older than me. He left school early to join the Air Force. He had been my hero. His interest in psychology made me want to know more. When I was 10 and he 19, I watched from a distance my parents' sadness at his decision to leave university for the military. It sowed the seeds of my own observation and examination of a family dilemma.

Brother David, three years older, and I were like bear cubs; we played and wrestled our way to puberty. David wanted to be an actor. He struggled for twelve years and used to say 'If I don't make it by the time I'm thirty-five, I'll continue.' My father was certain that acting was no way to become a man, business yes, acting no. I began to listen carefully to David's story. He felt he was the black sheep in the family. David's outpourings took precedence over a myriad of life's demands. They all seemed to pale at the importance of his words. We were connected by a deep caring. I felt my role was to listen to who he wanted to be not what he wanted to be. For David my father's non-acceptance of acting got translated into not accepting him. He was lost; I became the family runner, interpreting what he said to my parents and what they said to him. To me it seemed that if you nurture a person well they ultimately choose worthwhile activity.

The influence of my two brothers was enormous. One was a golden boy who made risk-taking seem fun and glamorous, and the other brother, David, was bleating into the dark night uncertain how to proceed. I think all three of us were more pursued and driven than listened to. This is both motivating and crippling. It makes failure and mediocrity anathema.

The question of why we were pushed and driven has its roots in the 'American Dream' philosophy. My father had come as an immigrant from Poland to the United States in 1907. He always had a fear of being deported, therefore he himself had a drive to do well. He worked for his father in a dry goods store, then later began to sell shoes in a department store. He joined a boot and shoe union but I suspect he was dreaming of private business. He survived the 1930s stockmarket crash and managed to keep his family intact. The motivation to sell more and to make it on his own was a dream that he began to pass on to his children. The generational trap was set and, as so many before us, and after us, we fell into it.

The rabbi

I was raised in a small town called Stevens Point, Wisconsin, USA. My father owned a family shoestore and was president of the synagogue. He was proud of both those roles and was continually improving them. The rabbi gave us Hebrew lessons and often ate Kosher food at our home. When I was about fourteen, the rabbi came into the living-room where my parents were sitting, stood in front of them and proclaimed 'Marcia is an intellectual.' The word 'intellectual' was usually reserved for men who had a seat near the eastern wall of the synagogue. Watching the role of women in the home, I had felt dangerously near to being chained to the kitchen. The rabbi had cut a link in the chain.

The heavens seemed to open with the rabbi's comment and I beamed. My parents were clearly delighted at the pronouncement. Whether I treated myself with more respect after that or they did, I'm not sure, but the road seemed clear to go to university. I wanted to be a psychologist.

Judaism played a strong role in my life as a child. Whenever I left home, my father would say, 'Remember you are a Karp and you have 2,000 years of tradition behind you.' I remember looking behind me one evening to see if the 2,000 years were hanging off my new dress for the dance. All I knew was that I wanted to have a good time. I hoped someone would dance with me. The pride of the Chosen People was immensely confusing. In a Gentile community it meant I was different, separate, and meant to be cautious. But I felt similar, together with my friends and carefree; what did it all mean, 2,000 years behind me? Did I have to wear the suffering of the Jews at every school dance? As much as I fought against this basic animal survival and dark Holocaust history, the sense that 'We shall survive' ingrained itself in my blood. The pride of a people surviving through rejection and extermination added strength to my backbone.

Why were some able to make it when so many others died in the concentration camps? Was it faith, strength, family? Our old rabbi said he remembered two symbolic determinants of his survival; one being marched with the work gang privately knowing he would survive it and smiling to himself at his inner reserve of strength, and the other was a dream he had on his bunk in the barracks. He was again due to be exterminated the next day and he dreamt that his father soothed his forehead, lifted a glass of wine and toasted 'Lechaim' (in English, 'to life'). The affirmation of his father, still toasting life with all its inequities, gave him the courage to keep going. He died of a heart attack only months after our last meeting.

The speech defect

From a young age I was plagued with a persistent lisp. I couldn't say my name properly. People asked, 'What's your name, little girl?' I would reply, 'My name ith Martha.' 'Martha, what a nice name,' they would say. 'No, ith not Martha, ith Martha,' I would insist. This went on for a painfully indeterminate time. My mother would sense my frustration and say, 'Her name is Marcia.' I would smile and take my mother's hand with great relief that the error had been corrected. Soon I was able to skip out of the geography lesson and meet with a speech therapist. Sometimes I would see her on my own, sometimes in a group of others who lisped. The therapist was kind and beautiful with straight white teeth and long clean hair. She made learning enjoyable. After many months my colleagues and I could say 'Sammy Snake sits still' without lisping. Being able to change a frustrating speech defect was a godsend. I could say my name. I experienced the process of therapy as a relief and therefore as something good. Perhaps this was my first introduction to therapeutic empathy. Both my mother and the therapist took seriously my inability to communicate the way I wanted.

High school choice

The next determinant was a career-choice in a class entitled 'American Social Problems'. I was 17. For the first time the word 'psychology' was explained in a text book. Each student was given the task of making a careers' notebook. My choice was psychology, at last. I have kept that notebook for twenty-seven years. The invitation to write this chapter has, for the first time, given me the chance to use the material in that yellowed sheaf of papers. What surprises me most about it is that the words I wrote when I was 17 I could easily be writing now. Below is a quote from the section 'Analysis of Self':

> When someone has a real personal problem it not only affects the one person, it affects everyone around him. If a person does not feel   .
> contentment and doesn't have peace within himself, it is hard to have world peace, as peace, in my opinion, starts with the individual.
> I think I have an unusual feeling of security and contentment. Knowing this, I'd like to see if I can transfer some of this security to other people. Curiosity is probably one of the things that will keep me studying and will help me continue my education in the psychology field. I want to know why we humans act and react as we do. Like most people, I don't thoroughly understand myself. By continuing in this field of the humanities I will not only learn how and why others do what they do but also I'll have a greater conception of my own actions. This to me should be one of the most important things in the world to everyone: to know thyself.

The next item in the notebook was an interview with my parents about why or why not they thought I could enter the career of psychology:

Question:	'Do you think I'd make a good psychologist?'
Mother:	'Yes, you have patience with people and you like people.'
Father:	'Yes, you have a natural aptitude for helping people.'
Question:	'Do you think marriage will interfere with my career?'
Mother:	'No, you're too determined.'
Question:	'Do you think my disposition and my personal characteristics are suitable for the job?'
Mother:	'Yes, you are a good conversationalist and quite sensible in your opinions and decisions.'
Father:	'You have a good sense of humour which will be appreciated by those you are trying to help.'
Question:	'Is there any field you'd rather that I go into?'
Mother:	'I would really like to see you go into teaching. This is a long range career as there will always be a great need for teachers.'
Father:	'If you went into journalism you could combine psychology with it and perhaps go into public relations.'

My reaction to this interview is two-fold. My parents were able to see the qualities roughly developing in me to be a listener and a sensible guide. They were honest about their own preference. I have no memory of being disillusioned by their lack of encouragement but rather I felt tolerated in my interest.

How did I become a psychotherapist?

By pure chance or divine ordinance I sat studying at the University of Wisconsin student library with the books of psychiatrist Jacob Levy Moreno perched innocently in front of me on a shelf. I had never seen or heard of them before. There were thousands of books in that library and I sat in front of those, not knowing that my career lay on the shelf, asking to be discovered. One title particularly intrigued me: *Who Shall Survive?* It was a question each student asked during the spring-time. The blossoms were on the trees, the sweet smell of end-of-term was in the air. There were essays to write and final exams to take before the longed-for spring break would take us to freedom once again. The book *Who Shall Survive?* – a massive tome of more than 2,000 pages – beckoned me to open it. It was much more inviting than all the books assigned to me for the final exam. I took it down and began to read. I felt quite devious and excited to embark on alien pages that had nothing to do with the subject I was meant to be studying. Moreno was a founder of group psychotherapy and originated a method called psychodrama. I sat and read the book for hours. I felt the author was speaking to me and for me. The themes that particularly struck me were Moreno's deep concern for the survival of humanity against a progressive use of automation and industrialization which brought with it a new robot mentality. What was to become of creativity and spontaneity, our greatest human resources? He developed a method of interaction called psychodrama, which enables people to use the resources of spontaneity and creativity to explore emotional truth in dramatic form. I don't actually know why I sat at that particular place. The fact that I did, and took an enthusiastic deviation from final exam studies, was to shape my career. 'The best things happen by accident,' Moreno used to say.

Up until that moment in the library I had been straddling two lives. By day I was a serious student of speech pathology. By night I was an ardent Thespian appearing in University productions of Strindberg, Brecht, Shakespeare, Ionesco, Arthur Miller and Tennessee Williams. I was a student of mime. My own emotional truth and the intricacies of humanity were revealed to me by playwrights and the world of theatre. By day, my clinical acumen was challenged and pathological truths were revealed in interactions with speech defectives and their families. People with severe communications disorders fascinated me. Moreno offered not a scripted actor but a spontaneous actor who played out his own life *in situ* showing us his scenery, his living space, and a cast of real characters. I was struck with the simplicity of taking real life as the drama to be performed. It allowed the protagonist or main character to be both the playwright and the actor. With a trained director, the protagonist spontaneously formed a working partnership to explore the truth of his or her own life. I thought Moreno must be a genius.

After my library encounter I told the speech professor of my psychodrama discovery. What interested me was a section Moreno wrote about working with stammerers. He had established fluency in stammerers by having them take roles other than themselves. I wanted to use this idea. With supervision, I spent the summer helping adults and children play roles such as aggressive aunts or belligerent brothers. The pattern of chronic hesitation was broken in those roles and fluency occurred. I then wanted the stammerer to establish a role repertoire within his or her own personality. It allowed fluency to occur by using internal power rather than external. I set about the work but I knew I needed more training. At that time I was looking into graduate programmes in speech pathology. There was one available at Columbia University Teachers' College in New York City. By good fortune, John F. Kennedy, President of the US, had made funds available at major universities for students who could not afford the tuition. I was one of those students. Kennedy had a sister who was mentally retarded and had recognized the need for more speech therapists; thereby the financial grants became available. I applied. For a young girl in Wisconsin, applying to Columbia was like reaching for the moon.

My interview was to be held in Chicago at the National Speech and Hearing Association Annual Meeting. The Department Head, Dr Seymour Ridgrodsky, was to meet me there to conduct the interview. I travelled 200 miles and arrived early at the three-day meeting. With my suitcase in hand I peered over the balcony of a big Sheraton hotel, surveying hundreds of people milling about the floor below. The sea of strangers, the big hotel, the prospective meeting, all made me nervous. 'There certainly are a lot of people,' I heard a voice say. 'Yes,' I replied, 'all gathered for a convention on communication disorders.' 'Are you interested in that?' the voice asked. 'Oh, yes,' I said and began excitedly to discuss my interest in the field. We stood for a long time sharing our ideas. The voice belonged to a man in a tweed jacket who puffed calmly on his pipe while being both humorous and knowledgeable on the subject. 'Well,' I said, 'I'd better go now because I must dress for an interview.' I told him all about the school in New York and my aspirations about getting in. 'Who are you meeting?' he asked. I found my piece of paper with the man's name written on it. 'Seymour Ridgrodsky.' 'That's me,' he replied. 'If you are who I think you are, you're in. I'll get my colleague and introduce you.' I almost fainted. Here I was about to face the difficult moment of interview and the warm-up for the meeting was the meeting itself. I met his colleague and we arranged for my entry into Columbia. I never saw them again in the three days of the conference. I thought again of Moreno's statement: 'the best things happen by accident.' I waited breathlessly for the letter of confirmation to arrive. Two weeks later it did, and the following term I had a small studio apartment in the Village in New York City. I was delighted to be a student at Columbia University. My choice of New York was to be near J. L. Moreno and his public theatre of psychodrama called The Moreno Institute on 78th Street and Broadway. My goals were to get a Master's degree in speech pathology, and, *en route*, study psychodrama and apply it to my studies. In graduate school I quickly became the student who was given patients with an 'emotional component'.

Graduate placement

The Metropolitan Hospital in New York provided me with a once-a-week opportunity to do dramatherapy with thirty-five patients. They were clad in their pyjamas. One particular day I threw puppets in the air for patients to catch. I went around to each patient and introduced myself. Some spoke to me as one of the puppets, some spoke as themselves. I stopped in front of one man who was neatly dressed in a dark suit and tie. 'How do you do?' he said grandly. 'I am Alexander the Great.' I was 24 years old, had never seen a delusional patient before and simply assumed this was a staff member with a sense of humour. 'How do you do: I'm Catherine the Great.' We smiled, he kissed my hand, bowed and said 'Charmed, I'm sure'.

The drama

One young patient, a drug addict who had difficulty expressing himself, came up to a small wooden puppet stage. He began to enact a scene showing us how he usually obtained drugs by manipulating his father to fill a prescription for him at the drug-store. We needed someone to play the role of his father. The young drug addict wanted 'Alexander the Great' to play the role. I said to the man, 'Alexander, would you grace us with your presence on the stage and play the father?' 'I'd be charmed,' he said, and up he came. He put the father puppet on his hand and played the father appropriately. They played out the scene. Soon the puppets were discarded and they played themselves. The young drug addict spoke truthfully about his intense guilt at using his father to get drugs. He used drugs to anaesthetize his emotional pain. It was a big step for the young man. I looked over at the psychiatrist who was in charge of the drug unit. She looked ashen-faced and intense. After the session I asked the psychiatrist if she was ill or if I'd done something wrong. She smiled and said 'Alexander the Great' had been a delusional patient for many years in the hospital. In all those years she had never seen him take part appropriately in any group work and was shocked at his responses. She praised my work and suggested that perhaps my naivité about his medical history allowed him to relate normally. I went home dancing inside, understanding Moreno's concept of spontaneity. The drug addict had produced a spontaneous drama. We included 'Alexander' in a spontaneous way, allowing him to become what was needed in the creative act. Psychodrama and language therapy were beginning to merge and make sense together.

Formal training

I was 24 years old when I began formal training in psychodrama at The Moreno Academy, a training centre for psychodrama in Beacon, New York. It was a living community in which to learn. We lived, ate, drank, studied and discussed psychodrama. The atmosphere was one of a family unit, a microcosm of society which allowed a certain continuity of study and discussion. For the first time in all of my training the major emphasis was on the work itself rather than on reading about the work.

There were two training sessions in the day, run by the director Zerka Moreno, and at night Dr Moreno held seminars in his living room. As a creator of the method and author of the books, he was there to discuss, consult, and review the day's work. Zerka Moreno was a good model as therapist and community leader. She was industrious, knowledgeable and interested in our work. Watching hundreds of therapists direct sessions had a profound effect on me. The method evokes many styles of tailoring the theory to personality. The training afforded me the opportunity to work on myself. It was in that close examination that I learned about my own family dynamics and the part I play in shaping my behaviour. The quest for knowledge about oneself and one's own reactions was sparked at Beacon and remains kindled. Each day brought new situations never before faced.

Inspiration

The greatest significance on my training was the inspiration of the founder himself and his partner, Zerka. Moreno had a genius for simplicity. He worked totally in here-and-now whether the scene took place in the past, the present, or the future. One learned to be open to the moment and to trust spontaneity, the gem which shapes it. He took a keen interest in each of us. In a rather breathless way, one never knew what would happen next. Two moments stay in my mind about his unexpected behaviour.

One morning at 2 a.m. my phone rang. 'Marcia.' It was Moreno. I yawned and mumbled. 'About what you said this afternoon,' he went on; 'you were wrong.' He proceeded to tell me why he thought I was wrong, said goodbye and hung up. I was stunned that he never made the usual noises about 'I'm sorry to wake you.' The afternoon conversation was being carried on at 2 a.m. in the morning as if no moments of life had intervened. I liked his taking the thread of it so seriously as to continue it. There appeared to be no strings attached but the fibres were cautiously explored.

Another moment was in a private tutorial about my work. He thought I was too 'nice'. He was right; as the youngest in the family, and a girl, I had learned to be the family sponge. I took in the hurts of my parents about my brothers and wiped up the effect by offering 'good girl' behaviour. It was not approval I was after so much as it was trying to make up for what my parents weren't getting. I became determined not to create any more hurt or disappointment. A nonsensical aim, really; one can only be what one is. Moreno observed in me a reluctance to see the shadow or darker side of what I saw and encouraged me to be more direct and confrontative. He modelled the courage to say 'what is' and to see it as it is.

Apprenticing to a psychotherapist is a good way to learn. Having a model and reviewing with peers the values and losses in that personality help to shape what a student will keep and discard. Seeing the model as just an 'ordinary' person is crucial. Without this balanced vision the student may idealize the role-model, making it an impossible role for the therapist to fulfil and for the patient to follow. Because, as students, we lived near to Dr Moreno and Zerka, we could see them functioning in their daily lives. If illness or circumstance intervened we were told the odd afternoon session was cancelled and we made our own programme. They were not indispensable. Another moment of 'regularness' was seeing the reaction of Moreno after a frustrating session with a couple in therapy where nothing seemed to go right. Afterwards he became very quiet and did not want to talk about it. It was not until days later that he could bear some of our queries about what did not work. I think he avoided us partly because he was displeased at the outcome and partly because he was formulating his own thoughts. Moreno became defensive about what he had done and called the male in the couple 'a spoiled child'. In fact, we were less interested in Moreno's success with the couple and more interested to hear what happened psychodynamically. Ultimately I learned something more important. Great men also have their pride hurt, and pride can get in the way of seeing clearly what goes on between patient and therapist.

Informal training

My informal training comes from life experience. Negative learning as well as positive gains have been instructive. Two situations come to mind: (i) sorority rush; (ii) the death of a neighbour.

(i) Sorority rush

A painful experience for me during the first year at university was being denied an invitation to join a Greek sorority (women's organization). The pain was not because I did not get in but because of the sheer amorality of how it was conducted. For example, my childhood friend was told her father's financial status was being reviewed before she could be considered for entry. I was told I should mention the name of a cousin who preceded me in the organization in order to get in on the 'old girl' ethos rather than on my own worth. We were treated to rounds of sorority house visits where we were casually socialized by hawk-eyed young ladies looking for *faux pas*, stockings with snags and any other basic screening criteria. The process began to be annoying and though my new-made university friends assured me that this was all very normal and part of the fun, it seemed a poor way to relate to each other. The day arrived when the round of invitations was to be delivered to our dormitory mailboxes. These invitations were called 'bids' and each sorority could bid for the girl they wanted. The anxiety and pandemonium in our dormitory were astounding. The girls were like stalking panthers, claws sharp, and tongues panting. One student told me she was thinking about suicide if she did not get asked back to the sorority of her choice. That particular Sunday I was looking at a photographic report on Biafra during the height of its starvation crisis. I showed the photographs to my suicidal colleague and hoped that the Biafrans' struggle would give her the perspective it showed me. Her comment was 'They always make those pictures look worse than it is', and went on complaining. I decided, peacefully and calmly, that the Greek folly was not for me. I have never regretted the decision and feel it laid a cornerstone in the sanity of my young adulthood.

(ii) A neighbour's death

For many years I had helped patients handle grief. One day we received a phone call to say that the 19-year-old son of a neighbouring farmer had died suddenly from an unsuspected heart condition. My partner and I decided one of us would go to them and one of us would stay with our baby. The decision was made by the toss of a coin. We had both wanted to go. It was to be me. I walked five fields to our neighbours' farm. It was a smallholding where they'd lived as sheep farmers for twenty-five years. The son had been working with them in preparation for taking over the farm. As I approached the small farmhouse all was quiet except for the barking dog.

My heart pounded. What if my neighbours felt my entrance was an intrusion into their grief? It was now 9 a.m. Their son had been dead on arrival at hospital at 7 p.m. the night before. What could I possibly say or do? It was not my son, so how could I understand? How dare I ... The door was open to their kitchen which was usually filled with laughter, new-born lambs, and freshly-baked flapjacks. The mother was curled in front of the Rayburn stove, the father was head in hands at the table. The son's boots, still muddy from the day before, were tucked under the mother's chair. I stood in the doorway and cried at the sight of their quiet staring. They looked up. I held out my arms. I had nothing to say. They got up and we three embraced and cried together. After a few moments the father threw back his head and said, 'Whatever made you come?' I cried again and sat down. They began to talk for hours about their son, laughing as they told stories spanning nineteen short years. I vowed to stay until their other two children joined them. In those few hours I felt my life as a psychotherapist was deeply rooted in me as a person. There was a fusion between my ability to cope with grief professionally and the ability to meet a personal crisis. The work was transferable. My presence helped the boy to live a bit longer in them and we three began to make the transition from life to death together. Their love would not die. Eight years later even the family dog travels three miles to sit alone at the grave.

When did I become a psychotherapist?

The influence of children – 'Will you be my therapist?'

I was a psychotherapist working in my first job at the Astor Home for Children in Rhinebeck, New York. There was a rather tattered ragamuffin girl of nine who lived at the Home as a ward of the court. She had been in psychiatric treatment most of her life.

I had been working only a few weeks and had not met her yet but had heard of her cunning nature. She knew the ropes and used them to her advantage. When I arrived at work she was waiting for me. 'Hey, Miss, are you gonna be my therapist? Please?' It was like a papal invitation. The moment stands out in my mind for several reasons. No one had called me a therapist before. The fact that she ranked me in line with many others past and present jolted me into the reality that I was no longer a student or an apprentice. In her eyes I was a therapist and with her instinct for survival she needed my professional blank slate to embark on her next hope in therapy. She became part of an adolescent group. I do not remember much about her except that she helped me, at 24 years old, to confirm the suspicion inside that I was becoming a therapist.

You be the problem

The next child who jolted me into the role reality of therapist was my daughter, Poppy. At five, she and her friend were having a discussion in the bathroom. 'Do you want to play therapy?' Poppy asked her friend. 'Yes; how do you play it?' Poppy said, 'It's easy. You be the problem and I'll be "mmm hmmm" then you be the "mmm hmmm" and I'll be the problem.' Her friend asked, 'What are you gonna be when you grow up?' Poppy said, 'I'm gonna work in a prison like my Mum did.' 'What do you do, give them bread and water?' asked her friend. 'Oh, no,' said Poppy. 'First you get a chair and talk to them. If they don't get better you just let them out.'

Another moment was when Poppy was 7 and she was left in the care of a baby-sitter. When I returned Poppy said to me, 'Judith needs to talk to you: she has a problem.' Judith was soon at my side and quietly told me the story. She had taken my children home with her where she had had a row with her husband in front of the children. When they got in the car to drive home, Poppy took Judith's hand and said, 'You need to talk to my Mum about this.' I was clearly launched as someone who could help.

What sustains me as a psychotherapist?

Being a psychodramatist is like moving mountains. It seems impossible. Before I begin, I look at the task ahead and wonder how I will gain the strength to do the job. As soon as I get my shoulder to the mountain, my head clears; I feel calm and focused. When the journey is completed I look back over my shoulder and wonder, 'Did we do that?' What keeps me going is my own vulnerability. When the emotions are genuine, I feel it. When I'm working with a protagonist, I rarely want to be doing anything else than exactly what I'm doing. The sense of being in the right niches, no matter how rough or spiky, is fulfilling. I am less comfortable socializing with people who are hiding from human emotions. I like to be with people who speak about what is true for them. The kind of patients I find difficult are the ones who dump their dilemma on to the therapist. They see therapy as a place to be cleansed, untouched by human hands, like a drive-in car-wash, aerial down and windows up. With that kind of patient, I feel unseen, unused and unwanted – though I am aware that all of those things are occurring. The challenge is to be mindful of the patient's generalized lack of trust for humanity, of which I am a tiny part.

Contrarily, the nourishing patient is one who gives many signals about what he or she is learning. The moment a light bulb goes on in the mind and the person has a light within – they mark that moment clearly. I am continually enriched by these moments when a person sows the seeds for change. They make me feel humbler and greater at the same time.

The dangerous sticking points for me are about my own personal energy. Too often I give more to my patients than to my family. The structure of a session seems easier to handle, the dimensions are clearer and less open-ended. When I have moved a mountain, I like to be left alone to catch my breath. Because I live and work in the same place, I am caught by role conflict. When the patients leave I am an available family member again. Sometimes I am not ready to be that. Though my heart is willing, my mind and body have just given birth and need to rest. It is nearly impossible to convince a 5-year-old that you are not there when you clearly are there. The guilt of being unavailable can become strong. Often I half-heartedly play the family member until I can catch my breath.

I have to remind myself about the concept of the 'good enough' mother and its adequacy. Being clear and satisfied with what I am able to do is a better message than 'I'm sorry for what I can't do.' There is a similar reality about the 'good enough' therapist. Perfection is not within the grasp of ordinary human beings. Trying to be perfect often gets in the way of being able to tolerate the imperfections of one's child, or patient, or partner. My husband and I, for example, often work together. Aside from our man/woman relationship we are business partners and co-responsible for groups. We play many tunes on each other's harp; sometimes they harmonize, sometimes the song is a solo with accompaniment, and sometimes they are simply different tunes. It is up to our creativity how we incorporate these different tunes. In some ways I had an easier time of it when I was the sole therapist in the household. There is an ongoing process of change and transition in our work together.

For many years Ken studied with me, and then became a colleague. During both periods we were partners, married, and shared five children including two of our own. We have had the usual realities that face couples who work together: if we are getting on well, the work goes well. The greatest gains of working together are: (i) the sense that we are not alone to share the load of training and therapy; (ii) when we create something by using what the other one has done, it is clearly a worthwhile co-operative effort.

Sharing decisions and opinions has been the most rewarding and the hardest part in accepting work with a colleague after so many years on my own. The habit of getting on with it unilaterally is hard to break. It is stimulating and helpful to see one's partner do a good job. Unilateral decision-making seems to pale and we are challenged to pick up where the other left off, directed by the content rather than by ownership of the task.

Daily life can be less dramatic. It is an occupational hazard of working with concentrated emotion that being an everyday citizen can feel anti-climatic. The people I meet at the post office or in shops don't know I move mountains. Often that is a relief: nothing is asked of me unless I offer it.

One of the constant sources of replenishment for me is my family environment. We live in the country. I like to feed the ducks, watch the lambs jump in the spring, and be surrounded by daffodils in April. I am a solitary person and need moments alone to be still and empty of thought. Some work days feel enriching, sometimes too draining or demanding. On those days I try to simplify what I am doing. Again, I do less in quantity, more in quality.

In the main, I enjoy the career I have chosen and am glad of the choice I made. Continual letters of reinforcement by people I've worked with spur me on to continue the struggle of uncovering human emotion. The doubts I have are the same as my mother's were many years ago: wondering if being around problems all the time is good for you. The query is a career in itself. When I am feeling strong myself it doesn't affect me. When I am in need emotionally, it takes enormous effort to give out in abundance. Often, after giving out, I feel better myself, having forgotten my own difficulties in the process. For a short time only, they seem less when I go back to them. This process of comparison happens periodically and it does make me wonder how much I have needed the work to rid myself of my own focus. I am currently learning to de-focus on me and to become more selfless in my life. Learning how and when to start and stop internal analysis is an art.

Implications for other therapists

My quest or journey is less about being a psychotherapist and more about living. My experience lately has been that I've learned too well about other people's lives and begun to be less generous to those around me, partly because of time and energy and partly because of a miscalculated balance of them and me. Therapists in training need supervision and a learned sense of talking about their own problems consistently. For each of us there are moments of clarity and balance, and moments of muddle and imbalance. As far as I can see, these continue until the last breath is drawn. The greatest professional hazard to which I have been prey is to feel unreachable and beyond help. It is in those moments I feel most desolate and would like to warn others of the danger signals to this irrational yet real condition:

1. concentration is lessened;
2. patients' problems cease to hold as much interest;
3. sleep patterns become disturbed;
4. drowsiness and exhaustion are apparent;
5. problems seem everywhere;
6. the needs of family or friends feel too big. (This is an interesting one. Therapists are unwise to rescue those close to them by using their therapeutic skills. Lack of compassion for the problem is a good signal that one is overloaded.)

Writing this chapter has also helped me refocus the enthusiasm for what I do and strengthen my greatest source of replenishment – the family. They renew my sense of belonging and give continuity in the long-termness of the commitment. Though I travel often, and have to leave them behind, my children and partner are with me.

I see myself working as a therapist all my working life. If on that journey to old age psychotherapy ceases to hold fascination, no doubt I shall do something else. My ideal self says 'Enjoy what you are doing or don't do it.' My real self is less hedonistic and more patient and says, 'Some moments you will enjoy more than others: stay with it.'

Chapter seven

My career as researcher and psychotherapist

Hans H. Strupp

I welcomed the editors' invitation to participate in this challenging venture; yet as I approached the task, I experienced some trepidation since of necessity it deals with highly personal matters.

Beginnings

Almost a quarter of a century ago, at a faculty party, I overheard a conversation between two colleagues, one of whom asked, 'How did you happen to become a psychotherapist?' The second answered, without a moment's hesitation but without rancour: 'You are asking a highly personal question.' I don't remember how the conversation proceeded, but for some reason I vividly recall the exchange. I had never thought about the issue in that light, but the riposte struck me as eminently meaningful. Indeed, when confronted with a question of this kind one is being asked to reveal thoughts and feelings one might share only with people closest to us. Some thoughts may be so private that we might verbalize them only in therapy, perhaps against strong resistances, and others we may not wish to verbalize at all. Thus I doubt that anyone in a chapter of this kind can ever be 'perfectly honest'. I pledge not to dissimulate, but the reader will understand that I shall use discretion.

I recall a statement in Freud's (1925/1959) autobiography in which he expressed bitter feelings about having shared too much of his 'personal affairs' with the world, which gave him small thanks (Freud 1925: 73). I shall try not to place myself in that position.

People often construct a mental image of a writer whose works they have read, a picture that usually has little resemblance to what the person is 'really like'. Some readers have told me that they had pictured me as a 'typical' German, perhaps with a crew cut, authoritarian, and forbidding. One exponent of a certain theoretical orientation with whose views I had publicly disagreed, but who did not know me personally, vented his spleen to a mutual friend by describing me as 'all brains and no heart'. Be that as it may, I hope that readers will come away with a somewhat more accurate picture of the person I 'really' am. I am also reminded of a statement by Goethe who said that the world had not really known him. How many feel that others really know us?

The problem of 'how psychotherapy works' has for me been a way of life for almost forty years. I have remained fascinated by the question of how one person can help another change and in the process alleviate to some extent that second person's neurotic suffering. I was initially attracted by the field of psychotherapy (and more specifically its subform psychoanalysis) because, in part, I was impelled to find answers to early traumas. In particular, I am thinking of the early death of my father (at age 45) when I was a little over 9 years old. The fact that my studies and my empirical research have brought me recognition has undoubtedly reinforced my enduring commitment, but the roots of my interest are deeper.

Exodus

Next to the death of my father, whom I remember as a stern disciplinarian, the second traumatic experience was associated with the rise of National Socialism in Germany. From 1933, after Hitler came to power, until my emigration (with my mother and younger brother) in 1939, life was filled with turmoil (from being a Jew to being a half-orphan). These experiences contributed to a persistent feeling of self-consciousness and alienation which in turn heightened my clinical sensitivity. As therapists, of course, we deal continually with hurtful experiences in our patients.

The subsequent years in New York (from 1939 to 1940) and in Washington, DC (from 1940 to 1957) continued to be troubled because again I felt a stranger (this time as a refugee in a foreign land). I strove hard to further my education, working as a bookkeeper and accountant by day and attending college at night.

During these years I earned a meagre living and contributed to the support of my ailing mother. By 1945 I had graduated with an AB degree (with distinction) from George Washington University, where I also earned an MA (in 1947) and a Ph.D. degree in social psychology (in 1954). My first job as a psychologist was with the Department of the Air Force (1949 to 1954). I served a second stint with the Department of the Army (1954 to 1955). Both positions were in the field known as 'personnel psychology'.

Through a teacher in Germany from whom I had taken private lessons in Spanish and English to prepare myself for emigration, I became interested in the history of art and philosophy, and when I started to enrol in the evening session of the City College of New York (CCNY), I took philosophy and German literature. However, a friend who was studying psychology at CCNY introduced me to abnormal psychology. I continued to take courses in psychology after moving to Washington, DC, but academic psychology held only limited interest; nonetheless, it seemed a safer way of preparing myself for a job than philosophy. Abnormal psychology, on the other hand, was more meaningful and relevant to me personally, although it too seemed fairly sterile.

The Washington School of Psychiatry years

I became acquainted with Freud's writings while living in New York. His towering contributions captured my interest in a personally meaningful way, as had, to a lesser extent, the works of Nietzsche somewhat earlier. Although academic courses had little to say about Freud, I pursued my readings in psychoanalysis and psychotherapy.

The turning point in my career came through a chance meeting, at a summer resort in western Maryland, with Dr Frieda Fromm-Reichmann. We took some walks together; I listened to her piano playing; and one evening we listened to records of classical music on a phonograph she had brought along. I also remember her feeding scrambled eggs to her cocker spaniel whom she treated like her child.

Some months later, I summoned sufficient courage to talk to her about my desire to undergo psychoanalysis. I harboured the secret hope that she might accept me as an analysand, but that was not to be. Instead, after an unpromising start, I began psychoanalysis with a young and inexperienced resident who was the brother-in-law of the analyst Dr Fromm-Reichmann had initially recommended. I began to see him on a low-cost basis (which was all I could afford) and, as I learned only later, he was being supervised. The analysis lasted from 1946 to 1952 and, as I came to appreciate only much later, it was a very constructive experience. Not only was it helpful therapeutically, but it prepared me for professional work as a therapist. Personal therapy, I have always felt, is an essential learning experience for virtually all therapists. In 1951 I married a distantly-related German refugee, and my marriage, I am proud to record, has lasted to the present time.

An important influence on my career was the growing involvement in the teachings of Harry Stack Sullivan, with whom Dr Fromm-Reichmann was affiliated at the Washington School of Psychiatry. I enrolled as a candidate at the School and studied with such prominent figures as Clara Thompson, Cora Dubois, Ernest Schachtel, Otto Will, David Rioch, Leon Salzman, Alfred Stanton, and others. As a budding 'academic' psychologist, I always felt somewhat out of place at the school but since at the time the school's door was open to non-medical trainees, I could reassure myself that what I was doing was not illegitimate. In 1952 the school conferred on me its 'Certificate in Applied Psychiatry for Psychologists'. As I said, I earned a Ph.D. degree from George Washington University in 1954, having completed an empirical study of psychotherapists as my doctoral dissertation. My mentors at George Washington University, to their great credit, were remarkably tolerant of my – somewhat unorthodox – dissertation proposal.

Becoming a therapist and researcher

Thus I had acquired a reasonable 'book knowledge' of psychotherapy and experienced a lengthy personal analysis. However, since George Washington University had no clinical psychology programme at the time, I had virtually no experience in the practice of psychotherapy. Being quite determined and goal-oriented, I presently took steps to remedy this deficiency. I apprenticed myself at two community mental health clinics, doing volunteer work in the evening and being supervised by senior therapists whom I had approached for this purpose. One of my supervisors was Leon Salzman, who previously had been my teacher.

Following the publication of my dissertation (in three papers that appeared in the *Journal of Consulting Psychology* (Strupp 1955a, b, and c), I began to think seriously about a research career in psychotherapy with some involvement as a practising therapist. The problem was that I had not completed a regular doctoral programme in clinical psychology and thus did not qualify as a clinical psychologist. I wrote letters to many universities and received as many rejections. In particular, I would have loved dearly to obtain a research position in the Laboratory of Psychology at the National Institute of Mental Health which was just then achieving prominence, both through its intramural and extramural programmes. Again, I had no luck.

But eventually fortune smiled on me. I had written a letter to Dr Winfred Overholser who was then both Superintendent of St Elizabeths Hospital and Chairman of the Department of Psychiatry at George Washington University. I inquired whether he might be willing to co-sponsor an application for a research grant to the National Institute of Mental Health (NIMH) which would allow me to carry forward my research and abandon my government position which held little interest. The proposal apparently appealed to him. For one reason, it involved no financial commitment on the part of George Washington University and in other respects it was also 'low risk'. I was contacted by one of Dr Overholser's lieutenants, a psychiatrist named Leon Yochelson, and after some discussions an application was submitted. It listed Dr Overholser as 'principal investigator' and I was named as 'project director'.

When the grant was reviewed by the appropriate NIMH peer review committee, I was approached by Dr Jerome D. Frank of Johns Hopkins University, who had been assigned the job of 'primary reviewer'. He asked me to visit him in Baltimore and apparently he was favourably impressed. (From my first meeting to this day, Jerry Frank has been one of my heroes and role-models.)

The committee recommended approval but not without a telephone call to Dr Overholser by one of the senior psychiatrist members. As he told the story, his friend and colleague said bluntly: 'We know you are not going to be actively involved in this research. Who is this guy Strupp, anyway?' The underlying concern was that a psychologist – and a novice at that – might become an embarrassment to a field which was largely the domain of psychiatrists. This concern was intensified by the fact that my research focused on the person of the therapist, a particularly sensitive topic. Dr Overholser must have given the necessary assurances, but it was decreed that a psychiatrist (who turned out to be Dr Yochelson) be appointed as a regular consultant, to keep an eye on the fledgling researcher. We began to meet on a weekly basis for about an hour, became friendly, and although he was not a researcher, he was able to make some valuable suggestions.

The approved grant (for three years) in hand, I resigned my government position and was given an office at St Elizabeths Hospital. I shared the room with the part-time rabbi who was housed with the chaplains in the new geriatrics' building. I was now a full-time researcher and had the luxury of a research assistant (Re Rieger, who became a good friend). It was a solitary occupation, but since I had no other duties I was able to accomplish a good deal in two and a half years (between 1955 and 1957).

The protocol called for the collection of data from a sizeable number of experienced psychotherapists, wherever I might find them. I was primarily interested in the study of therapy techniques and how they might be a function of the therapist's background training and personality. To accomplish this goal I used an analogue of a therapy session. This was a filmed interview with a rather difficult and unlikeable patient who complained of claustrophobia and anxiety attacks. The film was adapted for my purposes by splicing titles at twenty-eight more or less 'strategic' points in the interview. Viewers were expected to respond to each title 'What would you do?' by writing down their 'communications' to the patient. They were also asked to make diagnostic and prognostic judgements.

To obtain subjects, I solicited invitations from various organizations, carried a sound film projector to various centres and travelled as far as Chicago to collect my data. The analogue, while having obvious shortcomings, yielded valuable data. Although therapists' responses were written, they often seemed to come alive and portray the respondent's personality, attitudes, and style.

The work resulted in several journal articles (Strupp 1957a, b, and c) and my first book (Strupp 1960). It won 'honourable mention' by the Hofheimer Prize Committee of the American Psychiatric Association. It was the first honour to come my way.

Rewarding as my research turned out to be, the grant was only for three years and the job had no visible future. In 1957, I was confronted with the difficult choice between a lecturer's position at Harvard University and an associate professor's position (director of psychological services in the department of psychiatry) at the University of North Carolina in Chapel Hill. I chose the latter, partly because it offered greater security to me and my growing family and partly because it provided the opportunity for more significant clinical involvement. Harvard had no clinical facilities despite its psychological clinic which, as I discovered, saw no patients.

The North Carolina years: Psychologist in a department of psychiatry

Chapel Hill posed many challenges. I had not held an academic position before; knew nothing about administrative or supervisory responsibilities; and was grossly ignorant of academic politics, in particular the strife between psychiatrists and psychologists in a medical setting.

Within a few weeks after my arrival, the department of psychiatry voted that psychologists were not to conduct psychotherapy except for research purposes and even then only under psychiatric supervision. This vote was taken at one of the regular department faculty meetings, to which psychologists were not invited. (At that time, there were only a few psychologists in the department but their number was soon to grow.)

As might be expected, we psychologists made strong representations to have the new policy rescinded, and several meetings occurred, at which we were greatly supported by our colleagues in the department of psychology on campus. Eventually, the rule was relaxed and the responsibility for supervision was assigned to me. On the whole, this arrangement worked well for a number of years except that psychologists – we had faculty status – did not participate in the private practice plan available to psychiatrists. The latter doubled their academic salaries by treating private patients for about fifteen hours a week. In addition, the plan, from which clinical psychologists were specifically excluded, provided for journal subscriptions, travel funds, health insurance and other benefits. In later years, psychologists were permitted to participate in the plan to a limited extent. The net result of this private practice plan was that the most junior psychiatrist in the department had a greater income than the most senior clinical psychologist. Since status in our society is importantly related to earnings, the discrepancy in salaries underscored the second-class citizen status of psychologists.

The practice of psychotherapy was obviously the major bone of contention between psychiatrists and psychologists. Other mental health professionals in the department (e.g. social workers) also fought for privileges but they were less successful. The chairman of the department was heard to grumble: 'No one any more wants to do what he has been trained to do: psychologists, social workers, nurses, recreational therapists, etc. – all want to do psychotherapy!'

Here are some further vignettes that illustrate the struggle of a non-medical therapist to gain parity in a department of psychiatry. I was seeing a patient in twice-a-week psychotherapy, in face-to-face interviews and, along the way, my supervisor, an analyst, thought that this patient was a good candidate for classical analysis, and he suggested that I petition the chairman for permission. (Among other factors, it was unclear how this could be done physically since my office was too small for a couch.) I duly wrote a memorandum to the chairman, and the matter was considered at a faculty meeting. The answer was negative. The stated reason was that the patient needed a female therapist! I felt this decision was largely dictated by the policy of keeping non-medical therapists 'in their place'.

Psychoanalysis was the most prestigious form of therapy, and advanced residents were eager to be accepted as candidates for analytic training. This training was carried out under the aegis of the Washington Psychoanalytic Institute which conducted a joint programme at the University of North Carolina and Duke University. Since I had completed the programme at the Washington School of Psychiatry and had developed reasonable skills as a therapist (through supervision, coursework, and personal analysis) it was largely redundant to become a candidate at the 'official' institute. Nonetheless, my stubbornness wouldn't let me rest. Thus against my better judgement – it was known that no psychologist had ever been admitted – I submitted an application. One of the training analysts in the department with whom I was on friendly terms tried to dissuade me but I was not to be deterred. In due course, I was interviewed by a visiting committee. Three days later I received a curt note from the local committee which read, in full: 'Your application for psychoanalytic training has been rejected.' I reacted to this defeat with considerable rage. My analyst at the time (correctly) told me that the world of psychotherapy was larger than the American Psychoanalytic Association, and that I was free to study and learn with or without their blessing.

He also impressed on me that clinical psychologists are 'guests in the house of medicine' and if they elected to work there, they had to accept the limitations of 'guest status'. It took me nine years to learn that as a clinical psychologist I might be happier in an academic department of psychology. Thus, in 1966 I left North Carolina for Vanderbilt, a move I have never regretted. For the first time, I was a 'first class' faculty member in a college of arts and science. Before making this move, however, I seriously considered abandoning the field of psychotherapy *research*.

Several factors contributed to the transient desire to become a full-time therapist. For one thing, I had lost my grant support; an application for a research career award had been turned down by the National Institute of Mental Health, and I had no full-time research collaborators. Wisely, I later came to think, I never went that route.

Temperamentally, I consider myself much better suited to a research and writing career than to that of a full-time practising therapist. A research career in psychotherapy, combined with a small clinical practice, has allowed me to stay close to the clinical arena; it has satisfied to a much greater extent my desire to learn more about the process of therapy from a scientific perspective; to work collaboratively with graduate students, post-doctoral fellows, and colleagues; and, finally, I feel I have neither the patience nor the stamina to see patient after patient on a steady basis.

Renewed commitment: Psychologist in a department of psychology

While in North Carolina, I continued my research and also acquired clinical experience, both in psychodiagnosis (with Dr Gordon Rader) and in psychotherapy. In the latter area, Dr Wilfred Abse, an exceptionally able analyst, taught me a great deal about the practice of psychoanalytic psychotherapy.

By 1966, I had established a place for myself in psychotherapy research; I had become a tenured full professor; I had sponsored several doctoral dissertations; and I had developed reasonable skills as a therapist. I had also undertaken a second analysis (again with a male M.D. who later became a training analyst). In retrospect, this analysis, which lasted about four years, had been less than successful, for which I eventually came to blame my analyst who, not unlike my father, was an authoritarian, cold, and forbidding figure. Perhaps most damaging was the later realization that he cared little for me as a person. I probably sensed this but repressed the fact. He was generally disliked by psychologists who worked with him on a day-to-day basis. They reacted negatively to his pomposity and arrogance.

At Vanderbilt University I continued to research, practise, and teach psychotherapy based on psychoanalytic principles, in that order. I typically saw a few adult patients over a prolonged period, on a once or twice a week basis. I felt that therapy enriched my research and vice versa. Increasingly, I have striven to unify scientific inquiry, practice, and training. I have learned a great deal from my patients, second only to my personal therapy, but my first love has always been the empirical study of the therapeutic process and outcomes. I have remained riveted to the questions: What is psychotherapy? How does change come about? What are the essential qualities in patient and therapist that lead to success or failure? How can we improve training and practice?

The interpersonal perspective

In terms of my theoretical orientation I have remained faithful to Freud's teachings, but have also profited greatly from insights of Harry Stack Sullivan, Franz Alexander, and many others who have built on early psychoanalytic insights. I have always been much closer to Freud's writings on psychotherapy than to his contributions in other areas, particularly metapsychology. The latter I have come to regard as thoroughly antiquated and in need of reformulation. My current thinking is best reflected in my book (with Jeffrey L. Binder), *Psychotherapy in a New Key* (1984) which focuses attention on the transactions between therapist and patient in the here-and-now of the therapeutic relationship. In my view, Freud's conception of transference remains one of his most original and fruitful contributions.

To expand on this statement, I believe that patients' difficulties in living are most fruitfully seen as interpersonal. They give rise to interpersonal problems with significant others in the present, and they are presently enacted with the therapist as well. This tendency of patients to transfer unresolved problems to significant figures in the present allows the therapist to see transference phenomena *in statu nascendi* and to deal with them as empirical data in the here-and-now. As these maladaptive interpersonal patterns are identified and their meaning is better understood, the patient simultaneously has a good experience with a contemporary who has the capacity and commitment to understand and thus help the patient.

Therapy thus becomes a corrective emotional experience in which the patient feels understood in a way he has never felt understood before. In this process, early traumatic experience and empathic failures on the part of parents and other caregivers are relived and corrected. It may also be seen that the tendency of patients to re-enact maladaptive patterns of living with significant persons in the present is, in fact, the core of the patient's 'illness'.

From the behavioural approaches to psychotherapy I learned the need for close study of empirical phenomena and the necessity of maintaining an open mind about the nature of the therapeutic influence. I have respected Rogers' early emphasis on the importance of the therapist's empathy but have regarded client-centred therapy as a rather thin, watered-down version of psychodynamic thinking. Trying to keep up with the pertinent literatures has remained an encompassing activity. Next to my family, few things in life have absorbed and gratified me as much as my work and my students.

There is no doubt that Freud's life and work have had and continue to have the greatest influence on my development. Perhaps, like him, I have always been more interested in advancing scientific knowledge, rather than in healing. Still, there is a great pleasure in helping a fellow human being resolve struggles that one recognizes as related to one's own. Sullivan put it well when he said in his 'one genus postulate': We are all much more human than otherwise.

Throughout I have struggled against a certain ambivalence, on the one hand believing that psychotherapy can be immensely helpful; on the other hand, I have felt that therapy and therapists have very limited powers to combat suffering and unhappiness stemming from early and deep-seated conflicts.

Among my *bêtes noires* have been the cultist aspects of psychoanalysis, in particular the omnipotence and conceit of certain analysts, the orthodoxy of many older practitioners, and the grandiose notion that psychoanalysis is superior to any other science and therapy. It is easy for any therapist to fall prey to an omniscience complex, and a number of analysts, more than other therapists, have made a fetish of such beliefs. I don't think it is a coincidence that psychoanalysts as a professional group have performed or encouraged relatively little research (in the strict sense of the behavioural sciences) and that hard data on the effectiveness of psychoanalysis have been conspicuous by their absence. This is true despite the fact that thousands of analytic patients have been treated over the decades and a sizeable number of analysts have been trained.

What makes for a good therapist? I have no simple answer but I believe that a person needs to have passionate commitment and dedication, basic decency, an ability to empathize with human suffering (perhaps gained most meaningfully through overcoming one's own difficulties), intelligence, compassion, boundless patience, curiosity, a keen desire to learn, tact, reverence for life, and the ability to be constructive (that is, to keep one's aggressive and destructive tendencies in check). To this I would add the capacity to look for adequate evidence and to guard against premature interpretations or constructions. Needless to say, these are ideals, and few of us, if any, can lay claim to saintliness. It is more accurate to say that virtually any therapy session is flawed to a greater or lesser degree. It is also quite appropriate for patients to realize that their therapist is less than perfect (which simply says that he or she is human). In the service of this – often important – insight it is salutary to admit one's mistakes and shortcomings occasionally. For example, one might admit that one was distracted during a given hour or otherwise failed to do one's best. (This may seem self-evident and unnecessary except for the fact that among the occupational hazards of being a therapist are grandiosity and omnipotence.)

Just as the choice of a career is deeply embedded in one's personality, so is one's theoretical orientation. Thus I don't believe that one consciously chooses to become a member of a 'school', but one or the other fits more adequately one's inner needs. I have always felt the psychodynamic perspective did this for me. I started as a disciple of Freud, had formal training as a Sullivanian, returned to Freud, and eventually adopted an amalgam of psychoanalysis, interpersonal theory, object relations theory, and systems theory. I have been immensely proud of my students, particularly of those who embarked on careers in psychotherapy research themselves. I believe I have taught more effectively by precept and example than by formal instruction.

The crucial importance of the therapeutic relationship

I would like to say a few words about the therapeutic relationship, a topic that has held much interest for me. I am convinced that the *quality* of that relationship is the most powerful force in therapeutic change. What do I mean by 'quality?' Perhaps a good way to describe it is to refer to the crucial importance of how the therapist is experienced by the patient. For therapy to progress, the therapist must be experienced as someone who cares, is dependable, trustworthy, non-judgemental, helpful, constructive, benevolent, non-controlling, and kind. The patient must become convinced that the therapist is a person who is not easily bowled over or impressed, who maintains a high degree of objectivity as well as a certain distance. The therapist must also be someone who declines to participate in neurotic games the patient is typically impelled to play, who is not easily angered or inclined to retaliate even in the face of provocation, who seems to know his or her way through the jungle of the patient's conflicted feelings, and who is there when needed. All of these characteristics appear to fit true friendship and yet a good therapist is different from a good friend.

The major difference, in my opinion, is found in the *professional* nature of the relationship. The patient should always remember that he or she is engaging the services of a professional person and that this service should be paid for. The common currency in American culture is that of a fee for service. Beyond paying for the therapist's time, no other obligation is incurred. (Increasingly, the cost of therapy is borne by 'third parties', i.e. insurance companies or government.)

The fact that the patient's obligation towards the therapist is spelled out and sharply delimited allows the patient great freedom because he or she need not be concerned about the therapist's feelings, attitudes, or values. The patient enjoys the privilege of being permitted to experience (although not to act on!) any and all feelings towards the therapist without having to fear retaliation or retribution. The therapist, for his or her part, must live up to the contract I have described and must steadfastly resist using the patient for any purpose other than as a means of earning a livelihood and for the gratification that derives from exercising one's therapeutic skill. Thus the therapist's wishes, needs, fantasies, etc. must be assiduously monitored lest they interfere with the therapeutic work. The therapist must be acutely aware that the therapeutic relationship is a unique and highly privileged relationship. Because of the patient's vulnerability it is easier than in ordinary human dealings to influence, seduce, or otherwise abuse the patient. Thus any self-seeking departure from the sanctioned therapeutic role is doubly reprehensible.

Ideally, the relationship between patient and therapist should be a relationship between two equal adults, and if therapy goes well, such equality will eventually be approximated. Although it is instituted in that way from the beginning, the patient is recurrently impelled to engage the therapist on a childlike level, to recast him or her as a father, mother, sibling, and the like. That is, the patient has a tendency to 'regress' in therapy, to turn the therapeutic relationship into something it is not, thereby attempting to bring about the gratification of childhood wishes that were either unrealistic at the time or were the product of deprivations.

To some extent the therapist must gratify the patient's unfulfilled wishes in and through the collaborative work in therapy; in other respects the therapist must help the patient accept the fact that some deeply felt childhood wishes and needs were not satisfied and cannot be satisfied in adult life. Thus the patient is helped to accept certain limitations and frustrations that are a part of 'growing up'. In the end, the patient is strengthened to function more adequately as an autonomous adult. In sum: the therapist must understand what it means to experience neurotic struggles and to communicate that understanding through words and actions.

This does not mean that the patient is forbidden to derive enjoyment from the therapeutic relationship. On the contrary, to the extent that the patient comes to terms with his or her neurotic struggles, the patient can come to enjoy other close human relationships, including the therapeutic one. On the other hand, if the therapeutic relationship provides too many (or the wrong) gratifications, the patient will tend to use it as a substitute for relationships in 'real life'. Thus the therapeutic relationship must limit gratifications so that the patient will be motivated, as an adolescent is motivated, to leave the protected (but limiting) atmosphere of the home to seek his or her fortune elsewhere.

Just as 'real life' is not Utopia, neither is therapy. One hopes that psychotherapy represents one of the best relationships life has to offer, and in any case it should be an antidote to the kinds of relationship that the patient has come to dread and yearn for in childhood. Therapy is a means to an end, not an end itself. There are times when both patient and therapist tend to forget that fact. From the patient's vantage point, this is excusable; from the therapist's, never.

Without professional training, a therapist is unlikely to function effectively in what is basically a very difficult role. Negative effects in psychotherapy, as I was able to show (Strupp, Hadley and Gomes-Schwartz 1977), are ultimately traceable to deficiencies in the therapist, which should teach us that therapy should never be undertaken lightly.

The therapist must be human and humane

Although the patient–therapist relationship should always be a professional relationship, it need not be stilted, stuffy, or rigid. In recent years, thanks to the writings of Zetzel, Greenson, and Kohut, among others, therapists have been given 'permission' to be more 'human' than used to be the case when the 'classical' recommendations were followed. In other words, I believe that a therapist is not abdicating the professional role when he or she is natural and spontaneous. Freud's conduct, as is well known, can serve as an example.

The opposite of what I mean is illustrated by the following vignette. A patient, having overcome considerable internal resistances, presented his analyst with a small gift, a pipe, at Christmas time. He declined to accept it, ostensibly on the grounds that the patient's motives needed to be 'analysed' or that acceptance would muddy the transference. He lamely said something like: 'You can probably use it yourself,' which was hardly the point. The patient felt hurt because the analyst's refusal duplicated earlier experiences in which the patient had been made to feel that he had nothing to give. The analyst, following the 'abstinence rule', apparently saw the gesture as a 'manipulation' or as a form of 'acting out'. To be sure, therapists should guard against becoming enmeshed in a patient's neurotic scenarios, but they need to make a careful distinction between neurotic manipulations and a simple human gesture. The difference is one of empathy versus blind allegiance to a set of rules.

Perhaps it should come as no surprise that in my early therapeutic work I emulated various aspects of the 'neutral' stance mentioned above. In more recent years, I have been able to relax and make more sensitive distinctions. I have come to see therapy as an important 'corrective emotional experience'. I do not mean that the therapist should deliberately play a role opposite to the parental attitude that had been traumatic to the patient, but rather that the therapist should be human, in the best sense of the word. I see nothing wrong – and much that is right – when a patient develops a genuine fondness for a therapist whom he or she experiences as helpful, caring, and concerned. It seems to have taken analysts a long time – much too long! – to learn that basic lesson.

By the same token, I see it as a proper task for the therapist to encourage and support constructive moves by the patient in the outside world. Nothing the therapist does is ever 'neutral' and the patient always interprets the therapist's behaviour as helpful or unhelpful. It goes without saying that the therapist should avoid neurotic traps, e.g. when he or she is held responsible by the patient for the outcome of a well-meaning 'suggestion'.

I believe the role of 'interpretations' has been greatly overestimated. They may advance, as well as hinder, therapeutic progress. I have become particularly sensitive to 'pejorative interpretations'. By calling attention to some aspect of the patient's 'pathology' they do so in a way that undermines the patient's already shaky self-esteem. Certain analysts unfortunately seem to be adept at this nefarious game (Strupp 1982; Strupp, Hadley and Gomes-Schwartz 1977).

In Sullivan's felicitous term, the therapist should be a participant observer, a trustworthy ally. The therapist should allow the patient maximum freedom to reach his or her own solutions, and to keep advice and guidance to an absolute minimum. The therapist's communications should be succinct and simply meaningful. Despite the limitations of my early investigations, I was able to observe, even from the therapists' written responses, that there were substantial qualitative differences between the masters and the novices; the latter were often verbose whereas the former proposed communications that were 'crisp', to the point, and remarkably parsimonious. I have continued to admire the latter.

The essence of psychotherapy

What, then, is the core of psychotherapy? In my view, it is the special use of a relationship for the purpose of helping a fellow human being come to terms with the troublesome consequences of a traumatic past and the maladaptive learnings deriving from it. It means to become a companion to a fellow human being over a more or less extended period of time and to assist that person in extricating himself or herself from the painful and self-defeating hangovers attributable to earlier learnings. As it turns out, this is often a difficult and taxing assignment.

Curiously, there seems to be a fairly sharp dichotomy between people who become therapists and those who become researchers. Somewhere along the way, it seems to me, each of us has to decide which road to choose. Practitioners, of course, are far more numerous today than researchers. The latter may be said to entertain a more questioning attitude towards the phenomena in our domain; conversely, practitioners may have a deeper commitment to helping patients. The two, it seems, do not seem to meld very often. When they do, this is a happy coincidence. Psychologists, perhaps as part of their academic training, tend to be more cautious and less sure of their ground in making interpretations than psychiatrists, whose medical training seems to permit them to be certain, even in the fact of relatively meagre evidence.

To students of clinical psychology whose commitment to psychotherapy as a *science* is often ambivalent, I have recurrently remarked that, of all the mental health professions, psychology is the only one that is likely to advance knowledge through systematic clinical research. I believe this is so because our discipline, more than any other, equips students with the essential tools for becoming researchers. Exceptional psychiatrists who have chosen research careers have typically been self-taught. Efforts by the government to train larger numbers of researchers, through post-doctoral fellowships and the like, have had little effect on augmenting the cadre of clinical investigators. It is, of course, quite clear that the income of practitioners usually exceeds that of research specialists by a significant margin.

Although I have had to struggle against considerable odds to reach the point at which I am today, I feel that I have been extraordinarily fortunate, and do not wish to change my current role for anything in the world. I hope to remain in 'active status' as long as my health and circumstances allow. I treasure my collaborators, students, and colleagues in this country and in Europe, notably in Germany. A number of my colleagues have become good friends, and this fact, by itself, has been a great gift.

I feel that I have been able to make some contributions to the advancement of knowledge in psychotherapy and it is gratifying that some talented young people are continuing the work. If there is a lesson to be derived from my career, it is that recognition is more likely to come to those who once they have become committed to a field of endeavour – be it science or practice – persist in its pursuit for a considerable period of time, maybe a lifetime.

Research in this area has become specialized and demanding. One can no longer expect to be a full-time therapist and pursue rigorous research as an avocation. At the end of this century, research – particularly research focused on the therapeutic process – has begun to make noteworthy advances and I believe, more than ever, that significant progress lies ahead. Research has become at least as prestigious as professional practice. It is also heartening that research and clinical practice are showing signs of becoming integrated as the sharp dividing lines between 'schools' are being eroded. Perhaps the time is not far off when the growing *rapprochement* between clinicians and researchers of diverse orientations will bear fruit.

References

Freud, S. (1925/1959) 'An autobiographical study', postscript in *The Standard Edition of The Complete Psychological Works of Sigmund Freud*, edited by James Strachey, 20: 3–74, London: The Hogarth Press.

Strupp, H. H. (1955a) 'An objective comparison of Rogerian and psychoanalytic techniques', *Journal of Consulting Psychology* 19: 1–7.

Strupp, H. H. (1955b) 'Psychotherapeutic technique, professional affiliation, and experience level', *Journal of Consulting Psychology* 19: 97–102.

Strupp, H. H. (1955c) 'The effect of the psychotherapist's personal analysis upon his techniques', *Journal of Consulting Psychology* 19: 197–204.

Strupp, H. H. (1957a) 'A multi-dimensional system for analyzing psychotherapeutic techniques', *Psychiatry* 20: 293–306.

Strupp, H. H. (1957b) 'A multi-dimensional analysis of techniques in brief psychotherapy', *Psychiatry* 20: 387–97.

Strupp, H. H. (1957c) 'A multi-dimensional comparison of therapist activity in analytic and client-centered therapy', *Journal of Consulting Psychology* 21: 301–8.

Strupp, H. H. (1960) *Psychotherapists in Action: Explorations of the Therapist's Contribution to the Treatment Process*, New York: Grune & Stratton.

Strupp, H. H. (1982) 'Psychoanalytic failure; reflections on an autobiographical account', *Contemporary Psychoanalysis* 18: 235–58.

Strupp, H. H. and Binder, J. L. (1984) *Psychotherapy in a New Key: A Guide to Time-Limited Dynamic Psychotherapy*, New York: Basic Books.

Strupp, H. H., Hadley, S. W. and Gomes-Schwartz, B. (1977) *Psychotherapy for Better or Worse: An Analysis of the Problem of Negative Effects*, New York: Jason Aronson.

Chapter eight

A fight for freedom

Fay Fransella

Why did I become a psychotherapist?

It sounds ludicrous to start out by saying that there was no obvious reason why I became a psychotherapist. But that is so. It just happened. In fact, I really do not see myself as one; it is only because other people seem to see me in this role that I am in this book at all.

Such statements have intrigued me for more than twenty years. It can be paraphrased like this: 'I am not a stutterer, I am just someone who happens to stutter' (Fransella 1972); 'I am not an arsonist, that is what society calls me, *I* am purifying the sinful' (Fransella and Adams 1966); 'When I'm hallucinating, I'm not a hallucinator; when I'm vomiting, I'm not a vomiter. I do these things; I am affected by these things, but I am not the THING itself' (Fransella 1981).

Now I am faced with being put into a category and feel as they do. 'I am not a psychotherapist, I just happen to do what some people call psychotherapy.' This dislike of categories is one of my reasons for working so happily within George Kelly's (1955) personal construct theory – as you will see.

So, to avoid this being an overly short chapter, I have slightly changed the emphasis to 'how did I become a person who does psychotherapy?'

The process leading up to the decision

Having no ideals, motivations, fantasies, or longings to become a psychotherapist, all I can do is present a historical perspective which, maybe, will explain WHY I now do something called psychotherapy, and why I did very definitely decide to become a psychologist.

It always feels very pre-emptive to state that something started at a definite point in time, but this has to be in order to get anywhere in this narrative. My childhood, as I remember it, was one lived in secret. My mother had died when I was six and my father was in his sixties. I never had any doubt that my father loved me deeply, but the 60-year-old man found it difficult to communicate with this motherless 6-year-old girl. The succession of 'nannies' followed by 'companions' did not help me sort out who I was after the trauma of the disappearance of my mother. My life was lived secretly and internally.

Amongst other things, I had a secret longing to be a doctor, but I had learned at school that I was rather short on intelligence. I seemed to have a lack of desire to achieve. Having been put in a school form specially designed for those who were not expected to pass their School Certificate (roughly the equivalent of O levels at that time), it was clearly unthinkable that I should mention this grandiose dream to anyone.

One consequence of being with the 'dunces' was that we were not allowed to do mathematics. I thought of settling for being a nurse. But I saw this as being second-best. Even then I was never one to take kindly to that. Somewhere, dwelling within that passive, secretive child, there was another, more active one, struggling to get out.

So, at the age of 16, I left school with no encouragement from anyone to stay on. To the surprise of all concerned, I got enough passes to get my School Certificate. In fact, I received a piece of evidence that probably affected my life profoundly. Our headmistress taught history. At the time I was aware of having a near-photographic memory. It was therefore not difficult to take copious notes during her history lessons and to memorize these page by page. Not only did I get a distinction in history, but the headmistress wrote on the form giving the results 'you were top of all the Upper and Middle V's in history!' I nursed this piece of invalidatory evidence of my inherent stupidity silently. It takes more than one event to change one's basic personal beliefs. At some level I think that 'other self' was furious at being put in the dunces' form and decided to 'show them'. But I do not remember that this was a conscious decision.

So I went on and took a course in domestic science and went to evening classes in shorthand and typing. The former was at the wish of my family, the latter was for me. The norm for my family was for girls to prepare themselves to become wives and mothers. It sounds strange these days, but no women in recorded history in my family had ever had a job. So it was natural to follow the pattern and do domestic science while waiting for the necessary husband to come along. But that other self went to evening classes to learn shorthand and typing.

Somewhere within this period, someone told me about occupational therapy. This seemed quite interesting. It was in the medical world and yet appeared different from nursing – the second-best. Apart from not being considered high on brains I was also considered to be good at 'doing things with my hands'. The other self now came truly to the fore for the first time. I rebelled publicly against my background and the future that was laid out for me. Instead of staying at home to house-keep for my aged father, I became an occupational therapist (OT) and remained one for more than ten years.

In the psychiatric hospital where I spent all this time as an occupational therapist, I was lucky to be there just before it changed from being a war-time emergency hospital back to being a psychiatric hospital. This meant that I remained on the top of the pile as more OTs were employed. I was therefore in a position to develop the several departments in the hospital to fulfil my implicit notion of what occupational therapy was about. Occupational therapy was not just about doling out cane to make baskets or knitting needles and cotton to make dishcloths. It was about helping patients develop themselves as persons in spite of the all-pervasive effects of institutionalization on them. I became particularly interested in helping those 'long-stay' patients who formed the major part of our departments' clientele develop themselves psychologically. To me it was very much therapy and not just occupation. Perhaps there was some feeling below the level of conscious awareness that each of these people also had another person trapped inside struggling to get out.

There was Brenda whose ever-present vacuous smile only left her face when she passed a piano. She would never speak, only be the quiet, good 'patient'. One day I so arranged things that she and I were alone when we went past a piano. We sat down at it together. The smile left Brenda's face. In its place there was a look of someone who was in touch with the world again. She played. After some days she even began to try and speak on occasion. She was not 'cured' but she had started to become Brenda again.

There was Peter. I started a percussion band for these forgotten people. They did not agree with the need to beat their instruments in time to the music, but they were exploring their world in a different way. Peter thoroughly enjoyed himself. He masturbated to the music. As one psychiatrist put it 'he played his own organ'. We had patients meeting in groups to discuss 'things'. There were beauty classes for female patients who had been in hospital for more than twenty years – and so on.

Looking back, it is clear to me that what I enjoyed in the work was this aspect of helping people elaborate themselves in relation to their otherwise very restricted world. I was certainly not a psychotherapist. We had two amongst the psychiatrists who specialized in psychotherapy, but they were the people who consistently refused my invitations to come and see their patients 'at work' in the occupational therapy department. This was not thought possible on their part as it would destroy the psychotherapeutic relationship. That always puzzled and saddened me. A psychotherapist came to be someone who talked alone with patients behind closed doors and who saw him- or herself as being the one who brought about the 'real' psychological change in patients. These psychotherapists restricted themselves to the articulate ones – not Peter or Brenda. But we occupational therapists worked also with large numbers of people who were 'short-stay' – or 'neurotics' – and we felt quite strongly that we sometimes helped them. A psychotherapist was, for me, a distant figure, and someone who made you feel uncomfortable to be with because they were able to understand things about you of which you were not aware. I think they were also people of whom we were jealous.

I enjoyed being an occupational therapist. But there was a niggling question that would not go away. How did I know that what we actually did produced any useful results? There was a clinical psychologist at the hospital so I went and asked her how to go about answering that question. It proved to be relatively easy and quite fascinating. You take two groups of patients, give one group the drug, largactyl, and the other, a placebo, and give both groups a 'total push' occupational therapy programme – that is, a varied programme of events that filled the day. If occupational therapy is any good, both groups should improve.

This is precisely what we did and, indeed, the control group did about as well as the drug group. In fact, some of the control group did better – a couple even left the hospital. I learned two other useful things from this experiment. One was the inherent difficulty of a double-blind experimental design. Here were these two nicely matched groups of patients with only the psychologist knowing to which group each patient belonged. One day the sun was shining and I thought how nice it would be if we all went outside to work. Within one hour about half the patients were like beetroots. One of the drug's side-effects was skin sensitivity to ultra-violent rays. It did not seem to invalidate the research as we were well into it by then, but it did make a point. The other thing I learned was the nature of the professional hierarchy in research. I had formulated the question, been responsible for carrying out nearly all the work, collected all the data. It was quite a surprise to find that a paper was published on the research without my name on it at all. This motivated me to publish my own first paper (Fransella 1960).

How did I become a psychotherapist?

The carrying out of this research was one of the turning points in my life. I suddenly wanted to do those things that the psychologist had done. My fascination was with the designing of the research. How did we get to the point at which we knew what to do in order to answer the question 'how do I know that occupational therapy does any good?' It coincided with some dissatisfactions with my personal and working life. Also, the occupational therapy department was now quite large – three of the large wards had been given over to it not to mention many small rooms, and there were fourteen various members of occupational therapy staff. I would argue that the occupational therapist in a large psychiatric hospital, at least in those days, had a greater quantity of concentrated interaction with individual patients than any other staff. Added to this experience is the involvement with people suffering from virtually every type of psychological problem.

I was at the top of my profession in my early thirties both in status and financial terms. The choice was to stay put and know more and more about less and less or do something radical, like trying to become a psychologist. The other self had escaped the trap and now had to find out just what the limits were. So, I chose the later. But there were obstacles. I had no A levels and no Latin. So, in order to get accepted for a degree in psychology I sweated away for two years at evening classes. But I won and found myself at the place of my choice – University College, London.

I enjoyed every minute of it. But it was very different from what I had imagined it would be. There was virtually nothing that seemed to be about the individual person. It was intriguing how 'the person' was dragged in, such as in 'person' perception. My lack of mathematical knowledge proved no handicap. I had not developed any reaction against numbers. In fact, I found statistics quite easy as I simply had to understand how to apply the formulae. It was those with A level mathematics who had difficulties as they kept wanting to know *why* the formulae were the way they were.

One of my favourite courses was comparative psychology. This turned out to be the study of small creatures such as amoebas. How fascinating to learn about their phototropic behaviour. What more amazing antics can there be than those of the male three-spined stickleback? Not to mention the sheer beautiful complexity of the dances of the bees. I think I have come back to this fascination in my attempts to formulate further George Kelly's invitation to look upon all living creatures 'as if' they construe. Even the amoeba can be said to construe. If single-celled organisms construe, why not the cells of our own bodies? If the cells of our own bodies construe then perhaps we have a theoretical rationale for inviting the client with cancer to 'get into' that part in which cells are multiplying abnormally and encourage *them* to reconstrue. But that is behaving as a psychotherapist and I have not got there yet.

So, although somewhat unhappy that there was not much to do with individual persons, only people, I was most content to be studying for a degree – something which, on leaving school, would have been a ludicrous ambition. Of one thing I was certain though – I was never going to go back into the psychiatric world. I had left occupational therapy, after all, to move on. In retrospect, it seemed to cause me little surprise to find myself applying for a clinical psychology course at the Institute of Psychiatry in London. I got my psychology degree and a place on the clinical course. So started my period of postgraduate training in the place where Hans Eysenck was professor of psychology and the course's reputation was of the solid empirical, behavioural, psychometric study of abnormal processes.

This course started me formulating what exactly it was that I wanted. As is so often the case, it did this by showing me what I definitely did *not* want. I did not want to do the kind of behaviour therapy in which talking to and trying to understand the patient played no theoretical role. At best this was seen as 'establishing rapport' and 'motivating the patient'; at worst it was deemed to interfere with the therapeutic process. I was finding that the patient and I did a great deal of talking as I encouraged her to climb up her hierarchy from most feared to least feared situations. I imagine I was quite good at it. After all I had had ten years of close contact with a very large number of people suffering from a very large range of problems – from schizophrenia to agoraphobia.

At some point on this course I came across the repertory grid. Coming from his background of physics and mathematics, Kelly had felt strongly that psychologists should be able to put numbers to things at some point in time. He devised the repertory grid to enable numbers to be put to the relationships that were said to exist between the units of his theory – 'constructs' (repertory grid technique is described in Fransella and Bannister (1977)).

Here I felt was something that could be used with individuals yet also kept one's feet firmly on the ground by producing numbers. It was freed from the constraints imposed by the norms one has with intelligence or personality tests. I decided to use grids as part of my Ph.D. – which was on the effect of rhythm on the speech of stutterers. This was good, hard-nosed Institute of Psychiatry research. The grid part was like an add-on, a bit that made the work just vaguely personal to the person being studied. Use of repertory grids almost inevitably leads to a desire to struggle with George Kelly's theory of personal constructs (see Bannister and Fransella (1986) for an account of the theory and its applications). One gets the feeling that the potential of the grid data is greater than its empirical use allows.

On completion of the clinical course and my Ph.D. I spent some time as an assistant lecturer at the Institute. Then I applied for, and got, a three-year research grant from the Mental Health Research Fund to study the application of personal construct theory to the treatment of stuttering. It was not research into the efficacy of a treatment itself but of the relationship between construing and behavioural change. My continuing search for an understanding of how people change was well under way.

I remember having no doubts about my ability to 'treat' people who stutter. My clinical training at the Institute of Psychiatry had given me, as well as others, great confidence in the right of all who successfully completed the course to carry out whatever form of treatment they thought a client required – always along behavioural lines, of course. My struggle was to formulate a theory of why people continue to stutter in personal construct rather than behavioural terms. It was hard going but I ended up with a formulation which could be put to the test (Fransella 1972). Since the theory one has about a disorder determines what one does about trying to alleviate it, the therapeutic strategy was clear. It looked very behavioural but it turned out to be what people call psychotherapy.

How and why did I choose this particular theory and type of therapy?

It is especially true of *The Psychology of Personal Constructs* (1955) that one's theory dictates the therapy and Kelly made therapy the central example of the use of his theory. As I struggled to come to grips with the enormity of the theory I increasingly felt I had come 'home'. It was full of personal meaning.

In general terms, personal construct theory was in glaring contrast to the behavioural, empirical, psychometric environment in which I had studied clinical psychology. Personal construct theory helps one understand individual persons rather than people. I have always found people, in large lumps, rather frightening and only feel really happy with individuals. As Kelly put it:

> This term (person) is used to indicate the substance with which we are primarily concerned. Our first consideration is the individual person rather than any part of the person, any group of persons, or any particular processes manifested in the person's behaviour.
>
> (Kelly 1955: 47)

As I struggled to develop my theory of stuttering, I was asking the questions, 'What does a person think he is doing when he continues to stutter? What experiments is he conducting that lead him to behave in that way?' In my previous incarnation as a behaviour therapist, I would be asking, 'What are the environmental factors that lead this person to respond in this way? What triggers the behaviour?' and so forth. The personal construct approach appealed to me then as now because I believe that I have something to do with how life turns out – I do not just respond to events. I like the feel of asking why a person *chooses* to stutter or be fat rather than be fluent or slim.

Since we choose for ourselves that course of action (or pole of a construct) which leads to greater elaboration of our construing system, a person 'chooses' to stutter in that particular situation at that particular time. The choice is made on the grounds that the situation becomes most meaningful to him if he behaves in that way; he is able to predict what is likely to happen both in relation to himself and the other person's reactions to him. Needless to say, the choice is not at a conscious level.

I have never felt at home with the Freudian notion of an unconscious working away in my nether regions 'making' me do things I do not necessarily want to do and, at the same time, making it virtually impossible for me to 'get at it'. Echoes of the past again. Kelly's idea of having varying levels of cognitive awareness appeals to me much more. Those low levels of cognitive awareness are by no means easy to plumb, but at least it is possible. I particularly like the changed status of the 'experiment'. It became something that everyone does rather than something I, as a psychologist, *do* to 'subjects'. In Kelly's model, having construed a situation as, say, one in which a person *could* display their incompetence – an undesirable state of affairs – that person is likely to choose a way of behaving which will minimize the likelihood of appearing incompetent. This might be by stuttering, or by turning on the charm rather than the intellect. The person then (at some level of awareness) looks at the outcome of that behaviour to see whether it has had the desired effect or not.

What Kelly's approach does is make all our behaviour an experiment. Behaviour is the experiment we conduct to test out the validity of our construing. It turned behaviour therapy on its head for me. Kelly refers to this as the reverse snake-charming experiment. It is not the behaviour therapist who is leading the patient up his or her hierarchy of snake-related situations, it is the patient who is conducting his or her own experiments.

> He does not surrender his initiative to another investigator. He observes
> carefully what happens – how frightened he is ... and he notes how
> differently the snake appears as he approaches it. Finally, it is the
> patient, now a scientist planning his own actions, who decides what the
> next step in the experimental series will be. In this kind of therapy,
> behaviour is so clearly an experiment.
>
> (Kelly 1985: 12)

There is one more thing that I think drew me implicitly yet irrevocably towards personal construct theory. It denies that we are made up of bits and pieces. I had great problems during my degree course in holding myself together. That is, I would try and work out how motivation and memory and perception and personality and emotion and social psychology all held together to make up *me*. It was quite easy to blend two of these but not more. And here was Kelly stating most forcibly that we can and should only be understood as one, indivisible whole person.

This was so in contrast with my behaviour therapy training. There, we were concerned largely with learning new behavioural responses. Emotion appeared occasionally as in reciprocal inhibition. Where there is peace there can no fear dwell. It did not matter much whether the patient was worried to death about her husband's infidelity while she was away in hospital or anxious about how her husband would react if she were able to go out and about anywhere. My job was to help her feel relaxed in the context of that particular step on her 'going-out-and-about' hierarchy. Kelly told me that it probably *did* matter. He went further, and told me that it was possible that 'going-out-and-about' might not be the problem at all but rather that her anxiety could be about her own potential promiscuity.

I liked the requirement that one does not impose one's own construing on the client. The only thing that matters is the client's construing of the world – there are no 'shoulds'. It therefore, in my view, gives absolute respect to the integrity of the person. The relationship with the client naturally reflects this. There is no requirement that 'the relationship' is, of necessity, something that must be examined. It is there for examination if it seems useful to the client that such an examination take place. But the essential feature is that therapist and client struggle together with the client's problem. The therapist does not have the answer, the client does.

If I had to stick my neck out and say what, in my own construing, drew me to personal construct theory, I think I would have to say 'freedom'.

In all other theories I was made to feel trapped in some way; as a person not being wholly responsible for my actions; as being a rather poor, passive creature. I react strongly against history – my own as well as that which I felt was imposed on me by the social context in which I grew up and lived. Personal construct theory asked me to look upon life and upon myself 'as if' I had created the person I now am and, when I find aspects of myself I do not like, to take responsibility for that and attempt to re-create myself. The theory, as with life, says that this is by no means always easy. So it is with the client. He or she is not a victim of their biography. Re-creation is always possible.

Having partially at least escaped the deterministic trap I had early on created for myself, I feel involved in Kelly's philosophy at a very personal level. Although I did not formulate all this at the time, I have come to see that his comprehensive personal philosophy helped me understand something about my fears, anxieties, loves and hates and possible reasons for some of the seemingly irrational actions I had taken. Perhaps most importantly, it gave me a way to structure my search for the limits of myself.

The philosophy of constructive alternativism states that no one need be a victim of his or her biography; the past does not 'make' us, it is what we make of the past that matters. I came to see my need to be on the move when one thing was mastered as the active elaboration of myself. It seemed as if the first twenty years of my life had been lived in a trap, the next ten years as getting glimpses of the wider world inviting exploration but still fairly static. All that time I think I had no clear idea of who or what I really was. Using Kelly's notion that all behaviour is an experiment, I came to understand my behaviour as an attempt to test my limits. Kelly invited me to release myself from the trap of my past by coming to understand it.

Apart from personal construct theory having an explicit personal philosophy, it is a theory of the complete person. It is in this sense that I think its reflexive nature is so important. The reflexive nature of Kelly's ideas is one of the most difficult aspects to convey. For those who work (and sometimes live) within this model of the person, it involves a constant conscious or unconscious application to oneself. In writing this chapter, I have come to a greater understanding of 'my self'. It has been like using Kelly's other method of assessment (as opposed to the repertory grid) called the 'self characterization'.

The self characterization represents 'Kelly's first principle'. That is, if you do not know what is wrong with someone, ask – they may tell you. The person is asked to write a character sketch of themselves in the third person. The instructions suggest that the person writing it knows you better than anyone can ever really know you and is very sympathetic towards you and so forth. In a sense this chapter is an invitation to all of us to write a self characterization with mine starting 'Fay is a psychotherapist, she ...'. In this case, the editors (therapists) did put some constraints on the authors in terms of content, but the client is usually given complete freedom.

My self characterization led me to see that my passionate dislike of feeling hemmed-in by circumstances could be usefully understood in terms of threat (the awareness of imminent, comprehensive change in one's core structures). These situations remind me still, all too clearly, of those childhood days in which I could find no anchors or direction. There is an awareness that, if things go on as they are, then I shall be back in that existential vacuum. I had come to this awareness already but not in such clear terms. However, the further reconstruing it has lead to is to do with the 'core structures' that are involved in threat. These are defined as being to do with one's 'maintenance processes'. Clearly these operate at very low levels of awareness and are most often developed at an early age.

The connection I consciously made for the first time while writing this 'self characterization' was with a consistent pattern of illness that has been with me for years. Kelly suggests that it can be useful to think of psychosomatic illness as being related to core-construing. For me this is respiratory infections be they pneumonias, tuberculosis or just general upper respiratory problems. I can go for years without anything serious happening. During this time I seem able to ward off most viral infections and am known to say such things as, 'I have no time to be ill'. But when I look at the times when I succumb, they are all to do with a sudden feeling of being trapped – in my terms this means unable to see myself moving forward in any meaningful way. The construing is something like 'being free to elaborate myself versus being trapped and unable to move'. This is where I am at now. I plan to continue the exploration of this core-construing of mine and so hope to continue my personal development. The reflexivity of personal construct theory leads naturally to one being one's own therapist.

Formal and informal training

I have had no formal training as a psychotherapist whatsoever. Apart from going on a number of different sorts of workshops – gestalt, transactional analysis and client-centred – I have had very little informal training of the public variety either. But I did have a powerful influence in the form of Don Bannister, a fellow clinical psychologist. It was he who 'sold' personal construct theory to untold numbers of people. Although I had come across the theory and grids before I met him, it was within the context of his friendship that I developed whatever deep knowledge I now have of them both. Over twenty-five years we explored the theory, dwelt on its reflexive nature by looking at our own selves, tussled with explanations of apparently inexplicable problems relating to our clients and thought up more ways in which we might, together or separately, bring this exciting theory to the attention of others.

The excitement I first felt on browsing through Kelly's theory has never left me. It is this personal excitement that keeps alive what I consider to be an essential component of being a psychotherapist – curiosity. That unquenchable curiosity is behind the questions the personal construct therapist is constantly asking herself such as, 'What is the experiment this client is conducting that leads her to behave in this apparently strange way?' 'What are the alternative ways of construing this situation that are open to this client?' 'Is this apparent resistance I feel in this client a result of him experiencing threat or is it justifiable hostility in the context of what he has come to face?' 'Is there something in my relationship with the client that is impeding his progress?' Answers to these questions are what I seek to help me help someone else who is 'trapped' by their own constructions of life. It is the excitement and constant personal learning experienced by all those who become deeply involved in personal construct theory that I try to foster now that I have become a teacher of counselling and therapy.

When did I become a psychotherapist?

Being consistent with the present theme the answer must be 'never'. Perhaps the answer is 'I'm still in the process' – but I do not think so. I do not, and never have, earned my living at it. Psychotherapy has never formed a major part of my life – except once and that may be the important time. That one was in those early days when I did research into the relationship between construing and change from stuttered to fluent speech with those who 'stutter'.

For just under two years I had sessions with on average four clients a day, five days a week. Looking back on that now, some fifteen years later, it seems quite awesome. It was a strange situation for I did not really believe – in my heart of hearts – that you could help someone give up a life-long way of relating to others simply by talking with them. But the results showed that many did, indeed, change and a few became remarkably fluent. We were joint experimenters and many proved better at experimenting than I did. But personal construct theory is written in such a way that, whatever predicament I found myself in with a client, suggestions of what might be going on were to be found within it. If I were to stop resisting the title of psychotherapist, I would probably consider that I became a psychotherapist at the end of that period of working with those people who stuttered, coupled with the support, challenge and 'like mind' of Don Bannister.

I keep sounding audacious. But I believe there were three factors that enabled me to succeed in this transition to 'doing' psychotherapy without formal training – as many clinical psychologists have done before me and since. First, I was able to bring to the situation my wealth of experience from working with individuals with major psychological problems as an occupational therapist. Second, I found a theory which came so naturally to me that I was quickly able to use it intuitively; and third, there was the inspiration of Don Bannister (who also had no formal training).

Since that time I have continued to 'do' psychotherapy but never again on such an intensive basis. I have gained particular experience with those with other intractable problems such as anorexia nervosa, bulimia nervosa and obesity. I am now caused to wonder if my continued interest in those with long-term problems is related to my feeling that I have personal experience of escaping (partially at least) from such a trap. Otherwise my experience has been of a more general nature in trying to help those with depression, anxiety, marital problems and many others. I have tried to follow Kelly in attempting to change language, but it is difficult. In line with his theory he hoped to change the word 'psychotherapy' to 'reconstruction', for it is the process of reconstruing that lies at the base of psychological change. Anxiety and depression take on different meanings within the theory. Weight problems become something different when one looks at over-weight as a person's experiment – the excess weight is the person's way of validating some important aspect of the self – something that overrides the disadvantages of obesity.

I have worked increasingly with the model I formulated with stuttering. That is, that a person will not change unless they have some clear idea, *at some level of awareness*, of where they are changing to. One cannot give up stuttering unless there is an acceptable 'fluent self' to move over to; the obese person needs to verbalize what a 'normal weight' self would be; an alcoholic, what he would be like as someone who did not drink to excess and so on. Many people with long-standing problems seem to have a virtual void at the place they want to travel to. Others have something that prevents them moving; something that is unliveable with. There was the obese young woman who became aware that she thought all men would want to rape her if she were slim; the depressed woman who thought people who are not depressed are cold and hard; the person who stuttered who found out that he thought he would be unlikeable if he were fluent; the young man who suddenly realized that, if he were going to change, he would have to change such a lot that he would lose the 'me' that he valued greatly. The bi-polarity of construing has become a major focus of my psychotherapeutic work. Perhaps I, too, had to collect evidence of what that 'other me' would be like before I took the audacious step of becoming an occupational therapist.

I am much 'braver' than I was fifteen years ago. On two counts in particular. I have found that people are able to move far more quickly than I used to think they could. This means that I follow my intuitive sense that a person can face a particular aspect of his construing rather than build up to it slowly. In Kelly's sense I have become more aggressive.

The psychotherapist should be one who is not afraid to lay wagers which are collectable in the immediate future. He should be one who is disposed to try out his hypotheses and to encourage the client to do the same. This does not mean that he tries out hunches impulsively without first taking care to formulate them into hypotheses. He should have a clear notion of what it is that he is trying out and he should lay his wagers in terms which will get the most valid information with the least risk to the welfare of his client.

(Kelly 1955: 604)

So the result of these years of experience is that my clients stay less long in therapy than they did. If a client approaches the twentieth session I begin to wonder what is holding us up.

Another change has been the growing realization of the importance of the 'diagnostic' stage of therapy. I used to think, and it is a common feeling in those who do training with us, that I was falling down on the job if I was not 'doing therapy' at least by the third session with a client. I now know that this is not only stupid, but can also be counter-productive. Since the aim of personal construct therapy is to help the client reconstrue, and since one of the essential aids to this is the subsuming of the client's construing system within the set of professional personal constructs, then sufficient time must be allowed for this to take place. Kelly uses the term 'subsuming' in the usual way. That is, the placing of one thing under another. In therapy, the therapist attempts to understand the client's way of experiencing the world by placing a template of theoretical constructs 'over' the client's system. Until you have a sense of where possible channels of movement may be, where the client will resist change at all cost in order to preserve his core structures, where lack of structure lies and so forth, any positive intervention on the therapist's part can be damaging or, at best, useless.

Because I now give the client and myself time for this process of subsuming and diagnosis to take place, I feel more confident about 'pushing' the client and the whole reconstruction process is therefore likely to be shorter. For those not conversant with personal construct theory and therapy, I would add that the therapy process is seen as two people in a joint venture aimed at finding new ways of dealing with the world of the client. Thus, the first diagnosis is tentative, it has to be tested out with the client. As a result of these first experiments, the diagnosis will be up-dated. It is for this reason that Kelly always talked of the 'tentative diagnosis'.

The nature of subsuming is very important. It is not an admonition to the therapist somehow to take over and thereby manipulate the client's construing. Subsuming in the personal construct framework is achieved by the therapist being able to suspend – put to one side – his or her own construing, especially those relating to values. In this way you have a chance of 'getting into' the client's construing world. This is not to be confused with empathy. The subsuming of the client's world takes place within the system of professional theoretical constructs. These could be the identification of areas of preverbal construing (discriminations between events in the world established before the development of language); or tight as opposed to loose construing (the making of absolutely clear-cut predictions about events as opposed to the sort of extremely loose construing found in disorders of the thinking process in some of those diagnosed as suffering from schizophrenia); or areas of anxiety (when confronted with events we are unable to construe or make sense of), guilt (when we experience behaving in a way that is contrary to how we believe ourselves to be) or hostility (when we do not like the look of events and 'cook the books' so as to make things appear as we think they should); or pre-emptive as opposed to propositional construing (life is *nothing but* a bore as opposed to life is many things, amongst which it can be boring) – or those core structures.

In essence, personal construct therapy is the application by the therapist of Kelly's theory of human experiencing to the joint understanding of one person's construing of the world – the client's. Over the years I have developed Hinkle's (1965) process of 'laddering' as a major skill in facilitating the art of subsuming. This is a process in which the client (or anyone for that matter) explores their own construing system by moving to more and more abstract levels. When successfully used the therapist and often the client gain access to vastly important, superordinate, areas of construing in a very short space of time. I could no longer function effectively without this skill.

In conjunction with laddering, I have weaned myself off repertory grids as an essential feature of my therapy. I now only use a grid when it seems likely to serve the needs of the client or help me with my 'diagnosis'. That is, some clients gain greatly in confidence if they see their construing laid out before them; as one man said, 'I thought I was going mad and that my thoughts were so chaotic that they were making no sense. But I can see there is structure here which makes sense to me and I am greatly relieved.' Or if I cannot understand why a client does not seem to want to change – a grid might show that he feels his way of behaving is preferable to his perceived change.

Grids are therefore now one of the tools we have at our disposal when a client and I work together. Another big change for me is the increasing realization of the number of tools that are available. Because personal construct theory is pitched at such an abstract level, it enables the therapist to use methods originating from any other therapeutic model. This does not, of course, result in personal construct therapy being eclectic. Far from it, as all the time the therapist is working within a very elaborate theoretical system. But it does give the therapist great freedom in choice of therapeutic *methods*. For instance, if the tentative diagnosis is that this person cannot possibly countenance any useful change while his construing in a particular area is too tightly organized, then some method for loosening that construing will be used. This could be traditional relaxation, or sentence completion, or free association, or dream analysis, or guided fantasy and so on. These are tools employed to produce the theoretical aim of 'loosened construing'.

What sustains me as a psychotherapist?

Having written all this, I now know why I do not *and do not want to* see myself as a psychotherapist. Categories are one form of trap. Like the crab that shouts, 'I am not a crustacean, I am *me*', I want to say that there are lots more things about me than being a psychotherapist. I do what I and others call psychotherapy but much else besides. I do not even see it, and never have done, as a central part of my life. I know I would find being a full-time psychotherapist very claustrophobic. I do not think I would be good at it either because of the amount of concentration and energy personal construct psychotherapy requires.

I believe the unease centres on two issues. One is that I have the notion that at one extreme psychotherapists are people who start seeing clients at 8.00 a.m. and continue with 50-minute sessions until evening, five days a week. Also, that some psychotherapists see the same clients five days a week. From my personal construct perspective, both are undesirable. To do personal construct therapy requires very deep concentration in the effort to work within someone else's construing system. Over five clients a day would mean not doing the job properly. For a personal construct therapist to see the same client five times in a week would be very exceptional – it has certainly never occurred in my case. This is due to the fact that it is the client who has to do most of the work and who has the answers to the problem and not the therapist. It is the client who has to conduct new behavioural experiments and construe their outcomes and not the therapist. Thus, the client needs space in which to do this 'homework' and it is this that he or she brings back to the next session. The personal construct therapist will therefore nearly always have other work to do along with therapy.

My other concern seems to be something to do with the dreaded disease of 'hardening of the categories'. Occupational therapy was a category that had hardened – there were no alternative constructions allowed of what constituted an occupational therapist or her therapy. There was one diploma available. It is the same with being a medical practitioner, dentist or architect. I would not like psychotherapy to be like that. Since we know so little about the whole process of psychological change, there should be room for ideas, theories, methods and approaches that stretch beyond the limits of our imagination. So, I am happy to *do* psychotherapy but do not want to *be* a psychotherapist. I do not see psychotherapy as a profession. I think it will eventually become one. Then, no doubt, the categories will be hardened.

If I had my time again, I would certainly choose to include psychotherapy as one of my major activities. I hope to be able to continue working in this way for the rest of my productive life. It is one of the most exciting experiences of my day when I see clients. What greater human experience can there be than two people grappling with the disaster, pain, and the unknown of one of them? What greater pleasure than the experience of that other person designing a new life for themselves and putting it successfully to the test? What greater satisfaction than a person saying that she has changed and now feels able to go on with life; she does not know how it has happened but she is very busy and does not think she can spare the time to come and see me any more? What greater personal challenge is there than being confronted with someone who, despite one's best efforts, does not feel they are changing at all? Oh, yes. It is a part of my life I would give up most reluctantly.

Like all who do psychotherapy, I have those I feel I can work very well with and those who I find difficult or impossible. Those who nourish my sense of being a psychotherapist best have a predominant problem with important areas of over-loose construing. This will usually include much anxiety since they find themselves often confronted by events which they cannot construe. This means they are unable to get along with the business of living their lives as they would wish. Our main job is therefore to help tighten those areas so that life can be tackled again. I suspect that my validation from working with such clients comes from my personal preference for viewing the world from a loosened perspective – experience gained when I grappled with those early, unconstruable events. Over the years I have learned to tighten it up – for public consumption at least – but I really enjoy the loosened mode. I have most difficulty with clients who are at the opposite end of that dimension. Those whose favoured mode is tightened construing. Those people who border on the delusional; those who 'know' what is right and wrong. But, quite often, this tightened construing is protecting some areas that are threatening the client with apparent imminent chaos. Since I find this client the more difficult, perhaps it makes me work harder!

Implications for other psychotherapists

I have had a very great struggle with this section of the chapter. It seems so presumptuous to think that my own struggles and experiences have any implications for others. Many psychotherapists work within their own theoretical frameworks, and any implications I might think up would not seem relevant in other settings. But, with gentle but persistent prodding from an editor and discussions with my group of people studying personal construct psychotherapy, I put forward the following as tentative implications.

The first is about these theoretical frameworks. I have a personal commitment to theory. Perhaps this has to do with coming from where I have. There is no way in which I consider that I have enough knowledge/ experience/intelligence/imagination or whatever to work out my own framework. So I feel fortunate indeed to have found one that is so rich in ideas and comprehensive in coverage that it provides some suggestions whenever I turn to it with a problem. Someone pointed out after reading this manuscript that he now understood why personal construct theory attracted me so much. It tapped into that urge to move forward and not allow myself to be trapped again. Personal construct theory sees the person as a form of motion and its philosophy states that there are always alternative constructions available to choose among in dealing with the world. No one needs to paint themselves into a corner; no one needs to be completely hemmed in by circumstances; no one needs to be a victim of their biography.

Whilst I find one particular theory meets my own needs, 'there are always alternative ways of construing events'. Obviously others find other theories more useful for them, as individuals. What I do think important is that psychotherapists have a theory to which they can turn in times of need. This theory should live for them and should be something they feel they can both develop within and which they can develop.

Personal construct therapy has sometimes been referred to as an eclectic therapy. Nothing can be further from the facts. Critics confuse practical eclecticism with theoretical eclecticism. Because of the very abstract nature of the theory, a personal construct therapist can be eclectic in the methods he or she uses to help the client move on. This is very different from having no established theory and choosing therapeutic techniques considered appropriate to that client on a subjective basis.

The theory guides the therapist in many ways. One relates to cessation of therapy. Personal construct therapy has the goal of helping the client 'get on the move again'. To do this the client has to be given freedom to experiment and explore. This leads to a situation in which the client may attend weekly sessions for, say, three months and then come fortnightly, then monthly. Very rarely does it involve the client attending for more than six months. If no movement has been fostered, something is going severely wrong. Other theoretical systems see the length of therapy very differently. Our theories guide us in what we do.

In writing this account, I have become aware of how much stress I felt should be put on my ten years' experience as an occupational therapist, both in the sheer weight of numbers of people involved and in the variety of problems presented. The range of human distress is vast indeed. This was brought into focus by my clinical psychology training. Some fellow students had come straight from university after leaving school. I can see why they liked the behaviour therapy model. It enabled them to relate to patients from 'behind' their therapeutic techniques rather than grapple with the complexities and puzzles of the person. Not only had they no theory but they did not all have a richness of human experience to bring with them into the therapy room.

Apart from thinking that having a sound theory and experience is an essential requirement for helping those in trouble, there is another aspect that I believe is worth the consideration of others. This is the difficult issue of reflexivity. What I have written may give some idea of what this means in personal construct theory terms. It is the constant referring of the professional constructs back on to oneself. There is an awareness – at some level – that you and the client are two moving processes and that these two processes can be seen as being governed by the same 'rules'. There is an awareness that my construing may impose itself upon the construing of my client in such a way that I distort my understanding of what my client is understanding – and so on.

The reflexive nature of the theory puts an importantly different complexion on the issue of whether or not those in training should have personal therapy. I believe strongly that this should *not* be a requirement (just something that is available to anyone who may wish to have that experience.) My reason is simple. A student is constantly 'in therapy' as he or she progresses on our course. Whenever clients or theory are discussed or skills practised, students work on themselves at the same time. This is particularly so in supervision. No discussion of a client can take place without a detailed analysis of the student's construing of their interaction with that client. It is the reflexive nature of Kelly's theory that perhaps, more than anything else, opens up the opportunity to all who work within it to learn and develop ourselves both as therapists and persons as we move forward into the unknown, hand-in-hand with our client.

References

Bannister, D. and Fransella, F. (1986) *Inquiring Man* (3rd edition), London: Routledge.

Fransella, F. (1960) 'The treatment of chronic schizophrenia: intensive occupational therapy with and without chlorpromazine', *Occupational Therapy* 23(9): 31-4.

Fransella, F. (1972) *Personal Change and Reconstruction: Research on a Treatment of Stuttering*, London: Academic Press.

Fransella, F. (1981) 'Nature babbling to herself: the self characterisation as a therapeutic tool', in H. Bonarius, R. Holland and S. Rosenberg (eds.) *Personal Construct Psychology: Recent Advances in Theory and Practice*, London: Macmillan.

Fransella, F. and Adams, B. (1966) 'An illustration of the use of repertory grid technique in a clinical setting', *British Journal of Social and Clinical Psychology* 5: 51-62.

Fransella, F. and Bannister, D. (1977) *A Manual for Repertory Grid Technique*, London: Academic Press.

Hinkle, D. (1965) *The Change of Personal Constructs from the Viewpoint of a Theory of Construct Implications*, unpublished Ph.D. thesis, Ohio State University.

Kelly, G. A. (1955) *The Psychology of Personal Constructs*, vols. 1 and 2, New York: Norton.

Kelly, G. A. (1985) *Behaviour is an Experiment*, London: Centre for Personal Construct Psychology.

Chapter nine

Challenging the 'White Knight'

Eddy Street

It really is a strange business that leads a person to sit in a room with complete strangers and listen to their intimate problems and worries in what is an essentially one-way flow of personal information. There was a time when I embarked on this job for what seemed purely my altruistic desire 'to help people'. I had no understanding of how I had come to place myself in this position. As some form of awareness grew and was developed, I have seriously questioned whether I have the right to offer myself as a therapist to others and often I have wondered whether I wish to continue. At other times it has been important in some undefined way to keep working at the job as if to answer some internal questioning that cannot and never will be put into any verbal form. Often I feel that if it were possible for me to have complete awareness and insight into why I became a psychotherapist then I may no longer have the desire or interest to continue. If only for that reason I have to ask myself the question 'why' repeatedly, because each client who comes along demands and has the right to ask of me 'why you?'.

Why did I become a psychotherapist? My motivations

I was never prepared for a professional life. The family that I came from has no tradition or history of careers. One great-great grandfather was a clergyman, but that side of the family, my mother's, slipped down several classes. No, my family is essentially that of working people. My father was an engine fitter, his father an engine driver, my maternal grandfather a boilermaker – in fact, for three generations I have been the only male not to work on the railway at some part in my life – even my mother was working on the railway when she met my father. I remember my father saying to me when I reached the age of 14, the age he left school, that now I was on my own, that he did not know much about life in schools and colleges and qualifications, and therefore I had to make my own choices and decisions. That may make it seem as if what led me into this damn job were my own internal desires and caprices and that I did not follow any family tradition – on the contrary, the act of becoming a therapist was the result of following the role that was well laid down for me in my family of origin.

I grew up in a home in which three adults lived. My father never left home; he lived in the house he grew up in with his parents and he brought his bride to this house to live. His elder and younger brothers had left and his step-brother and sister from his father's first marriage had also left. Clearly my father had a very strong attachment to his father – my grandfather – a man who I never met in a conscious way, for he died when I was six weeks old. The household was therefore constructed of my paternal grandmother, my mother, my father, myself, and then a few years later my brother. I never knew, and still don't, whether we lived with my grandmother or whether she lived with us. My grandmother, 'Nan', ensured that we were not all incorporated into one unit and my father, although not supporting this directly, was reinforcing of the process. She maintained her own sitting-room, her own kitchen cupboard, her own bedroom, and nearly all of the time ate her own meals. But the confusion about the boundary around our family unit was con-founded by the fact that as a child until about the age of 5, I slept in the same bedroom as my grandmother, and so did my brother when I moved out.

Certainly in this early period of my life I was left with a number of clear messages and myths; that in my family there was some distortion of responsibility and obligation. My mother had left her family home and was living in what was for her a different environment; undoubtedly, she was lonely and miserable as a young wife and mother. And here was my father remaining close to his mother because of promises he is reported to have made to his father before he died. My mother felt herself to be down the list of the 'family's' priorities and my father felt himself to be torn. In such situations the bonds between husband and wife become strained and tensions develop. The individuals look to others to gratify some of their needs; if a father was still involved with his own mother, then would it not be natural for a mother to turn to her eldest son for some of her emotional support?

So I was given the task of dealing with some of the needs of an adult before my own as a child were satisfied. Closeness of this kind then leads the child into the inner world of adult fantasies, and as my father offered the model of attachment between mother and son, I became acutely in touch with my mother's thoughts and feelings. She felt that her family background was in some way 'better' than the life we were living. She felt we could and should rise above it and conduct ourselves in a more polite and mannered way and this would be a more appropriate reflection of herself. I was to represent this elevation of social status and so, instead of being named in the style of the age, I was given the princely name of Edward, to reflect the royalness of our station. I was therefore given the task as a child of putting others' needs before my own, of caring for those in need, and doing this in a respectful and honoured way that is found among those of high social status. Thus by this means the 'White Knight' was born.

Myth has it that the position of a knight is a good one to occupy. However, in real life it is not quite like that. He has to be dedicated to one cause and rise to serve that cause at a moment's notice. He has to learn that battles must be fought each and every day to protect what morality has decreed must be protected. He must be prepared even to fight the king or his champion if the lady that he serves so demands. A knight also somehow stands aloof from what is going on around him; he is apart, if not cut off, from some of the mundane elements of life. Aside from the moments of combat and service, a knight must sit to await the calling; there are no rules or expectations for these times, except for the ability to be in a state of perpetual readiness and it is during these times that a knight will have difficulty in working out exactly what a 'life' and a 'destiny' mean for him personally. At times like these a developing 'White Knight' will oscillate between strutting around as a gross example of masculinity or comically posturing in a Quixote-fashion. As a soldier of fortune, pressed into service for a 'cause', that cause (i.e. looking after somebody else) became a *raison d'être*. However, all knights discover that there are higher ideals, moralities, and ethics that can guide life, and in the moments of contemplation that grow from being cut off, I found myself questioning the meaning of existence and life.

White knights not only care for damsels in distress, and fight evil barons and dragons, but they must also search for a 'Holy Grail'; they must seek for something that is unobtainable in the hope of completing some higher moral task that has not just been offered to them by a family, but one that has developed from the sheer fact of living a human life. A family role was therefore created; a place to occupy in a way that all family members know what is expected from that person. A *modus operandi* for relating to the world was constructed; a way of being with others was set. From my family role, given to me as a young infant, added to the mixture of adolescent queries and questions, the process of becoming engaged in psychotherapy started.

How did I become a psychotherapist? Ways and means

I never at any stage of my school career set out to become a psychologist; with no model or guidance except, 'Do what you enjoy', from my father I pursued those subjects that I felt were no chore to myself. I felt attracted neither to science nor to the arts, a little of each seemed to be a good idea. Geography, as a subject, fascinated me, as it really was a case of strange sounding places with far-away names; besides I would need a map for my knightly campaigns. Perhaps it was also a case of 'anywhere could be better than here', but in a strange way I did follow the model of my father with his interest in the historical, for I became quite enthralled with the question, 'why is the land like it is?' and so began a lifelong interest in geology. It was these subjects I pursued in my final years at school. I seemed destined and was encouraged to undertake geology at university; there were, however, some diversions. The English master, after my performance in the school play, suggested seriously that I should pursue a course in drama and a careers master suggested that I had qualities that would make a career in law. Little did any of us realize that some of these elements would become incorporated in how I pursued my eventual profession.

I was just about to go to university to study geology when in a very definite clear way, I realized that I did not want to do it. I felt that I knew enough about it from formal education; to continue would destroy my interest in it. I decided that I would read 'social studies' at university and I knew this principally meant psychology. I did not know what psychology was. I had never discussed it with anyone, I had never read a book on it, but I knew that I wanted to study psychology. After being accepted at a university (thankfully without an interview) I read my first psychology book – *Fundamentals of Psychology* (Adcock 1964) – an introductory text with a definite Freudian slant. Consequently, my first formal acquaintance with psychology met elements of my fantasized notion of it; the subject was about why people did things as they did, about unconscious motivation, about relating, about sexuality, about maturity and emotional well-being. Psychology was about how to stealthily acquire an understanding of human nature that would lead to self-knowledge and wholeness – it was how a 'White Knight' could become content and even perfect inside his shiny armour.

Along with many other students, I found the study of psychology during my first degree something of a disappointment: instead of being about people and how they operate, it was about animals and statistics and complex method- ologies investigating peripheral issues. It was about compartmentalization when I was interested in wholeness. I remember my first ever psychology lecture at 8.30 a.m. on a Monday; I sat at the back with my pen poised to write about the wisdom and truth that psychology had to offer us as human beings, but all it was about was Konrad Lorenz and his imprinting ducks. In my notes for that day I did, however, begin with the fact that one of the ducks, due to his imprinting, tried to make love to Lorenz's wellington boot – well I was, after all, interested in sexuality!

I gradually accepted the inevitable themes of university psychology and looking back I believe I enjoyed most of it. I was eventually introduced to the work of Gordon Allport (1955 and 1961), Abraham Maslow (1962), and George Kelly (1955), and believed that I had found some psychologists who operated in a way that was appealing to me personally. Some time during these university years, an image formed in my mind of the male psychologist – he was attractive, always at ease, pleasant to everyone, with time to survey the world and the individual simultaneously, he was well grounded, in control of his emotions and free of problems and worries. I wanted to be like this. It fitted in quite nicely with being a 'White Knight'. I believed that I knew from an early stage that I personally would not quite manage to attain that state, but what was important was that if I were a psychologist, then others would believe I would have these qualities. Being a psychologist therefore meant I could use a different kind of armour.

As my university career came to a close I felt quite lost and confused as to how I would leave the capable environment of an educational institution and enter into the hurly-burly of real life. I was in danger of becoming lost in books in order to become a psychologist, but as a 'White Knight' always helps those in distress, then the way out of the confusion was to seek a way of putting to use my abilities of caring and meeting the needs of others. Belatedly I applied for clinical training, was unsuccessful, thought about other 'helping' professions, was generally depressed, worked as a nursing assistant but eventually began training to be a clinical psychologist in the NHS. The 'White Knight' had moved castles.

On being allowed access to individuals, who were classed as patients, I was struck with the awesome power that was given to me. A power that defined the relationship between me – as a professional – and them – as patients. I could ask any question that I thought important, I could lead someone on a convoluted journey through their life just so I could understand how they got to be where they were. I could demand (but, hopefully, never did) a respect that I did not deserve nor could warrant. I became frightened by the fact that patients would actually believe that I conformed to my own idealized vision of what a psychologist was. And what was more, I had the power to play up to this role, even though it was at serious odds with the turmoil that I felt behind my professional shield. I became acutely aware that those qualities I saw in 'the Psychologist' were nothing without an understanding. I was anxious for I did not have this understanding; psychotherapists had this understanding; I needed to become a psychotherapist. A true 'Knight' was a psychotherapist.

I am not sure if my training as a clinical psychologist met all my needs. It certainly provided me with a notion of how a professional should behave and it certainly provided a range of experiences for me to test myself. A variety of theoretical models and therapeutic strategies was provided for me and I was somehow expected to work out some personal integration. I did, however, learn that to be a skilful helper one needs a variety of means at one's disposal and I learned that I certainly did not have enough adequate 'means' at the completion of my professional training. I attended several workshop and study events given by psychotherapists and was always impressed by the ease with which they could evoke an emotional response, cope with its consequence and still remain themselves. I was particularly taken with the work of the late Don Bannister. I was always surprised at the emotionality that existed within me; at the intense and varied feelings that quite quickly popped out. I knew that my professional training merely placed me in a position where I could now begin to undertake psychotherapeutic training. I wanted the control that psychotherapy offered, not of the patient by way of power, but of myself. I wanted to become a psychotherapist so I could take the 'White Knight' on to a higher plane of existence.

Unfortunately, Britain does not offer many training opportunities for young therapists. I had by this time acquired a wife and defined her as a damsel in distress and this, unfortunately, meant that the search for the Holy Grail could not be pursued in other lands even though it was seriously contemplated. However, by some good fate I attained a position as a clinical psychologist which involved membership on a psychotherapy course. The course was based very heavily on the skills of client-centred therapy (Rogers 1951), though elements of the theoretical model were essentially grounded in a psychodynamic understanding of individuals; consequently we spent a significant amount of time studying Freudian thought. I had, during my professional training, a reasonable amount of contact with the Rogerian approach and therefore I did not feel I was entering into an alien environment. As with my first degree I somehow felt that I would be instructed in 'secrets'; that the key to understanding (and contentment) would be shown to me. Again there was disappointment on realizing that the theoretical component was just a study in depth of work that I had in some way already been introduced to. But what training offered was supervision – a weekly presentation of tape recordings of sessions combined with weekly group discussions about current cases.

For the first time I had to present all aspects of my work for the consumption of someone else, and someone 'better' than me. Individual supervision soon brought with it a mixture of excitement and dread. I was having to deal with my work in a disciplined manner and I had to have faith that my supervisor had some knowledge of how things would turn out if I kept pursuing the skills in which I was being instructed. It was this discipline and the belief in my superior that led me slowly to wondering whether or not a 'key' actually existed. It was also the realization that my own emotional response had an importance in the contact with clients and this had to be dealt with inside my own armour. In some way that seemed natural I sought a therapist for myself, but as I look back now on that first experience of being a client I remember very little about the themes I pursued or the insights I gained. No, my remembrances are focused on the development of my personal skills through my meetings with my supervisor. She was a woman and I believe she quite enjoyed the attentions of a young 'White Knight'; she, in fact, wanted me to take off my armour for her, but that seemed too risky and anyway it blurred the boundaries. My movements as a helper of others ceased to be gauche and blustering; instead they became more subtle and gentle. I gained an awareness of the multitude of choices that became available to a therapist at every moment and as my experience of the nuances of human emotion grew I enjoyed the challenge of trying to find the right response for the right client at the right time. There were, however, some feelings that my response was constricted by aspects of the Rogerian method. I was always aware of a brake on some elements of my spontaneity. In many ways, however, this training experience was steeling the inner man rather than removing the outer covering and it certainly provided a core element in my therapeutic development.

As a child of this particular training course, I felt attached and reasonably secure, but the world of human fallibility does not allow adults to remain as children for long. Problems developed, both on the course and in the department. It was decided that some of my time was to be spent with children and their parents. This was not so problematic for me as, having a young child by now, I too could consider myself a parent, and by now I could almost admit to myself that a way to deal with problems of my own was to go and help others. This work confirmed that the therapeutic method I had been taught was somewhat limited and rigid when faced with a different set of problems. For a while I felt somewhat confused. As the course finished, for me somewhat abruptly, the problems of the job increased, in some way a choice point came. With the prospect of another young child, it seemed I needed my family close. I ran for home rather than seek pastures new. A risk was taken, however, for instead of remaining in adult mental health, I took a job within a child guidance clinic. I certainly did not feel appropriately experienced as I made this move and I did feel that my skills primarily belonged elsewhere, but for my own benefit I needed 'to go home'. I needed the security of familiar surroundings in order to hold on to my new role in old armour as the 'White Knight' of a young family and I needed to keep close to those ties that valued that role in my family of origin. Even though I was questioning the need for armour in professional life, I needed it more than ever in my personal life.

For a little while I struggled with holding on to a Rogerian viewpoint whilst being a helper of children and parents. My work did not seem to hang together well and I felt it rather affected. But then I was introduced by a colleague to the works of Salvador Minuchin (1974) and Jay Haley (1976) – workers who were able to conduct the complexity of family sessions and who understood how families actually behaved. I was also introduced to the wonders of the one-way screen and the way in which it makes public what was once considered private. Somehow I was given permission to be different by my colleagues and I was allowed to realize that I did not have to take my work for weekly supervision to a supervisor who was interested in one model. I left behind my internalized supervisor and at some point I became my own supervisor. I entered my own head. I suddenly realized 'I can do this'.

Here I was in my own home town, with people whose language and experiences I automatically shared, who expected a certain type of emotional reactivity that was naturally mine. There, too, I was faced with families, and suddenly I realized 'I know about families'. I knew from that deep-seated intimate experience about belonging, about boundaries, about generations. I knew about conflicts resolved and avoided, about marital dissatisfactions rebounding on offspring. I knew about the effect of history and myth and the process of development. I knew about the struggle to be an individual in a family, as well as the struggle to be a member of a family, whilst retaining a sure core of identity. I personally was battling with these issues with my parents in one suburb and my family of marriage in another. Suddenly the experiences of the clients I was meeting were also my experience. I soon discovered that families have roles, and they are willing to offer particular roles to strangers; they want judges, scapegoats, lawyers, policemen, philosophers, and some even want a 'White Knight'. Oh how I struggled with those who wanted a 'White Knight'; for here I was placed by client families in a role which caused me difficulties in my personal life.

The one-way screen also allowed me to practise in front of an audience; it allowed me to be 'heard' in more than one way. If the family do not like or understand it – then my colleagues will. Family therapy became a reality to me, for somehow it tapped into that part of me that my own family had prepared well, as well as offering a freedom from that preparation. It allowed an emotional response and sanctity that felt truly my own. Somehow it allowed me to be a member of a group, a family, but at the same time I was different as an individual. It allowed me a control over a situation that I longed for, but on being given such control I found I did not want it. It offered me a power that I could just ignore and then turn into energy for others. Being with a family in struggle allowed me to care for and to help, but most importantly it allowed me to cease to be a 'White Knight' – but only if I chose. I had indeed discovered the 'Holy Grail' – it was myself. I had no need for armour. I soon saw that the skills I acquired became a part of my natural interaction and so technique became personal development. I had found something that had the quality of play in it. Helping others had become easier.

When did I become a psychotherapist? An identity

Shunryu Suzuki says 'In the beginner's mind there are many possibilities, but in the expert's there are few' (1970: 21). So did I become an expert – and is that expert a psychotherapist? At various times there do appear to have been some crucial points in my professional life when I have felt a movement towards a different way of being a 'therapist'. There was the moment of realization that within myself I had a range of responses that I could, at any time, genuinely choose for my client. I certainly felt that I had learnt something at that moment. There was the time when I realized that I could arrange to see a suicidal patient in a week's time and not feel personally responsible for what occurred to him during the interim period. There was the difficulty in clashing with my supervisor about the way certain processes should be dealt with; I experienced a different sense at that time, of me as a person able to stand on my own two feet. There was the time when it was no longer necessary to carry my supervisor around with me. I became truly responsible for myself at that moment. I knew that I was working in a different way, when I felt at ease about sitting with a family and dealing naturally with whatever it was they chose to throw at me. I might well have become a therapist when seeing families became 'play' instead of just hard work. Perhaps I am a therapist when I doubt what therapy is!

I believe there was a time when I called myself a psychotherapist, or to be more accurate when I called myself a family therapist. Some while ago I stopped calling myself it, primarily because I felt that I was unsure of what family therapy was and what it was that I practised. I am not sure for whose benefit it is to call myself a therapist. When I completed my formal therapeutic training, I wanted to call myself a psychotherapist, but I knew all the while that really it was to impress myself, to attempt to give out the aura that was associated with my idealized image of a therapist. When I first felt able to teach others family therapy, even though I had never been 'taught' myself, this too might have been the time when I did call myself a family therapist. But that time too has passed, particularly when I realized that it did not make any difference to how I behaved or how families treated me. I believe that I now prefer to think of myself as a person who attempts to behave in a therapeutic way for others.

So how do I now view my professional practice? It has undergone a number of major transitions. There was the move from the general eclecticism of my professional training to the Rogerian based adult individual therapy; from there was a move into family therapy based on structural/strategic formulations and then a move towards experiential and historical explanations and approaches. Each move has left its mark and each element is hopefully integrated into some whole. I am aware that each of these changes also marked important transitions in my personal life. I took up my client-centred therapy training at a time when I was trying meaningfully to leave my family of origin and establish my own identity in a family of my own. I entered the world of family therapy when I returned 'home' for support and from where I continued with the process of psychologically leaving home. This was also the time when I became aware that my newly acquired experiences of being a parent had a relevance to others. Finally, as I discovered that I had movement in the space of the therapeutic situation that was related to the emotional freedom in me, not fully realized elsewhere, I experienced some difficulties in my own marriage. As my marriage failed, the search for roots seemed even more important in order to secure me in the swirling currents of the post-divorce period and to provide a source of support as I took on the overwhelming demands of my single parent status. As I moved towards the experience of truly living my own history, I ceased to want to be a 'White Knight' for another and perhaps my wife ceased to want to be a damsel in distress. As I became acquainted with the work of Whittaker (Napier and Whittaker 1978) and Bowen (1978) I fully realized that my 'White Knight' template for relating had begun in my family of origin and that I need not behave that way any longer.

So what is it that defines me as a psychotherapist? Is it the intellectual appreciation and techniques that I have acquired via books and teachers, or is it my own growth in relation to a job of work? It seems that the more my practice develops, the more uncertain I am of what it is I practise. I gain a view of myself as a wounded helper, a person willing to share in the process of healing even though I have to deal with my own disabilities elsewhere.

What sustains me as a psychotherapist? Frustrations and sustenance

Like many other therapists, I suffer from the frustrations and tribulations of having to deal with agencies and bureaucracies that do not understand what I can do or what I can offer, and hence I do not feel valued as a person by my employers. As a consequence of this I have in the past been angry with those in power. Hopefully now, however, I have some sense of maturity and I am more likely just to continue with the job in my own way and generate my own validation. To some extent I feel as if I am less attached to my agency and colleagues. I no longer need the audience and so am quite happy to pursue my craft with the basic requirements in a far more quiet and unobtrusive way than I once did. I now feel I have much more of a sound connection to the values and ethics of what might be termed a psychotherapeutic morality. This is a morality that can be shared very readily, but it can only be shared with those who wish to share themselves. It cannot be imposed on helping agencies, neither can it be artificially constructed.

For many years I have felt frustrated in having to see many clients who just wish for an 'agency response' from me. In fact they do not wish to meet me as a person – they seek a solution to a problem and someone has sent them to me to provide it. Consequently, not all the time am I required to use myself, but then I suppose working for a public agency I have to accept work of this nature. I am sure that in past years the enthusiasm of a knight in shining armour would have lifted and even benefited some of these clients, but that kind of enthusiasm does not exist for me any more; it has probably been generated into a belief in life itself. Not every client who is referred to a child guidance clinic within the National Health Service in Britain is able to take this, for their immediate needs are far more pressing. I have discovered, however, that nearly all of these clients respond in a small way to a 'psychotherapeutic attitude' and now I have learned to appreciate very small changes in clients by offering this within the context of the required and the expected.

Over the years I have greatly enjoyed and been energized by engaging in clinical teaching to professionals-in-training. Every so often a trainee would come along who had the personal need to be a psychotherapist: and it was to these individuals that I found I had a way of offering something of value. I discovered a natural way of teaching and supervising that had a personal relevance to such trainees in their own struggle as well as being of assistance to the trainees' clients. For some time I often surprised myself with some of the things I said while teaching; it was as if it did not quite come from me, it was as if I only really discovered what I knew when I opened my mouth. More recently, however, this type of event has not surprised me because I do not believe I am bothered so much by what I know and what I do not know. I have a certain degree of security that I have 'knowledge' that is valuable to myself and others. It may well be that this security derives from the act of knowing rather than a particular knowledge itself. The growth of this security has implications for how much or when I teach, for clearly no longer do I need to teach to discover how much I know. I am sure, however, that the offering of myself as a clinical teacher will remain an area that continues to be sustaining for myself.

I do not really know whether clients in themselves are sustaining for me, as it feels more that it is the therapeutic situation itself that provides sustenance. I know I find some clients more exciting and some more challenging than others. I know I enjoy, in a playful way, being with a family where I can bounce around a variety of roles and allow myself a full range of emotional expression. I know also that I am attracted to the struggle that is found in doing marital work, the struggle of retaining an individual identity whilst being coalesced into a couple. I am also fascinated and enthralled by those couples and families who miraculously 'fit' the expression of 'my own theory' that is being verbalized at that particular time. I am also concerned about those families who fail to touch me and those who over-tax me. Ultimately perhaps in some unknown way, it is the tiredness that comes from the depletion of relating to people professionally that I find sustaining.

So where now is the 'White Knight'? Clearly I entered this profession to meet my own needs. I came seeking a way of relating; a way of being intimate with another, that was essential for me, but difficult for me to find as I behaved in the world outside the consulting room. I was attracted by the power and control that seemed to flow benignly from the therapist role. I needed an image to project for myself and others. I needed to feel worthwhile and important to someone – perhaps even someone who was not important themselves. I needed to try and find in others those things that were lost to myself. I wonder if all those who professionally engage in the therapeutic process have periods of feeling guilty because they are not there for their clients; it is for themselves that they undertake therapy. I sometimes feel angry with the damn job for trapping me in this way. On many occasions I have taken that guilt and anger to training events and experiential workshops and looked for something for myself whilst perhaps believing that it was for others.

I have always felt it important to 'work on myself', have enjoyed the luxury of being on the receiving end, and have often sought help from others when troubled myself, but only in small doses. To some extent I believe that life itself should be therapeutic and that individuals with a content and sustaining environment do not require therapy for themselves. But it was surprising to find that when I entered a sustaining and loving relationship, many old doubts, problems and worries returned in a new guise. So once again I sought therapy for myself, but this time for a more protracted period to deal anew with the fear that only a bag of wind existed inside the armour. This time the personal change has not led to a transition in my work, it has led to more of a deepening of my practice, for the growth has been in my personal life. I no longer need to be a therapist in quite the same way.

I am still very aware of my tendency to jump on to my heraldic-decked charger and gallop off saving everyone and demonstrating this to the public at large. But at least now I know that when that feeling comes, I am in trouble. I have to think again and then let a new set of feelings percolate through to me. Always in such situations I have something to gain for myself. With hurting nakedness I have to combat the 'White Knight'. It is at that moment that I now feel something happens for me. It is at that moment that I gain a new element of my own experience whilst losing that sense of self that demands experience for selfish needs. Even though this is painful and requires effort, it is also fun and enjoyable and this is why I continue at the job. Whatever degree of wholeness I have attained, I now use it for others; whatever moment of emptiness I achieve, I can offer its freedom to those who sit with me. When I started out doing therapy I noted how many writers on therapy drew attention to the links with Buddhism; I began with an intellectual study of Zen, but now I have developed a spiritual practice within the Buddhist tradition that has considerable importance to me in whatever I undertake.

I am now aware that my struggle as a therapist is about the attempt not to use the set of rules for relating that I was given as a child. I was set up with a blueprint of relationships that hampered some of my experience, responses and potentiality and now I no longer need this with the strength that once existed. Not surprisingly, I have found that a new depth to my work has grown since I established a new love with a woman; the love of a kind that once was unattainable for me. I now have a relationship that sustains me as an individual whatever I do and it may well be that I do not need psychotherapy, that I could give it up. Maybe this is a useful platform from which truly to undertake a psychotherapeutic practice.

Implications for other psychotherapists: For others

So what does this mean for other therapists? There are, of course, those issues of a political nature, that I sometimes take up on my soap-box when I need to spout forth. There is the need for all training courses for the helping professions to incorporate into their framework some psychotherapeutic practice and supervision. There is a need for all professionals-in-training to be given some type of individual assistance integrating all the different theories and strategies into a whole that fits for them as a professional self. There is a need for all those who supervise trainees to be offered some supervision themselves. Themes of this type, however, all concern professionals in some way coming into contact with themselves as therapists and hence into contact with themselves as persons. How a therapist thinks, acts and feels will be a mixture of the past and the present; there is beauty in the way that the historical processes of our lives interplay with the here and now experience. We neglect one at the peril of misunderstanding the other.

The other political themes concern the availability of psychotherapy within a public agency such as the National Health Service in Britain. If at some level it is seen as being a useful resource to supply, then serious thought has to be given to the ordinary working needs of those professionals who provide a psychotherapeutic service. However, it is not only psychotherapists who require the basic means to undertake their job, the time to do it well and the validation for doing so; every professional in the helping agencies needs this. Unfortunately the bureaucratic and market place ideology, that now tends to dominate, undermines the care an institution needs to offer its workers, before they can begin to care for others. Because of their view about assisting individuals to reach their potential, perhaps psychotherapists should directly indicate the nature of the environment that helping agencies could construct for themselves. But I am not sure if I want to take on such issues in an active way; for the moment it just seems important that I continue with my professional practice to demonstrate for those who wish to see that a sane way of dealing with people can be maintained in the face of adversity.

But this chapter is not about the politics of training and practice of psychotherapy; it is about a personal journey; it is about the search for identity in the context of an ordinary family; it is about relating to the past in a way that makes sense for the future to be continued. As I look back over what I have written, I do not feel that I have written about psychotherapy or even about becoming a psychotherapist – I have written about myself. I am aware now of the elements of my life's path up to the present that I have not been able to touch upon. Particularly I think of conflicts, confusions, and resolutions of the anima and animus elements of myself as I struggled with caring for two young children; I also think of the efforts I put in to acquire a new sense of individuation from my family of origin and of the new type of relationship I constructed with my father and mother. I wonder if I would have done these things if I had not practised psychotherapy; I somehow think I may have, but whether I could have put them into words would be another matter.

The 'White Knight' has been well and truly challenged. The spiritual combat that marks out the struggle for identity has been fully engaged in. It is now hard to stop writing because there can be no sense of an end point on a journey such as this. Every moment is just a point on a path and also the whole path at that moment. I know that once again I have presented myself to another – to you, the reader. I hope some element of my story has evoked a response in you. Thank you for hearing me.

Acknowledgements

Over the years I have been indebted to many individuals who have in some way made a contribution to the development of myself in therapeutic practice as well as to myself as a person. I would like to thank them for the personal gifts they offered me; the responsibility for the outcome is, of course, solely mine. I would particularly like to acknowledge David Lewis, Margaret Nuttall, Lynn Muir, Mary Bruton, Chris Evans, Andy Treacher, Paul O'Reilly, Wray Pascoe, Mike Shooter and Jeremy Hazell.

I would also like to extend my love, as always, to my family – to my Mam and Dad, to my brother Dave, to my children – Joe and Jenny – and of course, to Anna.

References

Adcock, C. J. (1964) *Fundamentals of Psychology*, Harmondsworth: Penguin Books.

Allport, G. W. (1955) *Becoming: Basic Consideration for a Psychology of Personality*, Yale University: Yale University Press.

Allport, G. W. (1961) *Pattern and Growth in Personality*, New York: Holt, Rinehart and Winston.

Bowen, M. (1978) *Family Therapy in Clinical Practice*, New York: Jason Aronson.

Haley, J. (1976) *Problem-Solving Therapy*, San Francisco: Jossey-Bass.

Kelly, G. A. (1955) *The Psychology of Personal Constructs*, vols 1 and 2, New York: Norton.

Maslow, A. H. (1962) *Towards a Psychology of Being*, Princeton, New Jersey: Van Nostrand.

Minuchin, S. (1974) *Families and Family Therapy*, London: Tavistock.

Napier, A. Y. and Whittaker, C. A. (1978) *The Family Crucible*, New York: Harper and Row.

Rogers, C. R. (1951) *Client-Centred Therapy*, London: Constable.

Suzuki, S. (1970) *Zen Mind, Beginner's Mind: Informal Talks on Zen Meditation and Practice*, New York: Weatherhill.

Chapter ten

A late developer
John Rowan

Why did I become a psychotherapist?

When I was born we were living in the married quarters of the RAF station at Old Sarum. My father was a squadron leader, and throughout my childhood he was moving from station to station. My mother was placid and stable, and adapted efficiently to all the moves and changes. We would move with him, but there was usually a period when he was away in the new place before we could join him, so that he was often not around in the home. It was as if he were the engine that kept everything going, but down in the hold somewhere out of sight. When he appeared, he was a strict disciplinarian, and believed in punctuality and the twenty-four hour clock. We had a nanny called Nurse Jacob, and a spaniel called Joseph. I was an only child until I was 6½ years old, when my brother was born.

Perhaps unusually, my father was the emotional one, and my mother the cool, contained one. I experienced him as manipulative and emotionally blackmailing and guilt-inducing. So in my adolescence I resolved to be different from him, and to be straightforward emotionally. At 16 I adopted the phrase 'education of the emotions', by which I meant having only those emotions which were convenient. The word 'love' in particular became very suspect, because of its associations with my father.

I did not know at the time that at an unconscious level I had made quite a similar decision for quite different reasons. This was that my mother had thrown me out of her womb, and taken away her breast, and cut off her love from me, and that I had to get revenge on all women, and all men too. My 'educated emotions' and straightforwardness turned out to consist largely of hate. I think it altogether probable that my mother, for reasons of her own, found it impossible to give love in any warm or personal way to me, and perhaps to others too. It felt to me as if I made various attempts to get her love, failed several times to do so, and retired hurt and lonely (the final shot in this coming with the arrival of my brother), and in the end turned loneliness into a virtue by claiming not to need people. In that way I could observe people in a way which was basically external, and calculated to cut me off from them very successfully. I then wondered why I never had much success with women. In other words, I had developed what I would now call the schizoid defence which I later found characteristic of so many men.

My father was interested in psychology, and particularly enthusiastic about the scientific approach of Cyril Burt. So at an early age I had some inkling of what psychology was all about, though I did not follow it up until much later. So what I am saying is that my approach to psychotherapy came from roots which were not really about caring at all. I was deeply suspicious of caring, partly because my father used words like love and care to manipulate and use others, and I was frightened of closeness, because I had tried to get close to my mother and failed, and got hurt.

My approach to psychotherapy was rooted in a different concept: I was always more interested in the notion of freedom. As I grew up, I had no interest in doing good or in helping people, and although this has changed now, it is still true that my main interest is in enabling people to realize their potential, and this may well be painful rather than soothing in most cases.

So there was no tendency towards psychotherapy in my early adulthood. Because of my father's occupation, and because I was called up in World War Two, I lived in thirty different places in my first thirty years. This increased my schizoid tendency, in that it meant that I never allowed myself to get too attached to anyone or any place, because I knew I would have to leave it and lose things and people sooner or later. Then when I came to start work, I did not know who I was or what I wanted to be. My jobs included tutor, agricultural engineering clerk, electrical factor's clerk, supply teacher, telecommunications engineer, telecommunications instructor, encyclopaedia salesman, office manager, library research editor, marine insurance clerk, and accountant.

During my Army service I spent some time in India, and was there introduced to the philosophy of Spinoza, which I found very exciting and liberating. Then when I came back to England, I was introduced to the work of Hegel by a friend of mine now dead, Harold Walsby. He pointed out that the work of Hegel was all based on the idea of freedom as the highest value. And he pointed out the connection between Hegel's famous statement, 'Being and Nothing are one and the same', and the scientific value of taking nothing for granted. I joined a small Marxist party, and soon became the editor of its internal theoretical journal. All these influences made me very suspicious of psychotherapy, though Christopher Caudwell, a marxist theoretician I had some use for, did have something to say about the importance of the unconscious, and Harold Walsby wrote about the connections between Marx and Freud.

It was about this time that I got married. I met my wife when I was teaching a course on cybernetics at Braziers Park Adult School, and Neilma was recording lectures by Joseph Needham on her Palantype machine during the same weekend. We played table tennis together, and it all started from there.

We got married at a registry office in Burnt Oak, and Peri was born a little over a year later.

The turning point in my discovering what I wanted to do really came, I suppose, when four of us, who had been expelled from the same political party at the same time, started to study together for the London University diploma in sociology. This was a four-year course, one evening a week, and at the time we did it, the four years were entitled social history, social structure, social psychology, and social philosophy. Our main intention was to know more about society so that we could start a political movement of our own. We had tried to start a movement under the title of 'Social Integration', but this had failed and we wanted to know why.

I found that I was particularly good at social psychology and social philosophy, and found it interesting and got good marks and awards. I even had a scientific article published in *Penguin Science News*. At the same time I had discovered that a possible career was in consumer research, and this quite appealed to me. It would develop my skills as a researcher very fast; it would pay well – I had a wife and two children to think of; it would give me a lot of knowledge of society and how it actually operated at grassroots level. Two social scientists had particularly impressed me – Mary Parker Follett and Ernest Dichter; both of these said that academia was slow and conservative, and that it was in commerce and industry that the live work of real change was pursued. Both of them took up the dialectical position I had learned from Hegel.

So I tried to get into consumer research, but none of the companies would have me without a degree. I decided, with a lot of help and prompting from the lecturers and my friends, to take a degree. I didn't have the required entrance qualifications, however, so in 1959, at the age of 34, I took the philosophy exam and the final exam for the diploma, an A level exam in logic and another one in English literature, and a scholarship exam to Birkbeck College. I passed all these satisfactorily, and duly enrolled for the joint honours degree in philosophy and psychology at Birkbeck College, under Richard Peters; I spent about three evenings a week for the next four years going to lectures and writing essays.

By the time I finished and got my degree, my wife and I had four children, so the pressure was even greater to get a well-paid job, and I duly went into consumer research. I liked the work very much, as I specialized in the psychological side, and this meant that I could use all my skills – in negotiating, in logic, in interviewing, in statistics, in writing – all at the same time. The views of Follett and Dichter that business people are much more alive, much more interested in experimenting than anyone in academia became truer for me than ever. I liked the feeling that my work was being used immediately, not placed on some shelf or dragged out with years of delays in the manner of some of my academic friends.

I went up the ladder quite fast, never staying in one job longer than two years, and at the beginning of the process described in this chapter I was managing director of the Bureau of Commercial Research and, at the same time, the London representative of Ernest Dichter International (interestingly enough, Dichter was a psychoanalyst who had gone over to market research – I was going to move in the opposite direction). I was well respected in the business, and had written papers and articles which had been published in the relevant magazines and journals. My main interest was in the objective measurement of attitudes and attitude change.

But I was not purely a businessman, as most of those in market research undoubtedly are. I had been a revolutionary, very much influenced by the ideas of Hegel and Marx, but had been disillusioned by the emphasis in the small party I had joined on having the correct case at all costs, and seeing the essence of the matter as winning arguments. As I have already said, I had tried with others to set up something better, but all our efforts foundered, and the group broke up. So I had been spending my spare time on the arts, working with Bob Cobbing to set up the Barnet Borough Arts Council, writing poems with the Writers Forum group, exhibiting collages and constructions with Group H, taking part in drama with Arena Theatre, helping to organize 'Happenings', getting together a magazine called *and* and organizing a poetry reading group called 'Soundabout'.

Three phases

The process of becoming a psychotherapist took twelve years in all, and went in phases. My going-in position was that I was interested in social change, but was frustrated because I couldn't see any way to achieve that. Phase one (1969 to 1971) was what could be termed a mid-life crisis, where I understood a new notion of politics, that it didn't have to be just about having the ideal political case, or just about getting out and acting militantly: it could be about feelings and relationships and the way you lived. Phase two (1970 to 1979) was where the crisis resolved itself and I found that groups were the best places for personal and political change. Group therapy was one of the main roads to freedom. Phase three (1978 to 1981) was where I found that one-to-one work was equally satisfying and more regular and reliable.

The only time I had any sort of ideal model of what a therapist should be like was in phase two, and here it was entirely a model of the group leader, not the individual psychotherapist. I was fascinated by group leaders like Fritz Perls and Will Schutz and the Esalen Flying Circus – people who would fly in, do their week or weekend group and fly out again. I still feel that this is much more exciting than one-to-one work, and I do it three or four times a year.

What tends to happen in such intense groups is that people who have been working for months or years in their individual counselling or psychotherapy, and have got really stuck and grooved in their method, may come to the event and allow themselves to be stimulated and shaken into some kind of breakthrough. So the visiting group leader harvests a crop which has been nurtured and tended elsewhere. This is great for the visiting leader and great for the participants, though it may be a bit disappointing for the regular counsellor or therapist, who sees his or her patient or client valuing something which is outside the regular meetings. This is the model which had real magic for me, though I later came to see that the regular therapist deserved just as much credit and acclaim as the visiting leader. I now feel that the ideal set-up for the client is to go to an intensive workshop to stir up deep and valuable material, and then go to an individual therapist to work through all the implications of this in detail over time.

So it was not really a question of why did I want to become a psychotherapist, as if that were the explanation of why I did become a psychotherapist, because the desire to be an individual therapist and the action of becoming one were all part of phase three, and happened more or less at the same time. Until I actually became an individual psychotherapist, I didn't really want to be one at all. By the time I wanted to be a one-to-one therapist, I actually was one. I was thrown into being a therapist.

How did I become a psychotherapist?

It all started with going to see a play. The play was *Paradise Now*, when it was put on by the Living Theatre at the Roundhouse in June 1969. This was an extraordinary play, which was partly scripted and partly improvised, and the improvised bits took up most of the time and involved the audience a great deal, either by the players coming into the audience, or by the audience coming on to the stage. It was highly political, but also had a spiritual aspect to it, mainly based on the Kabbalah and Tantra.

> The revolution of which the play speaks is the beautiful, nonviolent anarchist revolution. The purpose of the play is to lead to a state of being in which nonviolent revolutionary action is possible.
>
> (Rostagno 1970)

Joseph Chaikin once said: 'The Becks perform that special function which very few books and movies, some love affairs and great losses do – they can actually change your life' (Chaikin 1968). Well, I don't know how many people that is true for, but I am certainly one of them.

B NOW

I went with two friends who were also poets, Ulli McCarthy and Keith Musgrove. One of the lines in the play was 'Form a cell', so we thought we would. My loft had just been opened up, so we could meet there. We formed a group called B NOW, the B standing for 'Best society humanly possible'. Some of the best bits in the play had been the actions, which often took the form of the things done in encounter groups or microlabs – for example, one was the flying, where players and members of the audience had to get up on to a platform on the stage, and dive off into the arms of the waiting people, arranged in two lines with arms joining the lines. 'Breathe ... breathe ... breathe ... FLY!!!' – I remember it so vividly still (Malina and Beck 1971).

The meetings of B NOW all took the same basic form: part one was a series of non-verbal exercises, which went on for anything up to an hour (the exercises were devised at first by Keith Musgrove, who was working as a group leader at Centre 42 in Kensington, the first growth centre in London, and later by Rupert Cracknell and John Henzell, both of whom were art therapists); to open part two I would say 'All right: the revolution has happened; the world outside is just the way you always wanted it to be; what do we do now?' (we would go on from there into some very fascinating fantasies about Utopia, where we took nothing for granted about the way things had to be); and part three was the eating, where we all brought food and fed each other – the rule was that you must not feed yourself. This turned into a very sensual and delightful part of the meeting.

This was really my first experience of group work, and because it was my house we met in at first (though we went to others later) I could put in any of my own ideas that I wanted to; so in a sense I was a co-leader right from the start. Some of the experiences I had in that group stay with me today, and some of them were turned into poems, and it was an emotionally shaking thing to go through. The exercises often stirred up early traumas and were quite cathartic on occasion. My wife and parents-in-law and children (who lived downstairs) hated the group because of the strange noises (people crying, shouting, groaning, screaming, and so on) coming from the group. That was the main reason why we met in other places later. It may have been partly because of this beginning that Neilma always disliked my involvement with group work and therapy.

This group went on for about six months, meeting almost every Friday night, and then it gradually died – fewer and fewer people came regularly, and it petered out altogether. And I got interested in groups at that point – what made groups live and die – how did groups work exactly – what really happened in groups? So I started going to groups: I went to encounter groups, gestalt groups, psychodrama groups, Tavistock groups, psychosynthesis groups, T-groups, bioenergetic groups, movement groups – you name it, I did it. I read about groups, I studied groups. As a social psychologist, I was supposed to have read all the literature on groups, but I found I hardly knew anything, and in fact some of the best books on groups had not been written by then.

And in the process I came across the Association for Humanistic Psychology. This was an organization which had only been created in this country in 1969, though it had originated in the United States in the early 1960s. It existed to put across the theory and practice of just the kinds of groups I had been going to, at growth centres and elsewhere. The whole idea of a growth centre, I discovered, had come from humanistic psychology, as had the whole idea of having direct methods of developing human potential. And so I found it very congenial, and invited myself to a committee meeting; within two years I was Chairperson.

It seemed to me that humanistic psychology was implicitly revolutionary, in that it was totally dedicated to the idea of freedom. It was quite scornful of the idea that therapy was about nurturing people or supporting people – it was all about enabling people to take personal power and take charge of their own lives. It was very sympathetic to the ideas in the play, and indeed some of the exercises in the play had been taken from humanistic psychology in the first place. And yet there was something very solid about humanistic psychology; it worked.

What had been happening to me in the groups I had been to was that I had taken enormous steps in self-discovery. The first thing I discovered was that I was completely out of touch with my feelings – I really did not know I had such things, still less what they were. I remember how at one of the first encounter groups I went to, at one point the leader said, 'Let's just go round and see how we are feeling. How are you feeling right now?' When it came to my turn, I didn't know; I just had no idea of how to answer the question. If it happened now, and I had the same feelings, I would say 'I feel blocked', but I just did not have that vocabulary in those days.

The real self

The first clear and definite feeling I came up with in that first year was anger – I learned how to be angry, and how to express anger. The second feeling I discovered was grief – I cried and cried – I remember crying for forty-five minutes about how sad it was, all the tears I had never shed! Later came other feelings, such as love, hurt, neediness, and fear. Later still came the ability to open myself up to another person's feelings, and be intimate with them.

And with the healing of the split between thinking and feeling came, one time in a group, after a cathartic experience, a sense of being a whole person, of seeing people quite straight and undistorted. This only lasted for about half an hour, but it was something quite new, and I sensed that it was important for me. Later I had this experience again and again, as other splits were healed, and I started to label it as an experience of getting in touch with the real self.

The idea of the real self is very important in humanistic psychology, and it is always tied to actual experience, rather than being just a theoretical construct. I have written about it at some length elsewhere (Rowan 1983). It is the result of healing splits in the personality, and of the integration of the person which results from that. I have seen it happen many times in groups, and it is a marvellous experience to participate in in any way. The person can go round the group and say something to each person, and each of these interactions is completely unique and appropriate – no clichés, no old tapes playing, just fresh and direct perception and communication.

One of the most confusing things about the whole business was that in the growth movement there was this great emphasis on autonomy – on moving from other support to self-support. Gestalt therapy was particularly strong on this, and I loved gestalt therapy. Fritz Perls (1970) was the great facilitator of autonomy. Now I was great on autonomy, which to me was another name for freedom – I had specialized in autonomy, I was brilliant at autonomy, and so leapt at this and loved it. The whole idea of the real self even promised more autonomy. It was only later that I discovered that there is a pathology of autonomy the same as there is a pathology of dependence, and I had been feeding my pathology as much as doing genuinely good work in self-development. Autonomy is good, but emotional nourishment is important, too. With real intimacy I could get both of these things in a proper balance. This realization took a long time to dawn.

And, of course, all this led to an increasing interest in psychotherapy, although I still saw this as best done through group work. I was very suspicious of one-to-one therapy, as an expensive, middle-class, establishment sort of thing. I was also very suspicious of the Tavistock type of group, which I went to in 1970. I wrote up my experiences in that group in a series of thirty-eight poems, which I then delivered as a scientific paper on groups at the annual conference of the occupational psychology section of the British Psychological Society, and which later became most of one chapter in my book *The Power of the Group* (Rowan 1976a). This group, it seemed to me, was all about reinforcing the power of authority to put people down and keep them where they are. But what interested me was the process of change. How do people change? That was the question.

Radical psychology

At the same time, my intellectual interests had expanded and taken a new turn. I still pursued humanistic psychology, which was my positive path, so to speak, but now I also started taking a parallel negative path. I went in 1970 to the first Radical Psychology conference, organized by Keith Paton at Keele University, and out of that came a magazine called *Red Rat*. I helped to produce the first issue, and stayed with it until it was overtaken by a better radical psychology magazine, *Humpty Dumpty*, which I later helped to originate and produce. I got involved in other activities – some of us produced a big pamphlet called *Rat, Myth and Magic*, and started to invade and militantly disrupt various psychology conferences. We were very critical of the way in which academic psychology misled and demeaned people, reducing them to the level of stooges or inanimate things in order to study them. We felt that no human psychology could be developed in that way, and that it was all a big confidence trick.

I remember the excitement I felt in picking up on a second-hand bookstall the original American edition of Charles Hampden-Turner's (1971) book *Radical Man*. This was an account of what personal growth was and how it took place, right within the boundaries of humanistic psychology as I understood it. Later I met Charles, and liked him very much, though we have never seen eye to eye on the question of patriarchy. What the book said was that the personal and the political are one – that personal growth leads to political radicalism. And the book made it clear that authenticity in the existential sense (a combination of self-respect and self-enactment) was the major factor in any real self-development; it was the key to where one was going and also the key to getting there. The strong feeling of the real self which I had had in groups connected up with the philosophical idea of authenticity, and I felt a real connection there – that authenticity was one place where the personal and the political came together. One could not be authentic and experience alienation or anomie at the same time. This brought together the two paths (the positive path of personal growth and the negative path of radical psychology) in a way which I found very satisfying.

At first all this apparently made no difference to my daily life. In 1970 I moved to a better job in market research, as director of psychological research for one of the biggest companies. But the thing was working beneath the surface, and it came to the top when the company asked me to conduct an investigation of the validity of a big survey which was on a yearly contract and one of the biggest sources of regular income. My answers were so disturbing (showing that the figures we published were in certain ways seriously misleading) that the crucial lines in my report were reworded by the managing director and buried in a remote part of the report, not being mentioned in any of the summaries issued to the client. After some discussion of this, I resigned.

The year 1971 was an extraordinary one for me. I left my job, and did not take up another one, but went freelance. I got a contract to write a four-volume textbook of social psychology. I left my wife and went to live with a revolutionary woman in a political commune in Holloway, and wrote a series of poems about the experience (Rowan 1973). I spent a good deal of the summer doing street theatre, where I played the role of Mr Busy Bigness, in a piece called *The Allo Allo Allo Show: An Everyday Story of Ghetto Folk*. I went to more groups and found out more about myself. I was investing myself very intensely in my own life. Mid-life crisis, here I was!

Phase two

At the end of 1971, the political group I had been working with fell apart, and I broke up with the woman I had been with. This was an extremely painful time for me. I went back to my wife, and the whole story which is unfolded in my book *The Horned God* (1987a) began. I started to take a much more intense interest in group work as such. It seemed to be a natural development, as if one chapter had closed and another one opened. I started leading groups, just following the methods I had picked up bit by bit, as we all used to do in those days, because there were no training courses to speak of. My first paid workshop was at Kaleidoscope in 1972, and was specifically on creativity: since then I have done many workshops around that topic, and still regard it as one of the central issues in all growth and self-development.

It is marvellous to see people in these groups dropping their assumptions about what they are capable of, and finding their own creative centre. I find this one of the greatest satisfactions in the whole field, just of seeing people blossom and come forth. You can see their whole body change and become more open, more energized, more relaxed, more approachable. Very often there is an experience of ecstasy, and I myself had more and more peak experiences around this time. I found I could even lay myself open to experiences of ecstasy quite deliberately, along the lines suggested by Joanna Field in *A Life of One's Own* (1952). It was as if I had hit bottom and could now start coming up again.

This is perhaps a suitable point to say that I regarded then, and still do now, personal growth, counselling and psychotherapy as all really the same thing under different labels. They are all based on the twin ideas of unhindering and unfolding. Unhindering is about removing the blocks which people have put up in the way of contacting their own centre, and unfolding is about encouraging people to allow that centre to take over and to follow their own process of self-development with confidence and trust. Along the way the issues around existential choice arise again and again – as Maslow (1973) used to say, at every moment we have a choice between the joys of safety and the joys of growth. And as Mahrer (1978) was to say later, it is all a question of doing justice to our deeper potentials, and really choosing to do that.

So in the second phase of my development into a psychotherapist, I was mixing with highly experienced and trained people, some of whom were certainly quite radical, and learning as much from them as possible. One of the most exciting events I attended was in 1973, when I went to the AHP Annual Meeting in Montreal. Here I met some of the people I had been reading about and admiring, and actually saw them in action. In the same year I also went to an international workshop on co-counselling, where I met Harvey Jackins, and again learnt a great deal about myself. I was really getting in amongst a stimulating crowd.

The Council of Group Studies was an interesting group of such people, who decided in the end to start up a diploma course. This was adopted by the Polytechnic of North London, under the able and continually innovative leadership of John Southgate, and I duly joined this course and eventually (in 1975) got my diploma in applied behavioural science. This covered group work, individual counselling, theory and research, organization develo~~~~~~ and so on. This was my first introduction to one-to-one work, whic the form of co-counselling, because that was more politically acceptable than any other form. In the same year I had an important breakthrough in therapy, all about my mother, which I wrote up in *Self and Society* (Rowan 1975) a little later, and which made a big difference to my whole life. I could now relate to women as real people.

At this point I wrote a book called *Ordinary Ecstasy: Humanistic Psychology in Action* (Rowan 1976b), which put a lot of what I had discovered into print and made a sort of milestone in my progress so far. In a way it put me on the map as a person seriously interested in the whole area of personal growth, counselling and psychotherapy. I had already written a critical chapter on research methodology for a book edited by Nigel Armistead (one of the other people on *Humpty Dumpty*) which came out from Penguin (Armistead 1974).

Red Therapy

At the same time (1973 to 1978) I was working intensively with a self-help group called Red Therapy, which was dedicated to finding out more about the relationship between therapy and politics. It had started as a result of a meeting put on by Quaesitor, then the biggest growth centre in Europe, and was an interesting example of personal growth and radicalism coming together once again. In 1978 it produced a big pamphlet about its work, which I helped to write and put together. I learned a great deal in this group, both about myself and about the political implications of psychotherapy. Many of the lessons of this group were written up later in the excellent book by Sheila Ernst and Lucy Goodison (1981) – *In Our Own Hands*.

What I finally learned from this group was that personal change and political change could both be worked on in the same group. Often it seems that the growth person is opposed to the political person, and the politico is opposed to the groupie – in the US they called it the conflict between the 'Wheelies' and the 'Feelies'. I also learned the same thing in another organization which existed at about the same time called Alternative Socialism. Here again we found that the two things could be combined, rather than having to be contrasted with one another. Of course, the women's movement had discovered this for themselves long ago, but men were rather left out of this, and had to make their own (our own) discoveries.

So at the end of this phase I had run the full gamut of group work, and had made many discoveries there. I was by now a fully developed and functioning encounter group leader, specializing in work on creativity, sex roles and sub-personalities. And I was also a researcher, now having seen that the old paradigm of empirical research most used in psychology actually reduced people to something less than human, so that anything that might be discovered in that way could not really be about human beings at all. In 1977 I initiated the New Paradigm Research Group to push forward this insight, and this later led to the production of a big book (Reason and Rowan 1981).

Phase three

But it was in 1977 that an important turning point came, when I interviewed Bill Swartley for a special primal issue of *Self and Society*. It was as a result of that meeting that I discovered that he was just about to start a training course in primal integration therapy in London; I promptly joined it, and found it an absolutely extraordinary experience. The course was a very intensive one, with one weekend every two weeks; these later became residential, which made them even more intense. On the Friday night there would be a lecture or seminar, where we would examine some theoretical points, do tests, look at a case or whatever, usually with written notes supplied by Swartley. The Saturday and Sunday would be simply an experiential group, where we would work spontaneously with whatever came up out of the initial go-round. As well as seeing Swartley in action himself, plus guest leaders such as William Emerson, Jack Painter, and Paco, we worked with each other in small groups, learning how to do it ourselves. I did some deep primal work which was very important to me, including a lot of work on my father, and perhaps most of all working through my Oedipal material in a vivid, face-to-face way.

Primal integration therapy is a holistic approach, which says that the four functions which Jung speaks of – sensing, feeling, thinking, and intuiting – all have to be dealt with and done justice to in any therapy worthy of the name. So we all had to work in all four of these modes, learning how to use body work, cathartic work, analytic work and transpersonal work, all in their proper place at their proper time. It was a deep and far-reaching discipline which put tremendous demands upon all of us. I have described it at length elsewhere (Rowan 1988).

This training seemed to put together everything I knew and give it a coherent framework. As a result of this training, I felt ready now to work on my own. But I was working hard at other things, first of all as a freelance market researcher, then spending a year as a researcher for the British Psychological Society located in the occupational psychology department at Birkbeck College, and then another year and a half heading up the behavioural science unit at the Greater London Council's headquarters in County Hall. In 1978 the radical psychotherapist Giora Doron had the idea of starting up a psychotherapy training centre running a three-year part-time course, and very kindly asked me to take part in running the seminars for it. This I did, and quickly found myself more and more involved in the Institute which it later became. But it was still difficult to have more than a very minor private practice as a psychotherapist, because of the demands of my work and other interests. For example, I was on the committee of the Association for Humanistic Psychology, and also helping to produce the magazine *Achilles Heel* at this time, as I still am.

It was also at this time that I was meeting and going out with Sue, and at the end of 1978 I moved in with her. This relationship has proved to be one of the most important parts of my life, and Sue has encouraged me enormously at all the turning points which came from then on. This was helped very much by another breakthrough which came about in my own therapy in the primal integration group.

What happened was that I seemed to go back down the channel of time to a fork in the road where I had made a decision about how to live my life. It was as if I had decided to do without other people, and to make it on my own. It was a lonely, thumbsucking sort of a decision, and had led to what I called earlier 'the pathology of autonomy'. It seemed incredibly early, as if it were the first decision I had ever made, not to rely on anyone else. And I just went back to that fork in the road, and took the other path. The phrase that came into my mind was, 'I don't want to be alone', and it even came with a tune – an old tune from the 1930s called, 'We don't want to go to bed'. And as I came back up, clutching as it were this tune, it became louder and louder. And I could feel, as it were, relays clicking and connections making and unmaking themselves all through my brain and my body, as if the implications of that changed decision were working their way through the system. And when I came back from that weekend I found that my relationship with Sue was much more meaningful; that I could let her in to my deepest places in a way which I had not known was possible before. I could experience intimacy with her.

This may not sound very impressive. What is so new or remarkable about intimacy? But for me it was an enormous change. It was like opening up a whole other side of my brain and body, so to speak. The ability to let go of my fixed boundaries, which I first found with Sue, later extended to others too, and I found it extremely valuable in my work as a therapist. I could actually allow myself to know what other people were feeling, from the inside, as it were. So that when later I discovered a form of psychotherapy which necessitated just this opening of boundaries (Mahrer 1986) I was able to take it on and practise it with relatively little difficulty. But let us get back to the story and see how all this fitted in with my becoming a psychotherapist.

The thing happens

The big breakthrough took place at the end of 1980, when the GLC decided it no longer needed a behavioural science unit, and I was suddenly out of a job. This was a very painful experience, and the actual sacking took place in a hurtful way. I developed a bad back which ached so much that I could hardly walk. I went to my psychotherapy group with my bad back, and we discovered that I felt as if I had been stabbed in the back, and also that I had a burden of responsibilities which also weighed heavily on my back. So I dealt with both of these things, and my back went back to normal.

I wrote off for job after job, but nothing seemed to turn up, and it became clear that my age (55) was a problem. I did not fit neatly into any of the pay scales which people seemed to have. In January I spent more than I earned; in February I spent more than I earned; in March I spent more than I earned. But in April I turned the corner. I had found that the absence of a job had freed up my time so that I could go into psychotherapy full time, and after one or two false starts this is exactly what happened. I took on more work with the Institute, starting to run groups and do supervision as well as leading the seminars on humanistic psychology. So now I was acting as a full-time therapist, and also teaching psychotherapy. I had arrived. It was 1981.

When did I become a psychotherapist?

I became a psychotherapist proper in November 1980, when the tenant down-stairs moved out, and I took over his room and turned it into a therapy room. It still had the old wardrobe and chest of drawers in there, but I installed a mattress and a futon and two chairs and some big cushions and a tennis racquet and a baby's bottle and some massage oil and some boxes of tissues, and I was in business. Before that I had taken individual sessions in various hired premises, but this was now my own place, and I began to see more people and more regularly. It seems that I was already regarded as a therapist by many people, so it did not make any great ripples in my circle of acquaintances. It was more or less expected. It was as if the only question was – 'What took you so long?'

As an individual therapist, I did all the same things I had done in groups. In the kind of groups I was most involved with, much of the work is done with one person at a time, with the rest of the group looking on and sometimes participating in various ways. So there was no fundamental difference between working with one person in a group and working with one person on their own.

In theoretical terms there is an important point here, in that it is generally laid down that people shall not practise any form of therapy which they have not been through themselves. And I had not been through the long-term one-to-one therapy which I was now offering. But it seems that there are exceptions to every rule, and I found no difficulty in adapting what I was doing in the way required. I had certainly done several years of work on myself in co-counselling, which is a one-to-one method, and I suppose this must have helped too, though the assumptions are significantly different. I don't really know why it worked so well, but I seemed to find that I could do it adequately. However, there are some qualifications, which we shall come to shortly.

One of the main ways in which I learned more about psychotherapy was by teaching it, through seminars, group leadership, and the supervision of trainees. In a way there is no quicker way of learning something than by teaching it. And as I learned the lessons, I tried to pass them on again. In this way my 1983 book came about, which was all about how to be a humanistic counsellor or psychotherapist. People keep telling me it is a very practical and useful book, and it was certainly very useful for me to write it.

However, it came home to me after a while that there were certain clients I did not like or do very well with. And it seemed that I did not do well with them because they did not respond to the dramatic techniques which I prefer. They seemed unable or unwilling to take up more active roles, and insisted on staying passive and being the victim. Now, of course, this was not their fault, and I began to wonder if the reason I was so bad with them was that I had not experienced myself the extended one-to-one therapy which I was trying to practise. I seriously considered going into some very orthodox therapy just to see whether this were the case. It seemed that a Jungian analyst might be the most suitable. So that is what I did, and I am still carrying this on. It is too early to say whether this is the answer to the problem, however.

I suppose one of the main changes which took place between starting to be a therapist and now is that I acquired from 1982 onwards a new appreciation of spirituality. I began to acknowledge myself as a spiritual being with a path to be followed. This has led to an increase in the extent to which I work in a transpersonal way, using symbols rather than words. I actually believe that this ability to use symbols and to live and breathe symbols is what is meant by the phrase – 'Opening the third eye'. It really is a different way of perceiving the world. I found Ken Wilber the best guide into the whole field of spirituality, and have continued to gain benefit from his thinking, though I do not believe his map is quite complete or adequate.

But I combined this with my continuing interest in sexual politics, and what came out was a deep appreciation and some understanding of paganism. The old religion of paganism holds the Great Goddess to be primary, and links her with the earth and with the underworld. I particularly liked the approach of Monica Sjöö (Sjöö and Mor 1987), who also links feminism with paganism. Seen in this way, many of the usual transpersonal symbols are unwittingly patriarchal: for example, the identification of height with spirituality and depth with the primitive unconscious is a patriarchal distortion of the earlier conception of spirituality being essentially a downward movement. I have written about this at length elsewhere (Rowan 1987a).

In the earliest days when I started to practise psychotherapy people came through word of mouth, and they still do. One of the biggest differences between what I was doing then and what I am doing now is that I have much greater ability to empathize and get inside another person's experience. I also think I have become more adventurous and imaginative, as I have explained in some detail elsewhere (Rowan 1987b).

What sustains me as a psychotherapist?

I would need much more sustaining if I were to become the kind of psychotherapist who sees client after client all day every day. But I don't need much sustaining because my practice is very varied in all sorts of ways. On Mondays at the moment I start writing at about 5.15, have a bath and breakfast, have one two-hour session in the morning, then a staff meeting at the Institute, then a seminar there on humanistic psychology, then a two-hour session in the afternoon, and a one-and-a-half hour session in the evening. Except that once every three weeks I have someone from Swansea who comes for a three-hour session in the morning. On Thursdays after my writing stint I have a lecture for the London University Diploma in Psychology, followed by two one-hour clients, and some reading, followed by a two-hour session. On Fridays I generally spend some time reading and writing, and going somewhere with Sue. My other days are equally varied; usually I spend most of the weekend with Sue, but sometimes there is a group workshop at the weekend as well. Then there are committee meetings and magazine collective meetings to fit in once a month or so.

Another thing that sustains me is the feeling of success I often have, when something goes well. I can really see people changing in front of my very eyes, and that is very cheering. I remember one woman I worked with for a long time had a very dark undertone to her complexion, as if there were a sort of greyness under the surface. I said to myself that I would really believe she had got somewhere when this greyness disappeared. And sure enough, when she had worked through a particularly horrific and very early bit of her personal trauma, her whole complexion changed, quite dramatically and obviously. But more common are changes of mood, where people feel much more relaxed and able to take more risks in life.

Something else that sustains me is my membership of the International Primal Association, which was founded by Bill Swartley and others. I read the journal and newsletter of that association, and get tapes of important presentations, and this makes me feel that I am part of something bigger – a network of people with similar interests to my own, with whom I can share my practice. It is very sad, however, that not only Swartley, but also David Freundlich, whose ideas seemed very similar to my own, have both now died.

Another thing that sustains me is my membership of the Association of Humanistic Psychology Practitioners. This was something I helped to start in 1980, and it is the professional group within the Association for Humanistic Psychology. I have learned a great deal from this group over the years, starting with the Self and Peer Assessment programme initiated by John Heron and carrying on through various seminars and workshops – perhaps most of all through my work on the membership committee, which put me in touch with the work of most of the best people working today, and led to my involvement with the accreditation of counsellors and supervisors in the British Association for Counselling, and to my work with the Rugby Conference on the whole future of psychotherapy in this country.

Perhaps the thing that sustains me most is my work at the Institute. It was set up as a radical course, concerned not only with the technicalities of therapy but also with the social and political context within which all counselling and psychotherapy is carried out. We make sure that students are exposed to all the issues around exploitation, alienation, and oppression, not only on the global scale but also in the nitty-gritty details of therapy itself. One of the prime areas where this becomes obvious is sexism – the oppression of women by men. My own work in sexual politics (Rowan 1987a) becomes very relevant here. Therapists can put down women just as much as can any other authority figure – and even more effectively in some cases, because of the closeness of the influence. Alice Miller (1985) has written eloquently about the 'poisonous pedagogy' that can take place in the therapy session, reproducing and enforcing the oppressive relations that all too often occur in childhood. Hopefully the students we turn out from the Institute will not repeat these patterns. Racism, of course, introduces similar issues.

But because I recognize that the personal is political, I see all therapy as liberating. To the extent that a client can be enabled to work through to the stage of getting in touch with the real self, he or she will begin to see through the sham of roles and masks, and insist on authentic relationships. This is bad news for oppressors, because all oppression is based on mystification. And because the outcome of any adequate therapy is autonomy and the taking of personal power, it cannot be used to manipulate. There is no way that manipulation can produce genuine autonomy – and if by some miracle it did, the first task of that autonomy would be to confront the manipulator.

Of course, the liberation which comes through psychotherapy or counselling is slow and small in scale. But it is very sure, because it produces irreversible changes in people. And I believe that because of the availability of co-counselling and self-help groups, any time it needed to spread more quickly and speed up the process, this could be achieved.

I don't try to conduct my own therapy through my clients, and would feel that to be quite wrong. I have my own therapist, who I see twice a week, and also a supervisor, who I see regularly on a peer-sharing basis. It is essential to me to have somewhere to go with my distress or my lack of understanding, and be enabled to work through it and come out with some better awareness of what has been going on.

My main relationship is with Sue, and this sustains me considerably. I do not discuss the details of my cases with her, but I can exclaim about any particular triumphs or trials that I have had in the day, and she will listen sympathetically and share in whatever happens. And, of course, I listen to her day in the same way. The only strain is over time, when she has complained every now and then that we don't have enough time together, but we have that reasonably well sorted out at the moment.

I see myself as being a therapist for the rest of my life, because I am 62 now and this is a job which can be done even at an advanced age – it might even be that there is an advantage in being older for this kind of work. There is a feeling of stability and security that is quite useful in therapy, and which comes very naturally from an older person. But at the same time I want to make a bigger proportion of my income from writing, because writing is something which can be done at even older ages, and gives much more flexibility about where to live. I would like to run a live encounter group on television, but no one has yet asked me to do so.

Psychotherapy seems a good choice for me, especially in the varied way in which I carry it on. It gives me enormous interest and satisfaction. I only wish I could do more groups and less one-to-one work. But groups are much harder to set up and run, and I can't bear the hassle of organizing them myself, so I can only do them when someone else organizes them for me. Groups I find much more stimulating and much more satisfying than one-to-one work; usually in my groups a lot of things happen and people change a lot, and social issues come up much more. I particularly like the more extended residential group of five days or so, where people can really get down to deeper pieces of work on themselves with open-ended time to go through them fully, and other people to help out in various ways. And recently I have been co-leading groups with Sue, which has been marvellous and even better than running them on my own. It has been even more satisfying to see her growing and developing as a leader under my very eyes, and some of her comments and questions have deepened my own practice.

Implications for other psychotherapists

The one main thing I would like people to learn is a negative one – don't put all your eggs in one basket. I hate the narrow kind of therapist who was trained in one school, analysed by one analyst, and practises in one mode. I hate even more the narrow kind of 'therapist' who has never done any self-therapy at all. I very much like the open kind of therapist who has had many teachers and tried many modes, and has then settled on his or her own combination.

And this is not just a personal preference – there is a theoretical rationale for it too. It is that, as Freud said, therapists can only operate up to the limit of their own resistances. These resistances tend to be strongest in the areas which have not been reached by the type of therapy they did in their training. So when they get clients bringing up material which they did not cover in their training, they distort it and treat it as something else, which must be ineffectual.

It seems crystal-clear to me that the most important influence on any therapist is the personal therapy they have experienced themselves on themselves and for themselves. The second most important influence is the supervision they have had. And the third most important influence is the clients they have had; but this third one can be crucially and sometimes cruelly limited by the first two.

I would argue that every therapist who works in depth must be able to handle infant stuff when it comes up, must be able to handle perinatal stuff when it comes up, must be able to handle prenatal stuff when it comes up, and must be able to handle spiritual stuff when it comes up. Many training courses avoid some of these areas, and the beginning therapist will just have to get them somewhere else, or face being inadequately equipped.

Similarly, many training courses have quite an inadequate coverage of group work, and the aspiring therapist will probably need to go elsewhere for work on psychodrama, encounter, T-groups and so on. This work is needed to produce the kind of authentic human being which I think the therapist had better be. It has often been pointed out (Marmor 1974) that certain problems, as for example insensitive talkativeness, are never going to come out in one-to-one therapy, and need a group to become at all accessible. So I feel very strongly that a good training course absolutely needs to cover group work in some detail. And if an otherwise good course is not adequate in this respect, the aspiring therapist is just going to have to go elsewhere for such training and experience.

On the whole, the therapists I know myself are very conscientious in this respect, and do continue to work on themselves and expose themselves to new ideas and new experiences. But there should be more facilities for established therapists and counsellors to be properly taught about the new work as it comes along. Probably there are today more therapists who have never enabled their clients to go back to their early experiences before they were 5 years of age than there are any other kind. And yet all the implications of the work which has come along in the past few years, both in psychoanalysis and in the humanistic approaches, is that clients often need to go further back than that if we want to see substantial changes in the basic character structure.

Further, it seems to me that any course which avoids any discussion of the social context is going to let its students down. There is so much opportunity for manipulation by psychotherapists that it is crucially important to make sure that students are made aware of the necessity for this not to happen in their work. I believe that psychotherapy is a political act, and has to be taken seriously as a political act if it is not ultimately to do more harm than good. I have elsewhere (Rowan 1983) gone into this in some detail, in a chapter entitled, 'Listening with the fourth ear'. And this ear, the ear for the social and political aspects of the work, is more and more necessary each year. Good psychotherapy must do justice to this.

Possibly the biggest challenge is the spiritual aspect of the work. If we can take Wilber (1986) and his co-workers seriously, we have to devote much more attention than we normally do to this type of approach. The argument is that people operate on something like nine different developmental levels, some of which are completed, some of which are still in process, and some of which are as yet not visible at all. My own belief at present is that anyone who wants to be a good psychotherapist has to have their own spiritual discipline which they follow. Otherwise there are important and crucial human areas which they cannot help their clients with. This is to cheat people of part of their humanity, and it won't do.

As I go around the world, I often find myself introducing people to the idea of self and peer assessment (Heron 1981), which entails watching people do short sessions of 15 to 20 minutes using their own form of psychotherapy or counselling. And I am struck by the almost uniformly dismal level of expertise which I see and hear. I have come to believe that most psychotherapy and counselling that goes on in the world is pretty bad. I want it to be better. But it seems obvious to me that unless psychotherapists and counsellors are continually and quite humbly working on themselves to improve and develop further as professionals, no improvement will happen. As far as I can see, the reason for the lack of quality is that people do not really question themselves very much, once the training years are over. Kottler (1986) remarks on the way in which a depressing self-satisfaction seems to settle over so many therapists, such that they become blind and self-deceiving.

As can be seen from the narrative just completed, I had my first important breakthrough in therapy after five years of working on myself, and other major breakthroughs in the five years following. From that point on I was what Rogers (1961) calls a 'fully functioning person' and my spiritual path and growth became more important than my therapy. It seems to me that therapy really does take this long – something like a ten-year stint. And I think the experience of Jenny James (1983), who had almost continuous access to psychotherapy for long periods, and who still took ten years about it, bears out this view.

Obviously no training course could take this long, and this means that any psychotherapist, no matter how well trained, must continue to engage in personal growth work for a considerable time after the end of any training course. What I am arguing for is a substantial change in the way this further work is regarded – not as further deepening in the same method, but rather an extension into new and different methods and approaches which were not covered, or hardly covered, in the original training. Only in this way can we get the fully trained, fully functioning psychotherapist who clients so desperately need.

References

Armistead, Nigel (ed.) (1974) *Reconstructing Social Psychology*, Harmondsworth, Penguin.
Chaikin, Joseph (1968) 'A play on the stage...', *Village Voice*, Oct. 17.
Ernst, Sheila and Goodison, Lucy (1981) *In Our Own Hands*, London: The Women's Press.
Field, Joanna (1952) *A Life of One's Own*, Harmondsworth: Penguin.
Hampden-Turner, Charles (1971) *Radical Man*, London: Duckworth.

Heron, John (1981) 'Self and peer assessment for managers' in Tom Boydell and Mike Pedler (eds) *Management Self-Development*, Aldershot: Gower.

James, Jenny (1983) *Room to Breathe*, London: Caliban.

Kottler, Jeffrey A (1986) *On Being a Therapist*, San Francisco: Jossey-Bass.

Mahrer, Alvin R. (1978) *Experiencing*, New York: Brunner/Mazel.

Mahrer, Alvin R. (1986) *Therapeutic Experiencing*, New York: W. W. Norton.

Malina, Judith and Beck, Julian (1971) *Paradise Now: Collective Creation of the Living Theatre*, New York: Vintage Books.

Marmor, Judd (1974) *Psychiatry in Transition*, London: Butterworth.

Maslow, Abraham H. (1973) *The Farther Reaches of Human Nature*, Harmondsworth: Penguin.

Miller, Alice (1985) *Thou Shalt Not be Aware*, London: Pluto Press.

Perls, Fritz (1970) 'Four lectures' in Joen Fagan and Irma Lee Shepherd (eds) *Gestalt Therapy Now*, Palo Alto: Science and Behavior Books.

Reason, Peter and Rowan, John (eds) (1981) *Human Inquiry: A Sourcebook of New Paradigm Research*, Chichester: John Wiley & Sons.

Rogers, Carl R. (1961) *On Becoming a Person*, London: Constable.

Rostagno, Aldo (1970) *We, the Living Theatre*, New York: Ballantine Books.

Rowan, John (1973) *The Clare Poems*, London: Writers Forum.

Rowan, John (1975) 'A growth episode', *Self and Society* 3(11): 20–7.

Rowan, John (1976a) *The Power of the Group*, London: Davis-Poynter.

Rowan, John (1976b) *Ordinary Ecstasy: Humanistic Psychology in Action*, London: Routledge & Kegan Paul. A second edition of this book was published by Routledge in 1988.

Rowan, John (1983) *The Reality Game*, London: Routledge & Kegan Paul.

Rowan, John (1987a) *The Horned God*, London: Routledge & Kegan Paul.

Rowan, John (1987b) 'Siding with the client', in Windy Dryden (ed.) *Key Cases in Psychotherapy*, London: Croom Helm.

Rowan, John (1988) 'Primal integration therapy', in John Rowan and Windy Dryden (eds) *Innovative Therapy in Britain*, Milton Keynes: Open University Press.

Sjöö, Monica and Mor, Barbara (1987) *The Great Cosmic Mother: Rediscovering the Religion of the Earth*, New York: Harper & Row.

Vaughan, Frances (1986) *The Inward Arc*, Boston: New Science Library.

Wilber, Ken *et al.* (1986) *Transformations of Consciousness*, Boston: New Science Library.

Chapter eleven

Rhythm and blues

Jocelyn Chaplin

Why did I become a psychotherapist?

At the moment I feel as though I will always be 'becoming a psychotherapist'. I cannot imagine a moment when I would say, 'Aha, now I have arrived at my destination and here I will stay.' The word 'psychotherapist' comes from ancient Greek and means 'healer of the soul'. For me, helping to 'heal' other people's souls is intimately connected with the healing and development of my own. And I believe that this is a life-long journey.

However, I have been asked to look back over the path of my journey so far, and reflect on it. I have been given certain specific guidelines by editors of this book which I experience as both facilitating my task and yet also limiting its scope by providing me with headings. Another 'limitation' is the fact that I am now looking at the past through the spectacles of my own immediate present. The way I view and describe the past today may not be the way I would write about it tomorrow. Important facts or themes may be left out today because they don't fit with my present way of thinking about psychotherapy.

In a sense my story, like that of other therapists, started many thousands of years ago, when wise women and men took on the specialized roles of 'mind and body' healers. I believe that there have been psychotherapists for as long as humans have been conscious of psychological pain and a need to connect with and make sense of the world around them. But there have been many 'dark ages' when the intuitive wisdom, especially of women, has been denied and pushed underground, as in the medieval witch hunts. In the late twentieth century there seems to be a resurgence of interest in the kind of intuitive feeling and understanding that I believe most psychotherapists need, a so-called 'feminine' way of knowing. Perhaps this is a reaction to the overemphasis on the logical, so-called 'masculine' ways of understanding the world. As an individual, I am a part of this great tide sweeping across the world, the re-emergence of the 'feminine'. It is a movement that takes many forms. I, like millions of other women and some men too, have my own small part to play in this particular phase of history. So, to begin with, I see my own personal desire to become a psychotherapist and in particular a feminist psychotherapist as part of this historical swing.

I arrived in the world just after the Second World War into a period of optimism and the growth of equal opportunities encouraged by such events as the creation of the welfare state in Britain. As a child I experienced the tail end of the British colonial world in Africa and the growth of her (Africa's) independence movements. I grew into adulthood in the 1960s and was influenced by both the revolutionary politics and the 'hippy philosophies' of that period. All these influences led me towards the kind of radical feminist psychotherapy that I practise today.

Then there are also my personal origins, my family, my astrological birth chart, and my early experiences. I was born in the middle of one of the coldest winters Britain can remember, 1947, just two hours into the new year on 1 January. The bitterness of that winter may have provided a deep urge within me to strive towards the sun, both in reality and in its symbolism as representing emotional warmth, comfort and power.

I have also always had a sense of being between two worlds, the old year and the new year, living on the boundaries. Therapy is often to do with helping people make transitions across boundaries, e.g. from one stage of life to another. Being born on the boundary between years has given me a Janus image. I seem to be looking both backwards and forwards at the same time.

Astrologically, Pluto, the planet of the underworld and the unconscious, was sitting in the tenth house which is that part of the sky connected to vocation which strongly suggests a career in psychotherapy. Next to it in the same 'house' is the planet Saturn that brings both order and limitation. My urge to seek order within the unconscious, to analyse and contain it may partly come from this particular planet's influence. I also have a sense of being held back and limited in my career development which may again be connected to this pair of planets in that position. It is also the 'house' of the 'mother' which I have often experienced as 'dark' and limiting, both in a personal and archetypal way.

I will now consider my own real family and its effects on my 'becoming a psychotherapist'. My parents were both teachers, but my father had also fought in the Second World War. He was a captain and despite the horror of war had clearly enjoyed the companionship and status it gave him; returning to 'normality' was probably difficult for him. By the time I was born, he was the headmaster of a village school near Manchester. My mother, who had been at Oxford University during the war, gave up teaching to become a full-time mother, which must have been hard for someone who valued independence and mental work so highly.

Both parents had been brought up in strict, evangelical Christian families with a great deal of both emotional and sexual repression. My father who was a passionate man was torn all his life between the dictates of his religion and upbringing on the one hand, and his sexual desires and lust for life on the other. His own father had been a conscientious objector in the First World War and his family had been very poor for years. My father suffered, especially while at Manchester University, with a deep inferiority complex that turned him into something of a snob later in life. He hid these feelings by acting in a rather arrogant and dominating way on the surface. Like so many men, to help himself feel better, he consistently put down my mother. Although she was extremely intelligent, her opinions were rarely listened to and eventually it seemed that she simply shut up whenever he was around. It was as though she had been squashed flat by him. Yet it felt to me as a child that beneath her well-controlled exterior was a rage that simmered permanently, always threatening to boil over but never quite coming to the surface. I was afraid of my mother.

I was their first child. My mother wanted to keep me pure and clean and told me of her horror one day when some dirty smoke threatened to soil me as she was out pushing me in the pram. I always sensed that the messy, smelly, bodily, and, in particular, sexual sides of life secretly revolted my mother. I was apparently a 'good' and happy child. Perhaps I decided very young to hide my dirty bodily needs including the desire for cuddles. My mother had always found it very difficult to show physical affection.

But my first real trauma was when my younger sister arrived, screaming her way into life, full of demands. I was only eighteen months old. She was apparently a 'difficult' child but my memory is that she usually seemed to get her own way. After a short burst of jealous rage, I simply gave up trying to compete with her for attention. Something very deep inside me died. It felt as if the other three members of my family in their different ways were all overwhelmingly powerful, frightening, and cold. There were times in those early years when I hoped that my father, who had more ability to express love than my mother, really loved me best. I wanted to believe that secretly I was his favourite and I would try hard to please him. But mostly I retreated into books, drawing, and a fantasy world that soon became more real to me than the outside one, which I found too painful. Already the inner world was my comfort while the outside was too confusing and conflict-ridden.

My desire to please my father led me to read at the age of 3, and he enjoyed showing me off at his primary school. Of course, this made the other children hate me. So academic success has always filled me with fear of rejection from my peers. But my father was not around very much, however hard I tried to please him.

Then, when I was 4 years old we all moved to Africa, to the heart of Southern Sudan, where my father was appointed as principal of a missionary-funded teacher training college. My mother taught us at home for four years. She was an inspiring and enthusiastic teacher, but I was still afraid of her. My sister and I quarrelled most of the time.

We weren't supposed to play with the local African children, yet I remember wishing desperately that I was an African child living in the local village. The mud huts were comforting and womb-like. Life seemed so slow, contented, and in keeping with the rhythms of nature. I loved the drumming at night too. Once I was allowed to join in the dance and was given my own gourd to rattle. Several times I ran away or went to talk to my friend, the African cook. The cold spirituality of my Christian home contrasted dramatically with the everyday, warm and motherly spirituality of the African village. Already I sensed that there were other and perhaps better values and ways of living than my own family's. At this time I also had a dream. It was the only dream I remember from my childhood. The dream was of a vast flower with hundreds of pink and white petals, in layer after layer, going round and round. Later I thought that it was like a lotus flower often seen as a symbol of the harmonious self in Eastern religions. Certainly it must have given my unconscious some sense of hope, of a harmony beyond the conflict and pain of my daily life.

Then I began to long to be an ordinary little English schoolgirl. I didn't want to live in Africa and be different all the time. I was tired of being an outsider. So when I was 8, I went to live with my grandparents and attend-ed a preparatory school in Cheadle Hulme, Cheshire in England. I was ecstatic.

For three years I came out of my shell. I did well at school and had many friends. Then when I was 11, my parents brought me back to join the rest of the family in Ghana, where my father now taught at Legon University. Their marriage was not happy and my father was having an affair with one of his African students. One night, driving back from the airport where we had left my mother to return to England to have a baby, the car crashed. I was cut on the head. It was not serious, but left me in a state of shock and unconscious terror that my father had been trying to kill me because I suspected he was having an affair.

From that moment onwards I went back into my shell. I was sent to an all-African boarding school where I was the first white child. This was a rather traumatic experience that pushed me even further inside myself. I read avidly day and night. I discovered books on psychology and spirituality that spoke to me deeply. Jung's *Modern Man in Search of a Soul* was the first one that made me interested in psychotherapy, although I did not actually sit down and think, 'I want to be a psychotherapist.'

On the surface all this time I was apparently good and happy, but there was no one who I could talk to about my unhappy feelings. Yet I had some kind of inner strength, a faith in that harmony I had dreamt of as a child. Although I had rebelled against my family's Christianity by the time I was 15, I still had a sense of not being alone in a spiritual sense. It almost felt as though I had some kind of 'inner' guide, e.g. I always used to find the books that I needed to read at the time I needed them. But it would have been wonderful to have had another human being, a psychotherapist perhaps, who could have been with me, on that part of my journey. I would have liked someone who could connect with the spiritual as well as the emotional and sexual side of my life. Years later I realized that I wanted to be the therapist I never had.

This urge to fill the gap in my own life led me to study psychology at university. I thought that I was just interested in people and in what 'makes them tick' but I probably also wanted to understand and change myself. However, while at university I learned very little about people, but a great deal about rats. It was a disappointing experience.

After university I returned to Africa, to Makerere University for two years to carry out research on cross-cultural picture perception. It seemed a sensible thing to do, but my heart was never in research. My energies were more focused on my relationships with men and on painting. However, to please my father, I continued with research by taking a job back in London at the Royal College of Art, researching into print effectiveness.

While in London I started going to various humanistic groups such as 'B NOW' set up by John Rowan (see chapter 10) where everyone had to express their 'real selves'. I had already 'come out of my shell' in Africa with the help of a brilliant, but hard-drinking, African poet. I did not find it hard to know what I was feeling and it was always a relief to tell others about feelings. I was, in fact, a very 'good' group member. I made friends with other people who were interested in therapy and we used to talk about ourselves for hours while drinking endless mugs of coffee.

Through reading I 'discovered' psychotherapists like Erich Fromm and Wilhelm Reich who combined an understanding of the 'inner' world with a radical political understanding of the effects of society on people. I grew increasingly politically aware through my twenties. I became a socialist and later a feminist. Initially this process led to my rebelling forcefully against my 'bourgeois and patriarchal' family. I flew off to New York to live with one of a string of 'unsuitable' boyfriends for a year. I argued constantly with my father about politics. I left the world of research and went into community work.

Like my parents, I wanted to help people who were less advantaged than myself. It seemed the moral Christian thing to do! But I perceived my parents' way of helping as being essentially patronizing. Indeed it seemed that most forms of 'helping' such as social work took the stance that the 'helper' is 'OK' and the problem is with the 'helped' who is not 'OK'. At least in community work there was a more radical philosophy towards enabling people to 'help themselves'. But the old class and education hierarchies go deep, and attitudes towards 'the poor' or 'the black community' or 'mothers' were still extremely patronizing. Most of the people in the 'helping professions' had not examined their own motivations and personalities deeply at all. I worked in local government for some years and again found attitudes and lack of personal or political awareness appalling.

While I still believed that material 'outer' changes, such as improving housing, were the highest priority for social change, I began to feel more and

173

more that 'inner change' was vital too. The inner attitudes of both 'helpers' and 'helped' seemed to play a part in perpetrating the hierarchical systems. As Wilhelm Reich wrote, both economic and psychological factors are important. And I had had training and ability in the psychological area while my skills in community work were limited.

However, it was not until a very important event in my life that I seriously decided to return to psychology and begin training as a psychotherapist. That event was the birth of my daughter when I was 30 years old. In a strange way it seemed as if all my energies had, for the last ten years, been quietly working towards this new life. Until she was born I was unable to redirect these energies into a career. Perhaps it became also suddenly important for me to prove to myself that I was not 'just a mum'. Yet as I watched her growing and changing I learned so much about myself, about child development, and perhaps even about 'human nature' as it is manifest in this particular society. This new understanding also pointed me in the direction of psychotherapy.

I searched around for a training programme that would have some kind of Jungian framework without too great a financial commitment. I decided on the Westminster Pastoral Foundation in Kensington, London. It had a very spiritual atmosphere, a good reputation in the world of professional 'helpers', and was near my home.

Until this point my influences had all come from books. But at the WPF, I was helped by a Jungian analyst called Andrew Samuels. He was the first male therapist I was able to use as a target for the rage I had against my father and indeed against patriarchy in general. I shall always be grateful to him for playing this role for me. He also brought in the more earthy, sexual side of psychotherapy that can often get left out by Jungians, especially in a 'spiritual' environment like the WPF. He seemed to be able to combine both the symbolic and the bodily sides of human understanding. I was also impressed by Bani Shorter's (1987) model of the cycles and stages of life's journey.

In my last year at the WPF I met up with three women who became by far the strongest influence on my decision to be a psychotherapist. I had begun to doubt whether individual therapy work was really for me. The training had all been so inward looking, there seemed to be no awareness of the 'outside' world and the need for political change. It had begun to feel as though doing therapy was a 'cop-out' or escape from political action. But with these new women colleagues, Mildred Levious, Sara Gibson, and Ruth Popplestone, I was able to explore these feelings and contradictions. Sara and Mildred were also training to be psychotherapists and Ruth was a training officer in social services with a very strong feminist philosophy. We formed a group for support and growth, which eventually turned into a peer supervision group.

My fantasies about becoming a psychotherapist were influenced first by images of a wise old man, possibly affected by pictures of Freud, etc.! Then as I became more acquainted with feminist writings on psychology and spirituality I developed images more connected with women. The most powerful fantasy for me has been that of the 'Priestess', an ageless, beautiful, wise woman. I see her as a kind of guide to be available to people at those times in their journeys when they need her. She is somewhat detached, even cold, but also compassionate and 'knowing'. But she has another side that is completely untamed and wild, able to experience and therefore accept anything and everything from the most base to the most sublime. Whatever a client brings, she will accept. She is secretly passionate herself. She is queen of the underworld as well as priestess of some place in the overworld. Yet she can guide people on their journeys to and out of their own underworlds.

For me she has no name, but there are many ancient myths that could be associated with her, and goddesses that expressed her qualities. The many myths of descent into the underworld from ancient Sumaria to Hellenic Greece have had a powerful effect on me. The journey of Innana, queen of heaven, to the underworld where she dies and is reborn and returned is one of the oldest of such myths from summer. Persephone's abduction into the underworld and her mother Demeter's search for her is a better known later Greek myth. In many ways I feel I have spent much of my life 'in the underworld' and identify closely with Persephone. I remained 'ungrown up' too for a long period. And Persephone was the daughter aspect of the goddess. Demeter was the mother side, and in ancient times they were probably seen as one, having a dark *and* a light side. I too feel that I have both. For example, I can feel so-called 'dark' deep rage and pain and also analyse it with the 'light' side of reason.

As I get older I also find that the image of the wise old woman is becoming increasingly important. She has been represented as Hecate who 'governs' the crossroads which is a useful symbol for therapy. She has both dark and light, destructive and creative sides, but in patriarchy where such opposites are always split she is seen as all-destructive. It is vital for therapy that people are able to accept both sides of themselves and others. So these ancient 'dual' goddesses are valuable images for the modern world, and for psychotherapy in particular.

The black virgin is a surviving image in many parts of the world that I also find powerful and relevant. The original meaning of the word 'virgin', meaning a woman who does not belong to a man, has been important for me as well. I like to provide a model, especially for female clients, of a woman who is whole unto herself, who does not belong to a man, yet who also has a child and leads a fulfilling life that includes male friends and lovers. Most women I work with are deeply and fundamentally man-orientated.

I see psychotherapy as essentially a form of initiation into being yourself. Most people have remained being what their 'fathers' and the patriarchy expects and demands of them. For women this usually means marriage, etc. which often inhibits growth rather than facilitates it. So myths of initiation, rebirth, including some forms of symbolic death are important for me. The therapy room can be seen as a sacred place outside the everyday world, where people can go to visit their own underworlds and be guided through big and little 'deaths' and losses of childhood illusion, and then back into that everyday world with new skills and strengths and perhaps even new identities, as OK, 'grown up' limited people.

For me, the most important intellectual image of psychotherapy has been that of the snake or serpent, a symbol of ancient 'feminine' wisdom. The shape of the rhythmically-moving snake seems to represent the hidden forces in nature that connect the opposite energies and sides of everything. At the beginning of psychotherapy people tend to be stuck in one side of themselves and through the therapeutic process come to heal that split. Maybe they are always striving to be perfect or in control or hard working, and haven't recognized their opposites. The snake is a symbol of the power that heals such splits, and the snake, serpent or dragon features in many myths, usually being slain by some patriarchal hero such as St George. I believe that now is the time to bring back this ancient symbol and its wisdom. And I see psychotherapy as having a vital role to play in this process.

It is difficult for me to describe actual figures or models on which I based my notion of being a psychotherapist. I have already described my fantasy image of the therapist as a priestess, yet I do not personally know any priestesses. There are only male priests everywhere I look. But I am influenced by my reading about actual female priestesses, such as Starhawk (1982) and Stein (1987) who are involved in the new feminist spirituality which is much less hierarchical than most male-orientated religions. These priestesses do not act as superior beings who have a special relationship with god, but rather help to bring out the goddess within their clients, within everyone. They do not necessarily belong to any order, although there are organized goddess religions in some places. They work with the energies of mother nature, however she manifests 'herself' at the appropriate times.

The priestess (psychotherapist) focuses her love and concentrated attention on the client which is itself healing. She uses intuition as well as reason. So the role of healer is also important, yet for me it is implicit and 'in the background'. When I first decided to become a psychotherapist, I rejected the image of healer. The medical model of superior doctor curing a sick patient was not at all the way I saw therapy. But now I recognize that there are different kinds of healing that involve the 'patient' learning to develop his or her own inherent healing abilities. The body has its own self-regulating rhythms if only they are allowed to operate. I began to make connections between psychotherapy and other forms of alternative healing.

Another role that I connect with psychotherapy is that of educator. Again this was not a role that I would have included before I actually started practising psychotherapy. As trainees we were taught *never* to give advice or teach our clients. And yet when, for example, I am doing assertion training with clients I am in fact teaching them. I am also subtly suggesting different ways of thinking about themselves, e.g. more positively. I could be 'teaching' them this new way of thinking simply by listening to them properly. I am 'telling' them that they are worth listening to. I don't have to actually say, 'You must think more positively about yourself.' There may even be times when I do 'teach' them a skill or a tool for understanding themselves better, such as noticing whenever they overly idealize another person. I might even say, 'Just think of them as little babies. If you put that image in your mind it will help you not to be so overawed and scared of them.'

But I am also 'teaching' them my philosophy of life, however neutral I like to think I am. And the role of philosopher is another important one that I have always associated with psychotherapy. I feel a duty towards my clients to be constantly questioning the assumptions and frames of reference on which I base my work. I also believe that psychotherapy is intimately connected with our philosophy of human nature, how much we can or cannot change and with such questions as the meaning of life. My own interest in psychotherapy in fact started with an interest in these kinds of philosophical issues.

I also think that psychotherapy has a role to play in the transformation of society. Perhaps radical psychotherapists at least could be seen as revolutionaries, quietly undermining the main assumptions and structures of our deeply hierarchical society.

Despite, and perhaps because of, these grand and powerful images of psychotherapists, I was rather terrified of actually becoming one myself. The image and the ideal were fine, but was I personally up to it? It felt like an enormous responsibility to another human being to sit before them in this image of 'wise person'. I felt that I was not yet as 'wise' as I would like. My own life had been messy, painful, and full of 'mistakes'. Who was I to dare to help anyone else? I assumed that the psychotherapist could *never* be wrong, must *never* make mistakes. I also imagined that she wielded enormous power over the client. Anything that 'went wrong' with the client or in the sessions would be *all* my fault.

It was not until I actually began to practise that I came to realize that clients and my sessions with them have their own process. I can only trust that process. I am not totally *in charge*. In fact my original images of being a psychotherapist were horribly arrogant. Gradually I learned to be more humble.

I also imagined that it would be interesting to find out about other people's lives. The part of me that is deeply curious about people was looking forward to being a psychotherapist. I was even worried that this fascination with people's stories would lead me to ask too many questions and to be a bad therapist.

I also had an image of psychotherapists being rich and living in luxurious houses filled with books and priceless sculptures. My small flat in a rather run-down part of town was not the sort of place that I thought people would want to come to. Yet it has a lot of style, and besides, it shows people who

I am, without any shame or embarrassment. So eventually I decided that I was being a good model for the kinds of clients I wanted to work with. As a socialist I did not want to work with the rich. As a feminist I preferred to work with people who had not completely fitted in with patriarchy's expectations. This means that many of my clients are not well off and it is important that I should not be seen as vastly socially or materially superior. That basic human equality that I believe in so strongly would be more easily experienced with a therapist like me than with one who was richer. A good therapist needs to feel OK about themselves as they are, needs to feel quite ordinary and able to genuinely respect clients from whatever background or walk of life. I felt that these were all qualities that I had.

Other qualities that I felt were important were the ability to listen and empathize with people while retaining a clear sense of separateness. I had been a bit afraid at first that I might empathize too much and lose myself in the other person. But I soon found that the clearly defined boundaries of time and role in professional listening made it easy for me to detach and cut off when necessary. At the same time I felt it was vital to be warm and genuine and eventually to answer honestly any questions put to me. I would often explore the reasons for the questions first. But I could never be the 'blank screen' type of therapist because it would be too much of an act for me. I don't believe ideologically in that approach because it creates too much power inequality and can be non-genuine and even hypocritical.

A therapist does need to be able to use reasoning to recognize patterns in the client's behaviour and thinking. It seems to be important to be able to perceive with *both* intuition *and* reason the roots of the problems being explored. But the ability to allow this understanding to flow between the two of you in a form chosen by the client is even more important. It doesn't feel so helpful to give the client your interpretation in your own words the moment it occurs to you. I was afraid that my own excitement at having a perceptive thought might prevent me from staying with the client. I might be tempted to rush in too soon. So I would mentally 'file' the thought away in the back of my mind for future reference. I might write it down afterwards.

As I see 'containing' the client in all her confusion and emotions as a vital aspect of therapy, I was afraid I might not be able to cope. I used to see myself as a very vulnerable and not particularly powerful or motherly person. I am also quite small. I didn't fit my own image of a mother-figure. As I began to practise I learned to 'contain' despite not quite 'looking the part'. But when I'm feeling insecure I still worry about having the 'wrong' image. I suppose I see myself as a more intellectual than physical kind of container.

Most of my doubts about becoming a psychotherapist were centred on the fear that, in doing so, I was avoiding the more pressing external issues of poverty and injustice that I mentioned earlier. But there were other specific issues that I was unsure about. As a feminist, should I put my energies into seeing men as well as women? In the end I decided that I did want to see men as they have also been deeply damaged by patriarchy, and as they still have most of the power, helping to change them can have effects on lots of other people too. I also had dilemmas concerning charging money for something that I felt ought to be free. But I was also unconsciously wondering whether I was really all that valuable. Was I really worth £x an hour (50 minutes)? Another doubt was whether I was psychologically ready to be a psychotherapist. Had I arrived? Had I resolved *all* my own problems? It was not until I realized that very few, if any, other psychotherapists have resolved *everything* that I thought I was OK enough to do the work. I did not have to be perfect.

The main price that I would have to pay for becoming a psychotherapist was giving up the secure and fairly well-paid local government work I had been doing. Losing that security to become self-employed was somewhat daunting. At first I only had a few clients and feared I wouldn't make enough money to live on. But I also found teaching and training work to boost my income. Being isolated at work in the home could have been a sacrifice but because I balanced my client work with teaching, etc. and had weekly peer supervision, this did not become a problem.

Another price that I did not anticipate at first turned out to be the enormous amount of 'psychic' energy that I give out, often leaving me exhausted. Taking in energies including 'bad' feelings from clients is also tiring. I often feel drained after sessions. But as the years go by I learn to protect myself better; for example, by visualizing golden light around me in sessions, to create a psychic boundary between my client and myself.

How did I become a psychotherapist?

I chose the Westminster Pastoral Foundation (WPF) as the place to train because I had read their brochure and it appealed to me at the time. The reason for my decision to train at that point was that I was very disillusioned with the kind of community work I was doing for local authorities. I had lost my earlier naïve ideals. I wanted to 'help' in a different kind of way.

I decided to attend a 'respectable' institution although most of my experience of therapy to date had been in humanistic groups not linked to any accredited organization. And I was concerned about professional acceptability for the first time in my life. I had originally thought of doing the full Jungian analysis training but found that it was much too expensive and the people I met at the interview seemed very old-fashioned in their views and approach. Yet my interest in Jung was still strong and it seemed that the WPF did have a lot of connections with the Jungian institutes.

The WPF also provided the kind of calm and spiritual atmosphere that I needed to counteract the bustle and drama of my life outside. An interest in myths and symbols also drew me to the Jungians and eventually to the WPF. From an early age I have drawn and painted abstract images and people, often from African mythology. I have also loved reading stories of myths and analysing their psychological meanings. When I was around 13 I began to see the Bible simply as a set of such mythological stories and symbols. And at the WPF there seemed to be people who were 'spiritual' but also psychologically aware. Ideally I would have liked a training that also had the political radicalism of somewhere like the Women's Therapy Centre. But there were no courses of this kind available at that time.

I liked the relatively eclectic training at the WPF because I hated the idea of being in an institution that had just one guru, and one 'line' that everyone should follow. This patriarchal approach seemed to be a particular problem in many of the humanistic groups I attended. All too often there was one, usually male, genius figure who had 'started' the particular type of therapy, e.g. Fritz Perls in gestalt therapy.

My formal training at the WPF allowed me to 'jump in at the deep end' by giving me a client quite early in my time there. The supervision I had in a group with other trainees probably had the most impact on me. I learned not to rescue clients and to allow distance and silence sometimes between us. I used to find silences very difficult. Yet I felt uncomfortable with what I experienced as the staff's 'superior' attitude towards clients. It was as if we therapists had some secret, mystical knowledge that *they* didn't have. Yet as trainees we were never actually told directly what this 'secret' knowledge was. Much of this must have been my own projection. But there was also a somewhat precious atmosphere of secrecy in the building that others had noticed too. In fact I felt so uncomfortable with this attitude and the lack of political awareness that at one point I decided to give up and never become a psychotherapist. I did not want to be part of such an elitist profession! I rebelled.

I learned very little theory that I can remember during my formal training. Over the years I developed my own theory and body of knowledge through reading and experiencing different groups and institutions. But the confrontation with my own personal unconscious while training was extremely useful both in groups and later in therapy with a Jungian analyst who I contacted through the WPF. With her I began to be more realistic about my ideals. I began to bring 'down' my grandiose notions of 'changing the world' and bring 'up' my own self-esteem and everyday reality. I was able to start setting more realistic goals for myself.

Fellow trainees and colleagues were very important throughout my training in sharing fears and doubts about becoming psychotherapists. And for me, it was a new experience to connect with so many people from walks of life that I would previously have dismissed as 'too right wing' or 'too religious, rich, straight' ... etc. It helped me later to be more genuinely accepting of all kinds of clients.

Formal training also taught me to bring clear boundaries to the sessions, to write notes and to select major themes to talk about in supervision. It also enabled me to feel that I could contain the strong feelings I sometimes had about sessions for maybe weeks until it was my turn to share. Learning to contain my own feelings helped me enormously in the long term as a therapist to help clients to contain theirs.

Formal training also gave me the sense of being a professional and charging professional fees. It made me take the business of personal change and growth very seriously. Yet I found myself afraid of violating the WPF's unspoken 'rules', such as that we should not disclose any information about ourselves. This kind of rule went against everything I believe about authentic relationships between people. And while I realize that the sessions are not there to talk about the therapist, honest answers to clients' questions did not seem unreasonable. I felt that I could not be myself there. Even in supervision sessions, middle-class assumptions, such as 'marriage is desirable for women', were implicit in much of the discussion.

Informal training turned out eventually to be much more important. The peer supervision group I had after leaving the WPF taught me more than all the other formal courses put together. I could be completely honest with those women without fearing judgement. The others had a more humanistic background and we shared ideas and techniques with each other. We had a formal supervision session about once a month with a more experienced supervisor, Brigit Proctor, who helped us to really trust and use effectively our own intuitions and feelings about clients. With her I also learned how to be fully myself and yet stay in the role of therapist, how to care about someone but stay separate and professional.

I also learned a lot from my own life experiences, of facing my own aloneness, of reaching rock bottom, of years of low level depression and being with people who had faced their own 'dark night of the soul'. I gained enormously from having a child and watching her grow and develop, and from my own everchanging relationship with her. I have also learned from clients who have given me the privilege of accompanying them on their journeys. My own students have taught me a lot through their openness to ideas and willingness to share their responses.

When did I become a psychotherapist?

I vividly remember the day that I saw my first client while training at the Westminster Pastoral Foundation. On the previous evening, I had been elected as a parent governor at my daughter's school. It seemed that I had become a 'responsible member of the community'! Now I had to, at least pretend to be, 'grown up'. Now I had joined the 'establishment' and couldn't always play the role of rebel. I too had to become an 'authority'. Both events provided a turning point for me and I did begin to think of myself as a professional helper.

But at that time I still would not call myself a psychotherapist. In fact there was a period of nine months after leaving the WPF when I didn't think that

I would ever be a 'proper' psychotherapist. I would teach and run groups and perhaps occasionally work with one person, but actually to identify myself as a psychotherapist just felt too arrogant. I continued to work part time for local authorities, while full of inner conflict about my career.

Then my particular department was 'reorganized' and this provided me with a chance to leave the job with a small amount of 'redundancy money'. This gave me the final push to become self-employed as a teacher *and* for the first time I acknowledged that I was also a psychotherapist. A number of practical actions such as putting adverts in magazines and having cards made, helped me to feel that now I really was a psychotherapist. I had a hand-out printed about myself and my work. I registered with the local tax office as a self-employed psychotherapist. And so, two years after seeing my first client, I was ready to become a 'proper' psychotherapist.

At first I felt rather embarrassed telling people that I was a psychotherapist. New acquaintances seemed to be wary of me. People would joke about coming to sit on my couch. Men, in particular, seemed to be somewhat threatened. Perhaps they imagined that I could 'read' their minds and so would have power over them, or perhaps it was the reaction many men still have towards women with independent, professional careers of their own. It put me a bit apart from many of my peers.

But close friends were pleased for me and even rather proud of my achievement. Sometimes there would be small hints of envy from friends whose own careers or directions in life were less satisfactory than mine. But I had two close colleagues and friends who were at a similar stage to me in 'becoming psychotherapists'. There was a great deal of mutual support and encouragement in our group. All of us had times when we doubted our abilities or felt that we weren't 'doing enough' for our clients. There were often feelings that only *other* people were 'proper' psychotherapists, people who had 'secret knowledge' or 'superior social status'. Meanwhile we were beginning to work more confidently with more and more clients.

Over the years as my confidence increased, I began to feel less totally responsible for clients. Paradoxically I felt less powerful too. At first I had thought that I must seem all-powerful to the client and that my every word must be given enormous importance. But gradually I began to trust the process of therapy, of our relationship and of the client's own journey. Increasingly, I saw myself as a guide and container for small parts of the client's personal journey. And the main focus of the therapy is that journey. My role is a limited, albeit very important, one. I was learning to trust in some form of external process of which I was only a part. Some might call this process god or goddess.

I found myself working increasingly intuitively, following the client, rather than sticking to 'rules' or interpretations according to the 'bibles' of Freud, Perls, or anyone else. I was also more able just to 'be' with clients, witnessing their growth rather than 'managing' it. At first I would find long silences very difficult, but later I found that some silences were incredibly powerful and even proved to be turning points in more than one client's therapy. So many clients come feeling that they must bring a problem or topic of conversation to 'entertain' me with. In a sense I too used to feel that I should 'perform' for my clients. Simply being together in the present, quietly aware of each other's presence, I now feel is a vital aspect of psychotherapy.

Along with changes in my practice as a psychotherapist there have been changes in my thinking. Although when I started training I had already developed some theories about human 'nature' and a model of my own as well as various idealistic images of psychotherapy and its power to change society, these were unconnected with therapy practice. They were abstract. My model of rhythm or interconnected opposites was taken more from Taoism and Eastern religions than everyday therapy. It was based on the idea that everything has opposite sides, even if one side is hidden. In Taoism, there is Yin and Yang – the holding in and giving out of energy – sometimes wrongly expressed as feminine and masculine sides. What goes up must come down. Over-dependence can lead to extreme independence.

In psychological terms, a 'healthy' person is conscious of and able to express all sides of themselves, rational and emotional, strong and vulnerable, etc. Their energies would be able to flow between their various opposites at different times, as appropriate.

When one opposite is hidden, the energies do not flow. There is repression and perhaps projection of that side on to other people. Energy is stuck. If the opposites are too separated or extreme, such as the ideal self and the 'hopeless' real self, then a person will swing compulsively from one to the other. This would be a jagged movement as opposed to the winding flow of a rhythmic movement backwards and forwards. My image of the winding snake seemed to fit theoretically with what is supposed to happen in psychological change. Instead of being stuck in one side of themselves, people do move from one to the other as they learn to accept their hidden or unacceptable sides. I had even experienced it in myself. But it was not until I worked with live clients using the model in the back of my mind that I realized that it really did work.

It also helped me to have a very general framework into which most of the different therapy teachings fitted. I did not have to stick to one school of thought or another. I just looked for the opposites and their reconnection in all the theories. I also related the 'snake' model to the theory of dialectics, written about by Marxist intellectuals as the movement between opposite classes, etc.

It was some years after I finished my formal training that I discovered all the feminist literature on spirituality and ancient goddesses. A friend pointed out to me the connections between my model of rhythm and the 'female principle' at the heart of the 'old goddess religions'. Indeed one of the most important symbols attached to the goddess was in fact the snake! I then started reading everything that I could lay my hands on that related to the ancient (and modern) goddess spirituality. I travelled to ancient sites in Crete, Turkey, and Malta and these gave me strength and inspiration. I studied archaeology and anthropology as well as psychology (I was teaching a social anthropology class at the time). And I found myself becoming more interested in the questions of the relationship between matricentric or mother-orientated societies and psychological factors such as emotional expression.

How did the ancient mother-centred Neolithic societies of the Near East, Africa, and the Mediterranean all gradually get turned into warring patriarchies circa 3,000 BC? And what can we learn from this change, to help us in the changes happening today? I became interested in how we can use ancient images to help us gain confidence today as women. My interest centred on questions concerning how we can develop and understand the 'female principle' of inter-connected opposites and cyclical processes in terms of *today's* world. How can we use it to help us psychologically to grow and express our potential? I found that I was constantly contrasting the hierarchical structure of the patriarchal principle with the rhythm of the female principle. I even began to see clients' problems in terms of one 'internalized' hierarchy or another. For some, feelings about class inferiority, being fat or simply being a woman, were basic factors in their lack of self-esteem, which has such an enormous influence on psychological well-being. Everybody seems to have suffered from being at the bottom of one hierarchy or another. And, in a society where it is supposed to be your fault if you lose rather than win, or are at the bottom of any hierarchy, strong feelings of inadequacy must result. This kind of thinking enabled me to connect my political awareness with psychotherapy. I published a booklet called *The Mass Psychology of Thatcherism* (Chaplin and Haggert 1983), using these ideas to analyse the 1980s in Britain.

Since then I have written and published a number of articles, chapters for books and finally, in 1987, a whole book (Chaplin 1988). Writing has helped me a great deal to clarify my ideas and practice. As much of the writing has been about feminist approaches to therapy I have had to read, discuss with colleagues, and examine my own beliefs around such issues as, what is different about feminist therapy as opposed to non-feminist therapy? It is a whole different way of thinking, using the female principle rather than male hierarchies of thought. It is not, however, a particular school or technique of therapy.

My understanding of what I perceive as feminist therapy has not just come from one source or from particular books or theories. It has grown gradually out of many years of working within women's groups, running women's courses, exploring women's styles of management in institutions, involvement in campaigns for women's rights, visiting the peace camp at Greenham Common in Britain, and simply being a woman myself in today's world. When women organize we try to be as non-hierarchical as possible. We rotate our leaders. We weave connections between ourselves and ideas. Everything we do, we do differently from the patriarchal, hierarchical approach, if we have the chance. It is not enough to change our styles as psychotherapists, we are actually talking about a fundamentally different way of thinking about *everything*.

Yet this feminist way of thinking has quietly permeated many areas of the therapy world and indeed respect for intuition and other previously dismissed 'female' skills does seen to be increasing. I am at times encouraged by mixed conferences I attend or management training courses that I give. But at other times, I am discouraged by the depth of the influence of patriarchal thought patterns and behaviours. Today I see myself as a pessimistic optimist!

What sustains me as a psychotherapist?

I find that being a psychotherapist is a great privilege. Being allowed into another person's sacred inner space, to be invited to walk with them on their journey and in their dark places, to be present with another's self-discovery makes me feel honoured and proud. It is often quite awe-inspiring to be a psychotherapist. I often marvel at people's resilience in the face of dreadful life experiences, at the strength of the human spirit. Sometimes the changes that people go through in therapy can seem quite magical. They can be explained in psychotherapeutic jargon but there is another level at which the changes are profoundly mysterious.

The other side of this coin is my own fascination with people's lives and stories. Being a therapist can be like reading a novel. I want to know what the next chapter will bring! This can result in over curiosity about clients and a difficulty with holding back from asking questions. Many times I have wanted to ask questions out of my own interest rather than for the sake of the client and his or her immediate needs. With experience I find it easier to curb the questioning, but I am still aware of it as a danger. However, I do think that so long as a therapist keeps control of his or her curiosity, this fascination with people helps make the job rewarding.

It is easier to feel rewarded by those clients who show noticeable change, who connect this change to the therapy and show some appreciation, especially at the end. But, of course, many clients do not leave as changed people, to go dancing down the street into a future of self-fulfilment! It can be quite disheartening to let a client go when it does not seem as though they have changed at all. But again, after years of practice it became easier to 'trust the process' and not just blame myself.

Clients who are open to change and listen when I do occasionally make comments do nourish me, while clients who cannot take in my words, and sometimes not even my love, are not so easily rewarding. Some people are too afraid of letting in anything positive from another person to even allow themselves to listen. Such clients often talk incessantly. Others are too afraid of judgements to let go any control over the sessions. However, when these clients do eventually begin to trust or let go, the relief I feel can be most rewarding.

185

The clients that I find most difficult to work with are those who are deeply depressed and whose energies easily bring down my own. I can leave sessions with these clients feeling absolutely exhausted. Sometimes I need to protect myself 'psychically' from a client's energies; for example, by visualizing light around myself.

My own therapy or personal growth continues year after year and I keep facing new issues or new sides of myself. Often these are sides that have been looked at before, but I keep coming back to them as if on my spiral journey, e.g. issues centred on control or dependency. What I find amazing is that when I am personally looking at a particular issue, lo and behold that is the very issue that most clients will be coming with! Clients seem to find me at the right point of their lives. Or is it I who 'find' them? The work that they do on these issues undoubtedly helps me. But I also believe that the work that I do on the issues helps my clients. But I rarely feel that I have completely 'resolved' any of the issues brought to me by clients. Indeed many of them are essentially contradictions that cannot be 'resolved'. Rather we all need to learn to live with the opposites. At other times it can feel as though a particular client has gone 'further' than I have along a particular path and is 'teaching' me something. In a sense all my clients are teaching me about myself and about being human. I recognize parts of myself in every single one of them!

I personally like the kind of deep, but limited intimacy that therapeutic relationships have. As a woman who in her past easily found herself merging or wanting to merge with others once I became emotionally involved, I need to learn about boundaries and detachment. Being a psychotherapist has helped me work with the contradiction of longing for closeness but needing separation too. I find it a valuable model for other kinds of relationships. We all need our boundaries. I have also learned to sit quietly with another person in 'real' life, which I could not easily do before I became a therapist! It helped centre and stabilize me.

Most of my emotional support comes from colleagues and friends. My daughter is proud of the fact that I am a therapist, and working at home means that I can quite easily fit my hours around her needs. I limit the number of clients that I see in a week and try to see only one or two in the evenings. But it can still be a strain after giving out energy to others all day to have to give more to my daughter at the end of the day. At times she seems impossibly demanding! Relationships with partners and recently with men friends have suffered. I feel as though I am unable to give them very much. I want and expect them to give to me and become too much of a 'taker'. While years ago I was very giving, perhaps too giving in relationships, now I have gone to the opposite extreme. After being available for clients all day, the last thing I want to do is look after a man friend at night.

I need a balance in my life between 'taking in' and 'giving out, communicating my ideas'. In work this balance is now being achieved. Two or three times a week I teach psychology, counselling, and social anthropology.

I get considerable satisfaction from this work, as it is the opposite of sitting listening to clients. Intellectual stimulation, being listened to, and contact with groups, are all needs of mine that are satisfied through teaching and giving workshops. They also give me a chance to try out and discuss my theories with other people.

My painting also helps to sustain me. It is relaxing and I can lose myself in it completely. But it also helps me to express my own inner conflicts, fantasies and needs. Writing helps me to clarify ideas and also gives me a sense of being heard. Holidays are also vital. Recently I have been travelling to places of particular importance in the ancient world of the goddess – Crete, Turkey, and Malta. My outer journeys mirror my interior journeys. I am searching for positive images of women and female power.

I do see myself as continuing to be a psychotherapist but I seem to be moving more towards the spiritual and artistic aspects of the field. I want to communicate to the public about the feminist ways of thinking and the power of the female principle through writing and art as well as being a psychotherapist who is basically listening to clients. If I had my time again I would certainly choose to be a psychotherapist, only I would have started earlier in my life, because it would have given me a clearer direction during my somewhat confused twenties.

Implications for other psychotherapists

First, it has been my experience that formal training is only a small part of the process of 'becoming a psychotherapist'. Yet all too often it becomes the only focus. People often think that if they find the perfect training, after three or more years on the course they will turn magically into 'perfect' psychotherapists. Becoming a psychotherapist is more likely to be a lifetime's work and it needs to take its own time. A point will come when a person feels ready to practise, but this may or may not be during or immediately after finishing a formal training. A person's own emotional and spiritual growth is as vital a part of the 'training' as formal tuition. This growth can take place with or without the guidance of people labelled 'psychotherapists'. Friends, colleagues, lovers, even chance encounters can teach us so much about ourselves if we are open to them.

Second, it is vital to find your own individual way of working, using your own intuition. Adhering strictly to the rules of one particular 'school' may interfere with a therapist's own judgements and energies. Specific skills and approaches may be needed at some stage of the training to provide the discipline which is vital to the work. But once these have been learned, people should feel free and confident enough to develop their own style. For many people this might be largely intuitive and difficult to define or categorize in terms of any specific school of therapy. We need to really trust ourselves.

Third, it can actually be an advantage to have experienced a lot of psychological pain and conflict when growing up. Our own vulnerabilities can also be our greatest strengths as psychotherapists. And we do not need to be totally 'sorted out' with all conflicts resolved in order to be good psychotherapists. In fact, as William Blake wrote, 'No progression without contraries'. We too need to learn to live with the opposites and the contradictions of life and of being a psychotherapist.

Fourth, it seems to be important to recognize the small part we as individuals play in the growth of our clients. It is basically their journey that is the focus of therapy. We can help guide, contain and channel energy for them. But we are not in charge. We need to be humble.

In summary, the main themes of this contribution have been:

1. It is possible to combine an awareness and involvement in radical politics, feminism, socialism, etc. with work on the 'inner' side of life as a psychotherapist. By recognizing 'inner hierarchies' as the result of social factors and by helping to create a less hierarchical culture and way of thinking, therapists have a role in social change. My personal story was a struggle to connect these two sides of me, the spiritual and the socialist feminist.
2. Intuition and trusting the process of change are just as important as rational analysis and specific psychological theories.
3. We are the product of our times and of our personal histories. There are no absolutely 'true' theories or psychotherapy approaches. We need to have the courage to travel our *own* journeys, not those of Freud, Jung, or anyone else. We need to find our *own* 'truths'.

Writing this chapter has helped me to realize just how early in life the seeds of my desire to be a psychotherapist must have been sown. It now looks, in retrospect, like an inevitable path!

References

Chaplin, J. (1988) *Feminist Counselling in Action*, London: Sage.
Chaplin, J. and Haggert, C. (1983) *The Mass Psychology of Thatcherism*, London: The Socialist Society.
Shorter, B. (1987) *An Image Darkly Forming*, London: Routledge & Kegan Paul.
Starhawk (1982) *Dreaming the Dark*, Boston: Beacon Press.
Stein, D. (1987) *The Women's Spirituality Book*, St Paul, Minnesota: Llewellyn Publications.

Part three

Commentaries

Chapter twelve

The self and the therapeutic domain

Laurence Spurling and Windy Dryden

Our aim in this chapter is to outline some of the themes that run through the essays in this book, themes that seem to play a major role in how the process of becoming a therapist is made intelligible by our contributors. Such themes include the therapist's drive towards understanding and repair, the development of empathy, and the concern with the integration of different parts of oneself. We then pursue, in part two, a particular line of inquiry which, we believe, the essays in this book bring into view, namely that an important, if not crucial move in the process of becoming a therapist is the establishment of a particular domain in one's sense and experience of oneself, which is that of the inner world and the self. This domain is taken to represent both the field of the therapeutic endeavour and the source of therapeutic knowledge, skill, and intuition. We will consider how the notion of the self plays a key part in these accounts, and some of the ways in which it is described. In part three we suggest that the idea of the self serves an important function as a counterpoint to theory in psychotherapy. In part four we focus on the language employed by the contributors to describe both their development as therapists and the practice and nature of psychotherapy itself. We identify, in addition to the language of the self, three traditional areas of discourse – the religious, political, and narrative – which are used by the writers as a fund of metaphors and ways of thinking with which to try and describe the highly elusive process of therapy. We finally make reference to the view of therapeutic knowledge, as having a fundamentally personal and interpersonal dimension, which seems to emerge from what our contributors have written.

This chapter is not meant to give an overall review of the essays. Although we hope we have identified some of the more persistent themes that are common to the accounts, we have used what our contributors have written, and the way they have written, as a springboard to speculate about how both the process of becoming a therapist and the practice of psychotherapy can be thought of and written about. In so doing we have treated the different essays as though they constitute one, communal text, as our interest has been in what is common to these accounts rather than with how they differ from each other. To this end we have risked taking liberties with what individual contributors have written. We hope these liberties have not been too gross, and that, in our use of these essays for our own speculations, we have remained within the spirit of the real value of these autobiographical essays, which is that they will provoke others to think about how the desire to be a therapist, and processes of initiation, development, growth, and maturity within psychotherapy, can be both thought about and put into words.

Part One: The development of understanding and empathy and the drive towards repair and integration

Psychotherapy as a calling

In writing about why and how they became therapists, there seems to be general agreement among the contributors to this book that the profession of psychotherapy is to be conceived as no ordinary occupation. Being a psychotherapist is described in terms of being a 'privilege', as involving a special and unique form of interaction with one's patients. For example, the practice of psychotherapy is described as 'an art form for me, as well as a deeply-felt privilege and responsibility' (Mahoney p.28). 'The most common feeling I have when I think about being a therapist is one of awe' (p.47), writes Irene Bloomfield. As a kind of work which is so bound up with one's creativity and one's relationships to others, in short with who one is, it is seen less as something chosen than as a profession to which one is called. It is seen as the expression of a drive or need which brings the therapist into a special kind of intimate contact with others. Writing of his decision to seek therapy training, Brian Thorne writes of:

> ... a sense of inevitability mingled with something akin to dread. I knew I had little choice if I was to obey the voice within me. In short, my work as a therapist has in a sense been an act of obedience. (p.67)

Another, Paul Heppner, writes of the 'chance events' (p.73), especially meetings with therapists and counsellors who have proved inspirational, which seemed to have led him to become a therapist. This mixture of chance and underlying pattern contributes sometimes to a sense of uncanny predetermination:

> By pure chance or divine ordinance I sat studying at the University of Wisconsin student library with the books of psychiatrist Jacob Levy Moreno perched innocently in front of me on a shelf. I had never seen or heard of them before. There were thousands of books in that library and I sat in front of those, not knowing that my career lay on the shelf, asking to be discovered.
>
> (Karp p.91)

Somehow one's life is seen as having led to being a therapist; several contributors comment that they could not imagine themselves being anything else.

The drive to understand and repair

In this notion of psychotherapy as a calling, in which it is difficult if not impossible to determine whether one has chosen or has been chosen, there is implicit an idea that the nature of this calling, as well as to what one is called, is already moving beyond one's understanding. The therapist-to-be is called, without really knowing specifically to what he or she is called. But this lack of specific knowledge, about what one's future career as a therapist means, takes shape against a high value placed on knowledge itself. There is the sense that the wish to become a psychotherapist is born out of an insistent drive to *understand* other people and the world in which we live. The therapist is subject to a fascination, an 'unquenchable curiosity' (Fransella p.126), about people.

> Most of the time I find what patients are telling me extraordinarily interesting, and it still feels an enormous privilege to be admitted into their secret worlds.
>
> (Bloomfield p.46)

This notion of the secret world of the client, as a domain to which one seeks admittance, is seen as the particular object of the therapist's understanding. The practice of psychotherapy is thus a quest for some kind of hidden or secret knowledge. It is invested with something of the same mystery and passion with which the novelist Primo Levi describes his desire to be a chemist, in contrast to the more mundane concerns of his friend:

> We had no doubts: we would be chemists. but our expectations and hopes were quite different. Enrico asked chemistry, quite reasonably, for the tools to earn his living and have a secure life. I asked for something entirely different; for me chemistry represented an indefinite cloud of future potentialities which enveloped my life to come in black volutes torn by fiery flashes, like those which had hidden Mount Sinai. Like Moses, from that cloud I expected my law, the principles of order in me, around me, and in the world.
>
> (Levi 1986: 22–3)

The psychotherapist also looks for a key to unlocking the hidden ordering principle of the world, although the concern is with the behaviour of people rather than the structure of the natural world (a concern made more urgent in the case of those who have suffered directly or indirectly at the hands of others):

It was very important for me to try to understand why people behaved as they did; why my former best friends turned into bitter enemies because they were told to hate Jews.

(Bloomfield p.38)

Why were some able to make it when so many others died in the concentration camps? Was it faith, strength, family?

(Karp p.89)

This drive towards understanding the world in which we live is fuelled by a need or desire for a more personal kind of understanding to do with oneself and one's own life. In the words of Hans Strupp, 'I was initially attracted by the field of psychotherapy ... because, in part, I was impelled to find answers to early traumas' (p.102). This attempt to find answers to what might have gone wrong in early life is sometimes expressed in a determination and desire not to repeat the mistakes or deficiencies experienced as a child. As Eddy Street puts it, 'I am now aware that my struggle as a therapist is about the attempt not to use the set of rules for relating that I was given as a child' (p.145). Two other therapists express this in terms of the idea of wanting to be the therapist they never had:

Part of it may have been wanting to become the counsellor I had never had during my own stormy adolescence.

(Mahoney p.20)

... there was no one I could talk to about my unhappy feelings.... Years later I realized that I wanted to be the therapist I never had.

(Chaplin p.173)

What marks out these accounts is not the nature or amount of suffering or unhappiness but the attitude displayed towards it. Pain and misfortune are seen as having been survived, if not mastered. Even if 'rock bottom' (Chaplin p.181) is reached, suffering is conceived of as having reached a limit, and thus to have been tolerated and become tolerable.

Furthermore, and this is an insistent theme in these accounts, what is seen as having gone adrift in one's life is taken as an impetus to put it right again. The idea of having become the therapist one never had is an expression of having had an opportunity in some way to *repair* or make up for what went wrong or was lacking. Implicit in this kind of thinking is that, if one can become the therapist one never had, then one has already become a therapist for others. Thus the misfortune and unhappiness to which one was subject become the foundation of one's ability to be someone who can attend to the suffering of others. In other words, suffering or unhappiness are conceived of as having some intrinsic value, as having a meaning. Pain is seen as that which gives potency. This makes sense in that one cannot know about joy and happiness unless one has also experienced pain and unhappiness. But, more than that, is the idea that the therapist's vulnerability is precisely that which constitutes his or her strength. This is expressed explicitly by Jocelyn Chaplin:

> it can actually be an advantage to have experienced a lot of psychological pain and conflict when growing up. Our own vulnerabilities can also be our greatest strengths as psychotherapists.
>
> (p.188)

Another therapist writes of how the way she dealt with a painful experience of rejection 'laid the cornerstone in my sanity of young adulthood' (Karp p.96). Such a view is concordant with the ancient and compelling metaphor of the therapist as a wounded healer. This image expresses the idea 'that he who cures over and over, yet remains eternally ill or wounded himself, appears at the heart of the mystery of healing' (Groesbeck 1975:127). A persistent sense of having been hurt or wounded does indeed pervade the accounts in this book. But one's suffering is such, or is conceived as such, as to become a resource in that it sensitizes one to the suffering of others. For this to happen, for one's own suffering truly to become a source of strength and a means to understanding the plight of other people, the therapist must probably not have been too deeply wounded. He or she has been *wounded but not crippled*, or wounded but also healed. These essays are in accord, we believe, with Winnicott's idea about the degree of illness to which an aspiring therapist should be subject:

> One would rather have a really suitable person for doing this kind of work than an ill person made less ill by the analysis that is part of the psycho-analytic training.
>
> (Winnicott 1971:1)

Homoeopathic healing

We have suggested that a primary theme in the descriptions of becoming a psychotherapist is that of being called upon to understand the nature of suffering, and one's own suffering in particular, and to seek to repair what has gone wrong in one's own life through the attempt to heal others. Psychotherapy is thought of as a personal journey towards health, in which it is the therapist's own drive towards health and sanity which is healing for the patient. Psychotherapeutic healing is thus understood on the principle of *homoeopathic* healing (Groesbeck 1975:122–3). Unlike *allopathic* healing, which employs remedies which produce effects upon the body different from those produced by the disease, homoeopathic healing is based on the principle that like is cured by like, or that a cure is produced by giving small doses of a remedy which in a healthy person and in large doses would produce symptoms like that of the disease.

Psychotherapeutic healing can be seen as comprising both principles of healing. It is allopathic in the sense that the therapist offers the patient a different and better kind of experience, with a different outcome, to that of the patient's previous life history. In order to do that the therapist has to be in some way healed. Psychotherapeutic healing is homoeopathic in the sense that the patient is brought to re-experience or re-think, in small and safe doses, something of the original trauma or complaint which brought him into therapy. It is this idea of psychotherapeutic healing as homoeopathic which is given more prominence in these accounts. They stress the similarity between therapist and patient, the recognition of which is seen as a prerequisite for the therapist's ability to have sympathy for the patient in his suffering and to be able to empathize with him and accompany him on his journey towards health. For example: 'I became a therapist when I stopped being a technician and, ironically, when I literally adopted the client's role' (Mahoney p.28). The therapist knows what it is to suffer and to seek help because he has been there himself.

A sense of isolation and the development of empathy

What is the nature of the wound with which the therapist is afflicted, and from which he or she derives strength and understanding? Rather than any particular event or constellation of occurrences, the wound seems to consist of, or express, a sense of *isolation* or division from others. The various biographies convey an early and dominant sense of being on one's own – variously described as a 'sensed isolation', and of having been 'compulsively self-sufficient all of my life' (Mahoney p.27); as 'standing aloof' and 'being cut-off' (Street p.136); or as 'a persistent feeling of self-consciousness and alienation' (Strupp p.102). This feeling of aloneness and isolation results in a sense of being a 'stranger' (Strupp p.102), an 'outcast' (Mahoney p.19) or an outsider – 'a predominant feeling for me growing up was of being an outsider, and being different in some way ...' (Heppner p.70). This may be contingent upon, as well as compounded by, ethnic or cultural differences. The therapist can consequently come to take up a position of being an observer of other people, a looker-on of relationships, as described by John Rowan:

> It felt to me as if I made various attempts to get [my mother's] love, failed several times to do so, and retired hurt and lonely ... and in the end turning loneliness into a virtue by claiming not to need people. In that way I could observe people in a way which was basically external, and calculated to cut me off from them very successfully.
>
> (pp.148–9)

Such an attitude of external observation, of looking in from the outside, can become established as a habitual way in which one sees oneself and relations with others, as in the metaphor of peeking through a window employed by one therapist:

discussions with my friends have provided me with instances where I was able to peek through new 'windows' to learn more about life's experiences.

(Heppner p.77)

In whatever way the sense of isolation from others is dealt with, relationships with others become an object of inquiry and curiosity. One therapist refers to her 'observation and examination of a family dilemma' (Karp p.87). Such an examination, together with a wish for intimacy brought about by the sense of isolation, seems to produce, and be produced by, someone who is given or has adopted the role of attending to others in the family; for example, in having been 'given the task as a child of putting others' needs before my own, of caring for those in need' (Street p.135). One metaphor used is that of having been a 'family runner' (Karp p.88) who interprets what one family member says to another.

This sense of isolation from others, with its consequent yearning to become close, translates itself not only into a stance of observing, taking care of or interpreting for others, but also into a powerful need to understand the nature of relationships. Hence the concern, manifested in these essays, with the nature of the boundaries between people, shown as an interest in and aptitude for gauging the feelings of others, for being able to enter the other's world. This can comprise or involve a form of identification or role-reversal with the other, demonstrated by one therapist when he writes, after having told of his teacher begging him, with tears in her eyes, not to waste his gift with words: 'I share that story – *the tears now my own* – to emphasize the potential power of a well-chosen moment and a core message' (Mahoney p.18, italics added). This identification with the other can carry with it a sense of or potential for losing oneself in the other, or even of merging with the other:

I realized during my primary school days that I had an ability which seemed unusual and which was both a blessing and a curse ... I simply experienced, with alarming frequency, the powerful sensation of knowing what it felt like to be in someone else's skin.

(Thorne p.54)

To really know what it feels like to be in someone else's skin involves in some sense to have been there. It evokes the intertwined or symbiotic closeness of mother and child, in which the therapist must be able to become immersed, but from which he or she must be able to separate. The psychoanalyst Ralph Greenson describes this as empathy:

Empathy ... is a special form of nonverbal, preverbal closeness which has a feminine cast; it comes from one's motherliness, and men (and women too) must have made peace with their motherliness in order to be willing to empathize ... People who are empathizers are always trying to re-establish contact, like people who are depressed. I believe that

197

analysts who have been depressed and have overcome their depression make the best empathizers. One must be able to regress to empathic contact with the patient and then be able to rebound from it in order to check on the validity of the data so gathered.

(Greenson 1966:16)

The demands of psychotherapy as described by Greenson, the need to regress to a kind of preverbal contact with the patient, balanced by the ability to detach oneself in order to think and work with some objectivity, point to an area of fundamental tension for the therapist. The nature of the therapist's wound seems to lie in particular in the sense of isolation and separation from others, which drives or attracts him or her to seek empathic closeness with others in that 'life of intimate relationships' (Thorne p.56) which is psychotherapy. But the wish and drive for closeness with others carry with it the danger of becoming too involved with one's work and one's patients. Over-detachment and over-involvement are both cited as occupational hazards.

The greatest professional hazard to which I have been prey is to feel unreachable and beyond help. It is in those moments I feel most desolate.

(Karp p.100)

It has become increasingly clear to me that as a therapist it is critical that I pursue other interests and am able to separate myself physically and psychologically from that role for extended times.

(Heppner p.85)

Not to be able to separate carries with it the risk of losing one's bearings, if not one's very boundaries, as a separate person – what Brian Thorne characterizes as the 'curse' of empathy as counterpoint to its 'blessing'. The therapist can thus become caught in a conflict between striving for closeness with others, while simultaneously fearing the loss of separateness which might ensue.

This conflict, the two sides of which make up the characteristic rhythm of therapy as a form of detached intimacy, is not something which can be avoided – on the contrary, each therapist has to learn his or her way of recognizing and facing it. The point is that both sides of the conflict are needed, and have to be held in some form of balance or integration. One aspect of becoming a therapist seems to be the recognition that the different aspects of a situation, conflict or dilemma should not be met with by denial, avoidance or other such measures, but rather by an attempt to hold the different parts together.

The search for wholeness and integration

This notion of uniting or bringing together elements which are in conflict with or opposition to each other finds expression in the recurrent idea that psychotherapy is a concern with *wholeness*, with integrating the different parts of oneself (itself another feature characteristic of homoeopathic healing, which is more concerned with the totality of symptoms than with symptoms in isolation). 'At the beginning of psychotherapy people tend to be stuck in one side of themselves and through the therapeutic process come to heal that split' (Chaplin p.176). Becoming a psychotherapist is similarly conceived as a journey towards wholeness. On their way towards becoming a therapist several authors comment on their disappointment with academic psychology which only presents a picture of people as in bits.

> Along with many other students the study of psychology during my first degree was something of a disappointment: instead of being about people and how they operate, it was about animals and statistics and complex methodologies investigating peripheral issues. It was about compartmentalization when I was interested in wholeness.
>
> (Street p.137)

> I had great problems during my degree course in holding myself together. That is, I would try and work out how motivation and memory and perception and personality and emotion and social psychology all held together to make up *me*. ... And here was Kelly stating most forcibly that we can and should only be understood as one, indivisible whole person.
>
> (Fransella p.123)

The progress towards becoming a therapist is thus conceived as a move towards integrating the various parts of oneself. 'And with the healing of the split between thinking and feeling came, one time in a group, after a cathartic experience, a sense of being a whole person' (Rowan p.154). 'I like to provide a model, especially for female clients, of a woman who is whole unto herself' (Chaplin p.175).

Part Two: The psychotherapeutic domain: the inner world and the self

The delineation of an inner world

We have so far outlined some of the features that seem important in understanding the process of being a psychotherapist. Out of a basic curiosity and wish to understand how people relate to each other, coupled with some sense of having been emotionally wounded or injured which finds expression in a reparative drive directed towards the healing of such emotional wounds in others – out of elements such as these the therapist creates, as it were, a space or *locus*, which constitutes a particular kind of domain of experience and knowledge. This domain is taken to be of intrinsic and particular value in both understanding the process of becoming a therapist, and in constituting a particular domain to which psychotherapy addresses itself. This domain is conceived of as lying within; it is a form of inner space or inner world.

The various accounts of the therapists' early life portray a preoccupation with this inner world, a 'fascination with the richness of real, everyday "inner life" struggles' (Mahoney p.20). There are different paths which lead to this inner world; for example, it may be through a love of books or an immersion in fantasies. In speaking of his close involvement as a child with his mother, one therapist remarks that 'closeness of this kind then leads the child into the inner world of adult fantasies' (Street p.135). Another describes her childhood as one which was 'lived secretly and internally' (Fransella p.117). A third reveals one motive for such a move inside:

> mostly I retreated into books, drawing and a fantasy world that soon became more real to me than the outside one, which I found too painful. Already the inner world was my comfort while the outside was too confusing and conflict-ridden.

> (Chaplin p.171)

Here the move inwards is shown to be a consequence of a turning away from the world, which is experienced as too painful and bewildering. But the inner world need not only be a retreat from the world outside. It is also conceived of as a source of richness and hidden vitality, as a hidden part of the world which plays a vital part in unlocking some of the secrets of human life. Furthermore, the delineation of an inner space or inner world establishes a domain for that which is seen to constitute the core or kernel of our existence, and which might offer a key to unlocking the door to psychotherapeutic knowledge – the self.

The domain of the self

In our view it is the concept of the self, and a concern if not preoccupation with its nature, limits, realness and development, which runs as a unifying thread through the essays in this book. The nature of this self, an inhabitor of this inner domain, is explored in a variety of ways. For instance, the importance and problematics of seeking and receiving *recognition* and confirmation by others, as a fundamental step in how one's self is constituted and shaped, is given considerable attention. The essay by Hans Strupp charts his struggle to gain professional recognition from colleagues. Several contributors point to the crucial part played by their clients in affirming them as therapists. For example, one writes of a client whose desperation in seeking help, and willingness to trust him:

> compelled me to be real and not to deny the extent of my resources as a person and as a professional. She affirmed me in a way which no

amount of praise or encouragement from colleagues or success with less demanding clients would have done.

(Thorne p.63)

The therapist's childhood can be described as one in which this recognition or affirmation from others was lacking or deficient.

The influence of my two brothers was enormous ... I think all three of us were more pursued and driven than listened to.

(Karp p.88)

One consequence of not receiving the required recognition from others may be a sense of inferiority. For instance:

These feelings of differentness influenced me to feel inferior in some global way, and subsequently to be cautious with peers as well as to try harder to be liked and accepted.

(Heppner pp.70–1)

In linking his sense of inferiority with being different, Paul Heppner seems to imply that feeling inferior was for him consequent upon an appreciation of his own uniqueness and individuality. Irene Bloomfield writes of how a sense of inferiority as a result of rejection by those around her became transformed into a feeling of pride and conviction of inner freedom:

I can actually remember the exact moment when that bad feeling about being Jewish changed. It was like a sudden revelation. I was just walking along the street when it came to me that I did not have to buy all this stuff about Jewish inferiority which teachers, fellow pupils, and everything around us seemed to be proclaiming. I would go to Palestine and be proud to be a Jew. It was then as if a terrible, dark cloud which had threatened to engulf me was lifted and I felt free and somehow invulnerable. The latter was, of course, a delusion, as far as the external world was concerned, but something had changed internally.

(p.39)

This inner sense of invulnerability and freedom is reminiscent of the dizzying sense of limitless freedom, so well described by Sartre, which follows an awareness that many of the constrictions to our lives are self-imposed, or at least consequent upon our taking them as real. This may contribute to a sense of power, which is referred to by some contributors (usually in acknowledgement of its intrinsic dangers); for instance:

I knew only too well that I was a powerful person and anything which could have added to my sense of power might well have been to the detriment of my growth as a therapist.

(Thorne p.60)

The other side to a sense of inferiority is an intimation of *being special*. One therapist writes of being 'singled out' by one teacher and treated as special by another (Mahoney pp.18–19). Another refers to his 'unusual' ability to empathize and ability to share a 'warmth of companionship which I know now was exceptional' (Thorne p.54). A third writes, with delicate irony, of how extraordinary the practice of psychotherapy can sometimes seem:

> It is an occupational hazard of working with concentrated emotion that being an everyday citizen can feel anti-climatic. The people I meet at the post-office or in shops do not know I move mountains.
>
> (Karp p.99)

This sense of being special or unusual, which may lead to a view of oneself as in some way superior (cf. Marmor 1953), can be seen as a concern with the worth and potency of the self. As a counterpoint, another theme in these accounts is a concern with the *substance* of the self, and, indeed, whether the self has any.

> I was afraid that the next supervisor would really scrutinize me and find me out, that somehow I was hollow .... In a way, I feared I was a 'fraud' (i.e. the impostor syndrome).
>
> (Heppner p.78)

> once again I sought therapy for myself, but this time for a more protracted period to deal anew with the fear that only a bag of wind existed inside the armour.
>
> (Street p.144)

Such concerns and doubts about the substance or solidity of the self also find expression in a tendency, in some of the accounts, to *idealize* teachers or colleagues, who are seen to embody those aspects of self which are feared to be lacking in oneself. This idealization is, in fact, directly addressed in the two quotations that follow. The first is a description of how the therapist realizes, in hindsight, how he had idealized his first counsellor:

> He appeared to be a rational, scholarly man who was kind, supportive, accepting, self-aware, comfortable and enjoying the challenge of his work with people ... I remember at the time perceiving Dr Jesseph as 'having it all together', and clearly idealized him as a role-model. I liked him, and felt he not only accepted me but respected me.
>
> (Heppner p.72)

Another therapist gives an ironical description of how he initially imagined a psychologist to be:

> ... he was attractive, always at ease, pleasant to everyone, with time to survey the world and the individual simultaneously, he was

well grounded, in control of his emotions and free of problems and worries. I wanted to be like this.

(Street p.137)

The language of the self

What these essays show, we think, is that in order to try and describe how and why one becomes a therapist, a particular form of discourse or language is employed, which can be called the *language of the self*. Of course, since these essays are autobiographical, the authors can hardly fail to be writing about themselves! But our point is that this self, which is described in the language of the self, is seen to reside *within*. It inhabits a particular domain, that of the inner world. This is the domain of psychotherapy, which is taken fundamentally to be about experience and knowledge of the self – as one contributor puts it, psychotherapy is 'a form of initiation into being yourself' (Chaplin p.175). Hence, becoming a therapist is seen to involve becoming aware of and sensitive to this domain of the self, and to such features of this self as its nature, realness, potency, limits, and substance. The therapist learns or cultivates, we think, a certain form of *self-consciousness*, in the dual sense of this term. There is an intense curiosity about the self, and an awareness of its manifestations and vicissitudes. And there is also some apprehension or anxiety about this self, about how intact, powerful, or real it is.

Care must be taken not to extrapolate from this language of the self to making generalizations about the personality or character-structure of therapists and aspiring therapists. Indeed, our argument is more that the language in which these accounts are written constitutes a form of professional discourse, a discourse in which the therapist as a person, and his or her entrance into the world of therapy, can find adequate expression. As such there may be a polemical point to this language of the self. It may function as a counter-weight to the over-emphasis in much of the psychotherapy literature on techniques and interventions (see the Introduction by Gilbert, Hughes, and Dryden). This is captured in a statement by one therapist, which sums up this point of view:

I believe that what is most important in therapy is how we *are* with patients, and that this is more important than what we *do*. It is essential, therefore, that the therapist should go on working on himself.

(Bloomfield p.49)

The idea that what counts is 'how we are' rather than 'what we do', means that therapeutic discourse, in order to do justice to the practice of psychotherapy, has to concern itself with the self (what we are) rather than with techniques, programmes and interventions (what we do). The notion of the self is thus brought in to personalize or humanize the practice of psychotherapy in the face of impersonal or de-personalizing techniques.[1]

The self as an object

The concern with the nature of the self, which we have identified as a salient feature of these essays, does have one important consequence about how the self is conceived. The self is thought of as constituting both the *target* of psychotherapeutic interest and intervention and, at the same time, as the primary if not the only *tool* of the therapist. This ambiguity is expressed in the phrase employed by the therapist previously quoted, one that occurs explicitly throughout these accounts – that of *working on oneself.* One works on oneself in order to make oneself more responsive and sensitive to the client or patient. The formulation is simple and, indeed, essential to any responsible practice as a therapist. Yet it involves a tacit splitting of the self into self-as-subject, that which works, and self-as-object, that which is worked upon. *The self has thus become objectified.* It has become an entity, something on which work can be done.

It seems that this objectification of the self is a necessary step in the way the therapist comes to think and feel about himself or herself. The ability to relate to oneself as object, as well as subject, is an important step in the development of self-reflection, and of understanding how we are treated and experienced by others. In the practice of therapy one needs to be able to think of oneself as an object-figure in the patient's world in order to understand the nature of the patient's relationship to oneself and its transferential aspects. In writing about themselves the therapists in this book have to handle both sides of this therapist–patient relationship, as they are compelled to treat themselves as a form of object-figure in their own world.

The self-as-object appears in various ways in the essays. Most commonly a process of self-observation and self-monitoring is described. For instance:

> by observing and monitoring my own internal processes, I enhanced my understanding of human psychological domains. In addition I learned a great deal about the therapeutic process by being a client or participant in various self-help groups ... again closely examining my reactions and processes.
>
> (Heppner p.75)

This therapist makes clear that the process of self-observation becomes a crucial way into understanding other people, that the selves of other people can be grasped by analogy with one's own:

> My mother died from breast cancer during my fourth year in graduate school which introduced me to new life experiences, such as the grieving process and changing family dynamics when one parent dies. Only later did I realise that this first hand knowledge would be very useful to me as a therapist understanding clients with aborted grief reactions.
>
> (Heppner p.76)

The self-as-object is also described in quite different terms; for example, as the elusive goal of our striving, as in the metaphor of the self as Holy Grail:

Being with a family in struggle allowed me to care for and to help, but most importantly it allowed me to cease to be a 'white knight' – but only if I chose. I had indeed discovered the 'Holy Grail' – it was myself.

(Street p.141)

The ambiguities of self as subject and as object come to the fore in this passage, which gives the self responsibility for its own creation:

Personal construct theory asked me to look upon life and upon myself 'as if' I had created the person I now am and, when I find aspects of myself I do not like, to take responsibility for that and attempt to re-create myself.

(Fransella p.124)

These examples show, we think, that in fact the very notion of self-objectification, and the simple division of self into *either* subject *or* object, fail to do justice to the quite different versions of the self which are manifested here. Descriptions of the self as a kind of limitless, mysterious or self-replicating power, and yet as something that can be scrutinized, investigated, and for which one must take responsibility – such conceptions of the self resist easy categorization into subject and object. Here we come up against the presuppositions of our way of thinking about ourselves, and, indeed, of our very language, whose grammar turns on this simplistic distinction between subject and object; whereas the metaphors, ideas, and language of the essays in this book point to a way of understanding the self that goes beyond such distinctions.[2]

We have once again reached a point in our argument which is familiar, and which, we suspect, is a primary feature in thinking about psychotherapy, namely that it involves a balancing of opposites and contradictions. In a similar way as we have argued that the therapist can be seen as both wounded and as healed, and as involved while remaining detached, we now find ourselves contending that the way the contributors have written about and delineated the self, as that which above all constitutes the therapeutic domain, both serves to *split* the self into subject and object, while at the same time drawing attention to the fact that this very distinction is quite inadequate to do justice to what these essays seek to convey about the self.

Part Three: The self and the nature of therapeutic knowledge

The place of theory in psychotherapy

We have suggested that one feature in the process of becoming a therapist is the focusing of attention on to a particular domain, that of the inner world and the self, both in oneself and in one's patients. Psychotherapy would then be seen as a form of self-knowledge, or knowledge of the self (recognizing the ambiguity of the self as both subject and object). The most important kind of knowledge, it would follow, would be personal and interpersonal knowledge, knowledge about one's self and the selves of others.

However, psychotherapy is more usually conceived as a branch of *psychological* knowledge, and, as such, a form of *theoretical* knowledge. Several contributors in fact address the question of how useful psychological-theoretical knowledge can be in psychotherapy. Michael Mahoney, for instance, puts it like this:

> An adequate theoretical psychology will have to address the gap we have created between our heads and our hearts – between our formal mental maps and the complex, dynamic terrain of everyday experience.
>
> (p.32)

This need to find a way of describing the practice of therapy as bringing together both feeling and thought, both knowledge and experience, is echoed in the formulations of other therapists – that we need to perceive 'with both intuition and reason' (Chaplin p.178), or that psychotherapy is 'love with understanding' (Thorne p.64). There seems to be no one word which can adequately convey this quality of thinking with feeling or feeling with thought. The authors have recourse to descriptions of psychotherapy as an 'art form' (Mahoney p.28), as 'rhythm' (Chaplin), or as 'process' or 'dance' in which 'relationship' or 'experience' is seen to figure as central.

However, it is also recognized that in order for the therapist to think about his or her practice and development as a therapist a theoretical perspective is needed. Yet one can detect an uneasiness about theory, that it may render one's practice dogmatic and inflexible and stifle one's creativity. For instance:

> it is vital to find your own individual way of working, using your own intuition. Adhering strictly to the rules of one particular 'school' may interfere with a therapist's own judgements and energies.
>
> (Chaplin p.187)

As an insurance against theoretical thinking becoming dogmatic or too rigid, appeals are made for the 'flexibility' or 'openness' of the therapist. The strongest advocate of the need for theory, Fay Fransella, argues her case with this need for permeability in mind:

What I do think important is that psychotherapists have a theory to which they can turn 'in times of need'. This theory should live for them and should be something they feel they can both develop within and which they can develop.

(p.132)

This passage raises some interesting questions. If it is to theory that one should turn if things do not run smoothly, to where does one turn if things *do* run smoothly? Indeed, to where does one turn in order to know the difference between smooth and rough going, to know when it is time to look to theory? The answer seems to be that one looks to oneself. Thus the domain of the self can be seen as an alternative to theory and theoretical knowledge. It is constituted as a *locus* of creativity and spontaneity, and as a source of that personal knowledge which is counterpointed to theoretical knowledge.

The self stands for the impurity of theory

The idea of the self thus emerges as an antidote to theory, as a domain resistant to the imperialistic drive of theory. The language of the self is an expression of the need for theory in psychotherapy to be *impure*, in an analogous way to Primo Levi's celebration of the value of impurities in chemical analysis:

The course notes contained a detail which at first reading had escaped me, namely, that the so tender and delicate zinc, so yielding to acid which gulps it down in a single mouthful, behaves, however, in a very different fashion when it is very pure: then it obstinately resists the attack. One could draw from this two conflicting philosophical conclusions: the praise of purity, which protects from evil like a coat of mail; the praise of impurity, which gives rise to changes, in other words, to life .... In order for the wheel to turn, for life to be lived, impurities are needed, and the impurities of impurities in the soil too, as is known, if it is to be fertile.

(Levi 1986: 33–4)

Scientific theories aim to be pure, to be free from traces of 'subjectivity', 'personal bias' and the like, and resistant to change, so that they are valid for all people and on all occasions. But this purity of theory within psychotherapy is problematic because theory, which has to be cast in a language which is universalizable and transmissable, has to address the *particularity* of therapist and client and the therapeutic relationship and the *untransmissability* of what happens in psychotherapy as it is prior to or beyond language (and hence is best conveyed through metaphors such as 'process', 'rhythm' or 'dance'). Even where theory is conceived in more conceptual terms, paradox is not evaded as one has to use a universal theoretical language to do justice to the unique way of speaking and thinking of the client. Writing about psychoanalysis

François Roustang refers to the 'idiolect' of the client which the therapist is called upon to understand:

> If the analyst slowly begins to understand something, it is not so much because of his knowledge, which belongs to another dialect or consists of formulations that are too general to account for this particular language, but because by listening, he himself learns the dialect invented by the analysand's unconscious .... The language spoken by the analysand consists to a certain extent of an 'idiolect', a secret language invented for a single person by a single person. Little by little the idiolect comes to be heard, and this isolated peculiarity that needs to be given resonance enables the analysand to wake up.
>
> (Roustang 1982:69–70)

The therapist is thus involved in a bind. In order to listen to the client without prejudice and without imposing his own assumptions and values, and to hear the particular resonances and structure of the client's speech, the therapist has to forgo his theoretical knowledge so that he cannot know in advance the meaning of the patient's utterances. Yet the therapist must also bring his theoretical knowledge to bear in order to make sense of the patient's utterances and in order to communicate such understanding to other therapists.

> Analytic theory is thus confronted by an impossibly divided task: to bring out what is universal from a nonsensical peculiarity and to present what is transmissable on the basis of incommunicability (which is not the ineffability, but the unintelligibility of discourse itself) ....
>
> Prior theory, the certainty that one knows, forms a protective armour around the analyst which preserves his supremacy in the analytic relationship. Psychoanalysis is possible when the psychoanalyst has forgotten the theory, when the theory has been put aside, repressed, and when it can return from time to time during a session. For what distinguishes the analyst from the analysand is that the analyst, caught in the transference relationship, must nonetheless be able to theorize.
>
> (Roustang 1982:70)

Theory and theoretical knowledge thus need to be mixed up with what remains idiosyncratic and personal to the therapist – theory needs to be impure. Knowledge in psychotherapy thus has to have an inescapably personal dimension. The language of the self can then be taken as a reminder of the *limits* of theoretical knowledge, which attempts to render the personal and particular into what is impersonal and general (as one therapist remarks, 'there was very little in the [psychology] degree course which had much to do with people' [Bloomfield p.36]).

Knowledge in psychotherapy – what you know or whom you know?

In the thesis that psychotherapeutic knowledge has a fundamental personal dimension, by personal we mean knowledge which stands in contrast not to interpersonal knowledge, but to technical or theoretical knowledge. Indeed, the notion of personal knowledge in these accounts is very much linked to the knowledge of other people. This is exemplified by what we think is a striking feature of these essays, which is the giving of names of teachers, colleagues, friends, etc. This naming of names sometimes reads like a roll-call of those by whom the therapist was supported or inspired. This can be accounted for as a recognition of the importance of personal contact and colleagueship in the world of psychotherapy, and, perhaps, by a wish to acknowledge those to whose inspirational qualities one feels indebted. But this naming of names may also allude to the conviction that psychotherapy is not fundamentally something that can be formally taught, or that can be learnt from books. It is rather about a peculiarly personal knowledge, in which knowledge of the self is taken as the key to understanding the other, and yet only occurs in the intimacy and interchange of genuine relationships with others. So that one's practice of psychotherapy would, in the last analysis. turn on the quality of one's relationship to other people.

Part Four: The language of psychotherapy and the religious, political and narrative traditions

We have argued that the language of the self is one kind of language used by the authors to address that elusive, if not mysterious process of becoming a psychotherapist, as well as to address the nature of psychotherapy itself. The language of the self delineates the therapeutic domain, constitutes the self as subject and object of inquiry, and, furthermore, alludes to what in a way is the tool of the trade, in that the self is something to be worked on in order to render oneself more self-aware. Such formulations, which speak of the 'self' as an entity and a domain, are inescapably ambiguous, as the self, in a simple grammatical sense, is who we are. But the vagaries of such a language may serve to remind us of *how little we actually know about psychotherapy, and how and why it works.* We are in agreement with these comments by Leon Chertok, in his article '200 years of psychotherapy: the common curative elements in suggestion and affect':

> We may say that the patient–physician relationship is a common thread running through the history of psychotherapy. This relationship has taken many different forms and been called various things down through the ages: Mesmeric fluid, suggestion, transference, empathy, symbiosis, and so on. But the fact is inescapable that, in spite of its long history, we still know very little about it.

This state of affairs may be accounted for, [first] by the very nature of this relationship, which exists on a primary, psychological affective level, prior to language. Its study entails a degree of personal involvement which most investigators have shunned. The succession of theories put forward to explain it represents so many attempts to objectivize it.

(Chertok 1984:188)

Bearing this failure of theoretical or objective knowledge in mind, we have argued that the delineation of the domain of the self represents *one* way in which, in the communal text which makes up the essays in the book, an area of inquiry has been constituted. We wish, finally, to draw attention to *another* way, as revealed by the language in which these essays are written, in which psychotherapeutic practice and relationship, as well as the process of becoming a therapist, are addressed. Psychotherapeutic language borrows and transposes ideas, ways of thinking and metaphors from other traditions of thought – in particular from religion, from politics, and from the narrative tradition.

Psychotherapy and the religious tradition

Several authors in this book made clear and explicit reference to the centrality of religious and spiritual ideas in their work. For example:

myths of initiation, rebirth, including some forms of symbolic death are important for me. The therapy room can be seen as a sacred place outside the everyday world, where people can go to visit their underworlds and be guided through big and little 'deaths' ...

(Chaplin pp.175–6)

My brief counselling encounters, lasting perhaps two or three months, do much to remind me of the remarkable capacity of many human beings to discover their own resources and strengths once they have been offered a modicum of acceptance and understanding .... With those whose journey is more arduous and complex it is not always so easy to hang on to my faith in the process and it is in these cases that my religious faith becomes of such cardinal importance.

(Thorne p.65)

The description of the therapy room as a 'sacred' place is a resonant image, and the notion of faith is of central importance in understanding how drive, commitment, and tenacity in a therapist are possible. A term such as 'faith' transcends the usual distinction between personal and professional, which is a consequence of the enormous personal investment required by the therapist in order to believe in and sustain his or her work. This is alluded to in this quotation:

In those few hours I felt my life as a psychotherapist was deeply rooted in me as a person. There was a fusion between my ability to cope with grief professionally and the ability to meet a personal crisis. The work was transferable.

(Karp p.96)

Other concepts which are derived from or associated with religion are 'mystery' and 'awe' – these terms are used to designate the nature of the therapist's power or skill. Although this power or skill is recognized as emanating from the self, it is also sometimes described as coming from somewhere beyond the self, as representing, for example, a 'power greater than my own' (Thorne p.65). Such a recognition can make for an attitude of humility in the face of some process of which oneself is only a part:

It was not until I actually began to practise that I came to realize that clients and my sessions with them have their own process. I can only trust that process. I am not totally *in charge*. In fact my original images of being a psychotherapist were horribly arrogant. Gradually I learnt to be more humble.

(Chaplin p.177)

Perhaps the most frequently used image for psychotherapy in these essays is that of a 'journey' which the client undertakes with the therapist as guide or companion. By 'journey' is meant a kind of Pilgrim's Progress or spiritual search. Change and transformation in psychotherapy are thus understood by analogy with religious conversion or initiation.

Psychotherapy and the political tradition

In the same way as with religion, some authors draw explicit analogies between psychotherapy and politics. The world of politics figures in the foreground of several accounts. Some therapists trace their desire to become a psychotherapist from political awareness.

My years of part-time menial labour had also exposed me to frequent injustices against the poor and minorities, and my aspirations to help seemed to draw from those sources as well.

(Mahoney p.20)

Those who specifically refer to the political realm sometimes refer to an attitude of unease or distrust with the world of politics and of people in large numbers:

I entered college in 1969 ... and soon became a participant in the ferment and rebellion on many college campuses associated with the Vietnam War and the Hippie generation. These experiences taught me to believe in the possibilities of change, and affirmed my liberal and humanitarian values as well as my general distrust of politicians and administrators.

(Heppner pp.71–2)

Personal construct theory helps one understand individual persons rather than people. I have always found people, in large lumps, rather frightening and only feel really happy with individuals.

(Fransella p.122)

The link between politics and psychotherapy can be seen as a way of marrying up the therapist's concern for the inner world with the world outside.

The strong feeling of the real self which I had had in groups connected up with the philosophical idea of authenticity, and I felt a real connection there – that authenticity was one place where the personal and the political came together. One could not be authentic and experience alienation or anomie at the same time.

(Rowan p.156)

An alternative view expressed is that this link between inner and outer may be more in the way of a split which cannot easily be bridged:

Most of my doubts about becoming a psychotherapist were centred on the fear that in doing so, I was avoiding the more pressing external issues of poverty and injustice ...

(Chaplin p.178)

Where politics is directly referred to, the emphasis tends to be on what psychotherapy can contribute to politics and political activity.

I understood a new notion of politics, that it didn't have to be just about having the ideal political case, or just about getting out and acting militantly: it could be about feelings and relationships and the way you lived.

(Rowan p.151)

I also think that psychotherapy has a role to play in the transformation of society. Perhaps radical psychotherapists at least could be seen as revolutionaries, quietly undermining the main assumptions and structures of our deeply hierarchical society.

(Chaplin p.177)

But if one looks at the language of psychotherapy, what strikes one is how much politics has contributed to psychotherapy, how much the therapeutic discourse has borrowed from the language of politics. The passage quoted above, in which Paul Heppner acknowledges that his experience of politics at college 'taught me to believe in the possibilities of change', shows how psychotherapeutic change is modelled on political change. Terms basic to psychotherapy such as 'power' and 'freedom' are also political metaphors. Unhappiness in childhood is understood in terms of another political metaphor, that of repression. 'Both parents had been brought up ... with a great deal of both emotional and sexual repression' (Chaplin p.170). Hence the liberation or transformation of the self, and the integration of warring sides of the personality, which are taken as the aims of therapy, can all be seen as transpositions of a political discourse on to the psychotherapeutic plane. Extending this analogy, the self, as it comes to be described in these essays, can be compared to the state or society in political discourse, the political economy of which is the object of inquiry.

By way of afterthought on the relation between psychotherapy and politics, the following quotation by the anthropologist Victor Turner, concerning a shaman in a traditional society, may also apply to the contemporary therapist (especially those who, like the authors in this book, have achieved pre-eminence):

> In many ways, he was typical of Ndembu doctors: capable, charismatic, authoritative, but excluded from secular office for a variety of reasons, some structural, some personal. He was the typical 'outsider', who achieves status in the ritual realm in compensation for his exclusion from authority in the political realm.
>
> (Turner 1967:371)

Psychotherapy and the narrative tradition

What, following Donald Spence (1982), we call the narrative tradition, constitutes another fund of ideas and metaphors which go to make up psychotherapeutic language. This tradition is explicitly addressed by Marcia Karp, who links therapy with dramatic theatre, and by Michael Mahoney, where his practice of psychotherapy and his love of writing are seen to inform each other mutually. Other therapists refer to the importance of the world of theatre and of books.

But the narrative or story-telling tradition is crucial in a less obvious way. There is a dramatic and literary style to these essays, for example, in the use of stories or vignettes to illustrate or explain, which seems both to demonstrate and exemplify what psychotherapy is about. In weaving together the different strands of their life into a coherent and compelling story, the therapists in this book can be seen to show what it is that occurs in, and what in some fundamental way constitutes, the process of psychotherapy, as that setting in which the patient's own story comes to be told.

Notes

1 This opposition between the language of the self and the language of technique is over-simple, because it leaves out of account psychoanalytic language, with its concepts of the unconscious, the ego, narcissism, etc. Curiously, psychoanalytic language plays little part in these essays, even by those who identify themselves primarily as in the psychoanalytic tradition. Although we think that the language of psychoanalysis is analogous to that of the self in that it also constitutes and comprises an inner domain, the demonstration of this argument is not relevant to our present considerations.

2 It takes us beyond the scope of this chapter to consider whether more adequate forms of expression can be found, but see Michael Balint's imaginative discussion of the notion of substance, such as liquids or air, which resist categorization into subject or object, outside or inside (Balint 1959: ch.7).

References

Balint, M. (1959) *Thrills and Regressions*, London: Maresfield Library.

Chertok, L. (1984) '200 years of psychotherapy: the common curative elements in suggestion and affect', *Psychoanalytic Psychology* 1(3): 173–91.

Greenson, R. (1966) 'That impossible profession', *Journal of the American Psychoanalytic Association* 14: 9–27.

Groesbeck, C. (1975) 'The archetypal image of the wounded healer', *Journal of Analytic Psychology* 20: 122–45.

Levi, P. (1986) *The Periodic Table*, London: Abacus.

Marmor, J. (1953) 'The feeling of superiority: an occupational hazard in the practice of psychotherapy', *American Journal of Psychiatry* 110: 370–6.

Roustang, F. (1982) *Dire Mastery: Discipleship from Freud to Lacan*, Baltimore: Johns Hopkins University Press.

Spence, D. (1982) *Narrative Truth and Historical Truth: Meaning and Interpretation in Psychoanalysis*, New York: W. W. Norton & Co.

Turner, V. (1967) *The Forest of Symbols: Aspects of Ndembu Ritual*, Ithaca: Cornell University Press.

Winnicott, D. W. (1971) *Therapeutic Consultations in Child Psychiatry*, London: The Hogarth Press and the Institute of Psycho-analysis.

Chapter thirteen

Ten therapists: the process of becoming and being
John C. Norcross and James D. Guy

Multiple and converging sources of evidence indicate that the *person* of the psychotherapist is inextricably intertwined with the outcome of psychotherapy. There is a dawning recognition, really a re-awakening, that the therapist him or herself is the focal process of change. Second only to the severity of the client's symptomatology, the psychotherapist – not theory, not technique – is the most powerful determinant of clinical improvement. 'The inescapable fact of the matter is that the therapist is a person, however much he may strive to make himself an instrument of his patient's treatment' (Orlinsky and Howard 1977: 567).

This book, among others (e.g., Goldberg 1986; Guy 1987; Kottler 1986), stands firmly against the encroaching tide of the tyranny of technique and the myth of disembodied treatment. What an invigorating opportunity, then, it is for us to partake of the personal and professional journeys of these ten prominent psychotherapists. It is a rare privilege indeed to share in the process of becoming and being a psychotherapist. These rich case histories address fundamental questions of the therapist's identity. Why did I become a psychotherapist? How did this occur? When was this accomplished? What sustains me? What might be the implications for others in the ministering professions?

We would like to preface our comments by congratulating the contributors on their insightful, and occasionally moving, accounts. Readers are likely to be touched by the pain of early traumas, parents' deaths, World War Two childhoods, bewildering adolescences, annual relocations, deteriorating marriages – to name but a few contained herein. We admire them for the courage – and model – of self-disclosure in a profession that demands it from clients but discourages it in practitioners. In an age of escalating openness and electronic feedback, no other profession practises so clandestinely as we do (Burton 1972).

At the same time, we take to heart Hans Strupp's (chapter 7) doubt that 'anyone in a chapter of this kind can ever be "perfectly honest"'. Appropriate discretion should be exercised in matters of this nature. Risks of exposure, undesirable admissions, unconscious distortions, retrospective methodology, and constraints of present-day exigencies all detract from the possibility of uncompromisingly honest presentations.

This is how it inevitably must be, of course. As with most phenomenological works, these chapters are – as Paul Heppner (chapter 5) notes – working hypotheses, best estimates to connect the past with the present and to project into the future. The errors of omission, which can at best be intuited, are probably more revealing than the distortions of commission. We wondered, for example, how the book would have changed had spouses or significant others been asked to contribute one-third of the chapters. Better yet, perhaps the 'external validity' would have been enhanced had ex-spouses, former therapists, dissatisfied patients, and disowned friends independently contributed to the undertaking.

But, as more than one contributor reminds us, external perceptions of one's self do not necessarily correspond with his or her experience of that self. Mahoney (chapter 2) writes that 'there is often a gap between my identity as I experience it and the identities frequently projected on to me by my readers.' Strupp expresses similar concerns that the mental image of a writer constructed by the reader usually has little resemblance to what the writer is really like. In the words of Goethe, the world had not really known him.

As privileged as we are to be admitted into the inner sanctums, we find it necessary to move beyond voyeuristic pleasures and individual details (as well as the unavoidable comparisons to our own pilgrimages). It is not rabid confessions alone that advance our understanding of the therapist's contribution to the clinical enterprise. Rather, as is true of psychotherapy itself, it is judicious self-disclosure in the interest of the client that facilitates awareness and movement.

In what follows we attempt to delineate recurring themes and implications for the person of the psychotherapist. The objective of our chapter is to extract and amplify salient patterns in these disparate tales, all aimed towards an examination of becoming and being a psychotherapist. We draw, in this admittedly incomplete review, on the ten chapters themselves, the extant research literature, and the results of a survey of the ten contributors conducted in the autumn of 1987.

It is obviously not possible, in a chapter of limited length and a book of such wide scope, to address all the themes raised. We have selected six topics based, primarily, on their impact on the practice of psychotherapy. Secondarily – and unapologetically – we have chosen these themes for their personal interest to us. So be it. After a brief review of our questionnaire survey, we consider each of these six topics in turn: background information, family origins, career determinants, training influences, stresses and satisfactions, and personal therapy.

The questionnaire

In August and September 1987 we distributed an eight page questionnaire to the ten contributors. The covering letter read, in part, as follows:

We have been asked to contribute a closing chapter which summarizes your experiences as a group and compares them to thousands of psychotherapists we and others have surveyed in recent years. In addition to reviewing your chapters, we are conducting a survey of all the authors. This will enable us to further understand your life experiences and make comparisons to relevant 'normative' groups. In order to allow direct comparisons we must employ the identical questionnaire items, even though several of them may be overly simplistic or antiquated.

All ten therapists responded promptly. However, several understandably took us to task for trying to fit complex human experiences into discrete numerical pigeonholes. As Marcia Karp wrote,

There were a multitude of answers that could be given in different moments for different measures. I certainly can see that it can be helpful to tease out certain facts or opinions. I don't like giving mine out in this way. Sorry – but that's a reality for me.

Still other contributors occasionally omitted items, writing that 'it doesn't make sense' or was 'too personal'.

We aggregated the results of these questionnaires and used them as one basis for the following sections. The comparison samples are based largely on surveys of American, doctoral-level clinical psychologists practising psychotherapy. Since only three of the ten respondents are American and only seven are psychologists, these comparisons are obviously tentative and approximate.

Background information

In reading the chapters we were struck by the authors' willingness at times to make themselves emotionally transparent, but frequently at the expense of mundane socio-demographic information. With a few exceptions, such as the late developer's (Rowan's) statement that he is 62, we do not get a concrete sense of basic facts: chronological age, racial background, religious affiliation, political orientation, and the like. This lacuna is probably related, in no small way, to the aforementioned difficulty in fashioning realistic mental images of the respective authors. Freud (1905/1963: 32), the intrapsychic master, admonished us 'to pay as much attention in our case histories to the purely human and social circumstances as to the somatic and symptomatic data'.

Here we consider our questionnaire results on these ten therapists.

- 7 from Great Britain, 3 from the United States
- 4 women, 6 men
- 10 Caucasians
- 4 married, 2 remarried, 3 divorced, 1 never married

- age range from 36 (Heppner) and 38 (Street) to 66 (Strupp) and 68 (Bloomfield); average age = 50.8 years
- 8 self-described political liberals (4 strongly liberal and 4 moderately liberal), 1 'radical', 1 moderately conservative
- 3 agnostics, 1 Jew, 1 Protestant, 1 Anglican, 4 'other' (1 Buddhist, 1 God-in-oneself, 1 Goddess spirituality, and 1 humanist).

The latter findings on political and religious affiliation deserve further exploration and comparison. Earlier studies on the political orientations of mental health professionals indicated that they tend to be liberal as a group (e.g. Holt and Luborsky 1958). In Henry et al.'s (1971) chapter, 'Political biographies: genesis of liberalism', they report that psychotherapists characterized their politics as 38 per cent strongly liberal, 50 per cent moderately liberal, and 12 per cent moderately or strongly conservative. Their analysis, consistent with that of our ten therapists, also indicated that the liberal composition of the mental health professions reflected conversion rather than lifelong adherence. We thus asked our sample, 'As a result of becoming a psychotherapist how has your political orientation changed?' True to form, 50 per cent responded 'became more liberal' and 50 per cent 'stayed the same'. Among the many factors contributing to political liberalism, Henry et al. (1971) identified three of particular importance: process of professional socialization, process of selective recruitment, and upbringing in fairly liberal families.

Survey research has demonstrated that the religious are under-represented among (American) psychologists in comparison with the general population (Ragan et al. 1980). However, psychotherapists did not begin that way in youth; the personal pilgrimage often begets a 'genesis of apostasy' (Henry et al. 1971). A religious apostate comes from a religious background but currently identifies his or her own position as agnosticism, atheism, or none.

The transition from orthodox religious membership to individual spiritual identification accurately characterizes our sample as well. The religious identifications of their family of origin were 4 Protestant, 2 Jewish, 2 Catholic, 1 Anglican, 1 atheist, and 0 agnostic. But the authors' own religious orientations at this time are: 1 Protestant, 1 Jewish, 0 Catholic, 1 Anglican, 0 atheist, 3 agnostic, and 4 other. Hence, personal conversion and religious apostasy are far more prevalent than parentally transmitted non-belief among this sample.

The discerning reader may, from the chapter contents, have been able to glean the professional characteristics and activities of these ten therapists. Nonetheless, we restate this information and fill a few gaps below, all adopted from the responses to our questionnaire.

- 7 psychologists, 3 'other' (psychotherapist, trainer)
- 5 Ph.D., 2 masters, 3 baccalaureates in terms of highest academic degree

- 6 contributors viewing their primary professional roles as clinical practitioners, 3 academicians (Mahoney, Strupp, and Heppner), 1 researcher (Fransella)
- 4 primarily employed in university settings, 2 in private practice, 1 in an outpatient clinic, 1 in a training centre, 1 in own business, 1 in a child and family centre
- all 8 of those not in full-time independent practice engage in some part-time private work
- 10 regularly conduct psychotherapy, ranging from 10 per cent to 60 per cent of their total professional time (average = 42 per cent)
- 8 of the eight responding to the item were teaching and supervising on a routine basis
- 9 of the ten conduct some individual therapy (Eddy Street being the sole exception – 20 per cent marital and 80 per cent family – and Marcia Karp being a near exception – 5 per cent individual and 95 per cent group)
- 3 of the ten engage in some marital or family therapy
- all ten have published articles, ranging between 7 and 250+ (average = 67), and 6 report one or more scholarly books.

The primary theoretical orientations of these psychotherapists are presented in Table 1. Two of the authors selected the cognitive orientation as most like their current practice, two endorsed humanistic (including gestalt), and two Rogerian. Compared to a 1987 contingent of doctoral-level clinical psychologists, the present sample is conspicuously lacking in behaviourists and eclectics but over-represented by the 'third force' in psychology (40 per cent versus 7 per cent for humanistic/Rogerian).

Several contributors, notably Fransella and Strupp, evidenced a tendency to structure their autobiographical narratives in accord with the prescriptions of their theoretical orientations. In their descriptions of becoming and being a psychotherapist it was difficult for us, as readers, to separate them from their therapeutic traditions. The form, depth, and content of these 'self-disclosures' seemed to parallel closely the classical dictates of their therapy systems. Despite the editors' injunction against treatment or theoretical chapters, the pervasive influence of treasured theories was clearly visible (Norcross 1985; Norcross and Prochaska 1983). As a result, the theory overshadowed the therapist on occasion.

Theoretical allegiance, like personal identity, is defined not only by the 'me' but also by the 'not me'. Theoretical orientations *least* like the therapist's own approach are also presented in Table 1, along with comparison figures. The top three on the 'unlike me' list coincide with the traditional three schools of psychology – psychoanalysis, behaviourism, and humanism – for the present as well as the comparison sample. Our ten therapists did, however, evidence more negative reactions towards behaviourism and more positive sentiments

John C. Norcross and James D. Guy

Table 1 Theoretical orientations

| | Most Like Self | | Least Like Self | |
Orientation	Present Sample	Comparison Sample*	Present Sample	Comparison Sample*
Behavioural	0%	8%	40%	16%
Cognitive	20%	8%	0%	5%
Eclectic	0%	34%	0%	1%
Humanistic	20%	5%	10%	29%
Psychoanalytic	10%	11%	40%	29%
Psychodynamic	10%	18%	0%	3%
Rogerian	20%	2%	0%	4%
Systems	10%	7%	0%	6%
Other	10%	7%	10%	7%

* Adapted from Norcross et al. (1989).

towards humanism than the latter. Eclecticism elicited no nominations as the orientation most like or least like one's own in the present sample.

A crucial question in attempting to extract salient implications from these ten therapists' journeys is that of representativeness. Is the present sample, in some sense, representative of the experiences of psychotherapists now practising in developed English-speaking countries? Our answer is yes and no.

Yes, reasonably representative in the sense of gender distribution, marital history, age range, religious affiliation, political orientation, employment settings, and professional activities. If one were to consider the entire population of humans designating themselves 'psychotherapists' then the distribution of highest academic degree (5 Ph.D., 3 masters, 2 baccalaureates) is probably close. However, if one were to restrict consideration to the four core mental health professions in the United States – clinical psychology, psychiatry, clinical social work, psychiatric nursing – then the present sample is overweighted towards the lower end of formal education. Fortunately, as discussed in the next section, formal education exerts significantly less influence on career development than informal training and personal experience.

No, these ten therapists are not particularly representative of psycho-therapists in English-speaking, industrialized nations insofar as they are entirely Caucasian and less disposed towards behaviourism and eclecticism. The contributors are, in addition, established and prominent psychotherapists. They have all published professional articles, to the tune of an astonishing average of sixty-seven articles apiece, and were all sufficiently respected to be invited to contribute to this volume.

These are not your ordinary, run-of-the-mill psychotherapists. (Nor, parenthetically, would it be desirable for them to be so in an undertaking of this nature.) What seems to distinguish them from their colleagues, more fundamentally, is a passionate commitment to the art and science of psychotherapy. In their own words, these ten are 'stubborn', 'achieving', 'industrious', and 'adventuresome' people who could 'never resist challenges'. This, it seems to us, is how they are basically unrepresentative, distinctive, and how they are willing to confront the challenges posed by an autobiographical task.

Autobiographical studies can open doors just as they can close them. The concrete case study can serve as a portal to sensitivity and depth, or can confine us to meaningless particulars (Sacks 1985). We will try hereafter to synthesize the idiographic and the nomothetic, the particular and the general, the romantic and the scientific. A wedding to their mutual enrichment, we hope.

Family origins

When considering the family of origin of our master psychotherapists, one is struck by the diversity of people and early life experiences encountered by each. The formative years were typically threaded with a wide array of events and relationships which seem to defy categorization. However, when considered as a whole, several patterns begin to emerge.

The primary adult dyad of early family life is that between the parents. Our psychotherapists described the marital relationship in their family of origin in rather positive terms, with only one indicating that the marriage was a 'poor' one. This is in contrast to earlier surveys which found that, although divorce was rare, parents were often reported to experience pronounced marital discord (Henry et al. 1973). It would appear, from both the survey results and the individual autobiographies, that the marital relationships of the historical parents in our sample were at least minimally functional, if not entirely successful.

Fathers apparently held a prominent position of importance in our clinicians' lives. With few exceptions, they loom as rather impressive, dominant individuals with considerable influence on our therapists during their formative years. Psychotherapists' fathers have frequently been devalued as passive, non-interacting men who contribute little emotional strength to the family (Ford 1963). By contrast, the majority of our clinicians describe fathers who were more invested, empathic, and active. While certainly not described in idealized terms, the autobiographical narratives suggest that these individuals had considerable impact on our therapists during their formative years. Fully eight of the ten described their relationships with their father as a 'positive' one during childhood. As presented in Table 2, even during the stormy adolescent years, fathers were viewed in a mixed, if not positive, manner. Nearly all were involved in non-professional careers, few obtained advanced education or training, and half were employed as labourers. As shown in Table 3, most of these fathers were relatively uninterested in the humanities or social sciences, even to a lesser extent than the fathers of 'average' therapists.

Table 2 Psychotherapists' relations with parents during adolescence

Perceived Quality of Relationship	With Mother		With Father	
	Present Sample	Comparison Sample*	Present Sample	Comparison Sample*
Positive	38%	50%	44%	46%
Neutral	12%	2%	12%	9%
Ambivalent	38%	14%	22%	9%
Negative	12%	34%	22%	36%

*Adapted from Henry *et al.* (1973).

In a similar fashion, mothers were also uninterested in the humanities and social sciences (Table 3). Only two worked outside the home. Curiously, by and large they were portrayed in a less positive fashion than the fathers. While it is unwise to minimize maternal impact on our therapists, it is interesting to note that they were inexplicably omitted or barely referenced in several of the narratives. When mentioned, few accounts contain the type of description commonly found in the literature, where psychotherapists' mothers are portrayed as intrusive, narcissistic, insecure, depressed, dominant, and sometimes competitive (Ford 1963; Henry *et al.* 1973; Miller 1981).

Furthermore, there does not seem to be the pattern of maternal enmeshment so often described by other clinicians (Sharaf 1960). Because of its omission in several of the narratives, one is left uncertain about its actual emotional impact on our clinicians. Yet, there are some clues. For example, on our survey, only four indicated that they had a 'positive' relationship with their mother during childhood. As can be seen in Table 2, fewer were also clearly positive in their feelings towards their mother during adolescence than was true of the comparison sample of therapists. While this may not suggest the level of conflict sometimes noted between future therapists and their mothers (Henry 1966), it does suggest a considerable amount of ambivalence.

Significantly, with the exception of Karp, siblings were rarely mentioned in the accounts of our clinicians. This neglect is probably attributable to the fact that seven of our ten prominent clinicians are first-borns, while one additional is an only child. A pattern of over-representation of first-borns among psychotherapists has been discerned previously (Bruce and Sims 1974; Henry *et al.* 1971), but not to so great an extent. For example, in one recent sample, 40 per cent of practising therapists were first-borns, while an additional 12 per cent were only children (Guy *et al.* 1988). Our sample of clinicians seems to give added support to the frequently replicated finding that first-borns are largely over-represented among highly successful executives, administrators, and professionals (Goldblank 1986). Perhaps traits often associated with first-borns, such as preoccupation with power and authority, high affiliation needs, nostalgia for the past, and pessimism regarding the future, provided the personal characteristics and incentives necessary for later

Table 3 Major childhood intellectual interests of psychotherapists and their parents

Interest	Psychotherapists as Youths		Mother		Father	
	Present Sample	Comparison Sample*	Present Sample	Comparison Sample*	Present Sample	Comparison Sample*
Humanities	10%	48%	0%	19%	20%	30%
Social Sciences	30%	15%	10%	25%	0%	11%
Other Specific Area	40%	25%	30%	26%	20%	9%
General	10%	12%	20%	18%	10%	17%
None	10%	0%	40%	12%	50%	28%

* Adapted from Henry *et al.* (1973).

professional success for the majority of our therapists (Schultz 1981).

Consistent with prototypical psychotherapists (Henry *et al.* 1971), our select sample evidenced upward mobility in income and education. Their parents pursued a wide variety of careers, such as farming, retail sales, education, military service, and 'blue-collar' factory work. Most of our psychotherapists have surpassed both immediate and extended family in regard to standard of living, diversity of cultural experiences, and career success.

Career determinants

What drives a person to concern himself with the dark side of the human psyche? What is it that compels certain people to elect to help the suffering, the dysfunctional, the outcasts? Assuredly they are a 'special sort' since the average individual prefers to ignore or deny the psychic sufferings of fellow humans.

The question of motivation is obviously not a simple or entirely conscious one. Motivations are likely to be partly or completely unconscious and subject to verbal distortion. Not infrequently, psychotherapists report that they come to realize some of the reasons they chose their discipline only in the course of intensive, insight-oriented treatment (Holt and Luborsky 1958). Below we review a variety of non-exhaustive motives, including deep internal ones intertwining with reality constraints, that lead to the final choice of psychotherapy as a career.

The road towards becoming a psychotherapist was a circuitous one for nearly all of our master clinicians. While the humanities and social sciences were primary interests for four individuals during their formative years (Table 3), the majority pursued unrelated activities such as sports, theatre, writing, and the hard sciences. Indeed, eight of the ten seriously considered other careers before entering the field. Even more striking, several pursued vocational alternatives such as marketing, farming, occupational therapy, and speech therapy before finally selecting a career in psychotherapy. In some cases, such as those of Bloomfield, Fransella, and Chaplin, the switch to a psychotherapy career occurred in mid-adult life or later.

What factors influenced the final selection of a career in psychotherapy? Perhaps it is better to ask 'who' rather than 'what'. In the preceding personal accounts, virtually all of our therapists were able to identify one or more individuals who had a profound impact on this decision. When asked on our survey which single person most influenced their interest in this vocation, nine of the ten indicated that it was a non-relative professional in the field. The single remaining therapist noted that it was a family member in the field. These responses are in marked contrast to mental health professionals surveyed by Henry *et al.* (1971), who found that over 60 per cent of psychologists were primarily influenced by teachers and others completely outside the field. This may reflect the pronounced emphasis that our sample placed on supervision and modelling over formal instruction, to be discussed in the next section. Perhaps our talented clinicians were more impressed by modelling and integrated 'ways of being' than by lecture material and scientific data.

Immediate family members had relatively little impact on the final decision made by our clinicians to enter the field. The extensive research of Henry *et al.* (1971, 1973) demonstrated that parents and relatives typically have a profound influence on the decision to enter the profession of psychotherapy. Over two-thirds of those surveyed by Henry *et al.* indicated that their initial interest in the field was due to the influence of family members who served as role-models, overtly encouraged this career choice, or enthusiastically supported the future therapist's personal choice. However, in our select sample, this influence was less pronounced. Their parents, as depicted in Table 3, were less likely to have interests in the humanities or social sciences than is true of average clinicians. Indeed, only one (Bloomfield) had a family member in the psychotherapeutic profession. Perhaps the career choice of psychotherapy was made in a manner which reflects the strongly independent natures of our exceptional therapists, at least with regard to their family of origin.

Perhaps a more central influence in choosing a career was the emotional climate of the family of origin during the formative years. The literature suggests that future psychotherapists often learned how to serve as an 'emotional buffer' between parents, as well as siblings, actively facilitating communication, compromise, and family harmony (Racusin *et al.* 1981). They served as caretakers, parentified children, who became adept at sensing and satisfying the emotional needs of both parents and siblings (Henry *et al.* 1973).

In our sample, while there are some similarities with the above description, several differences are apparent. For example, since parental marital relationships were viewed more positively, it seems unlikely that most felt that they served as 'marital counsellors' at home. There is also little mention of serving as a buffer or family arbitrator in the narratives, even though the majority were first-borns on whom this responsibility would likely have fallen. Contrary to the findings of Racusin *et al.* (1981), who reported that virtually all of their sample had at least one physically or emotionally disabled family member in their household of origin, only half of our group indicated the same. While Strupp and Street were saddled with 'caretaking' responsibilities for family members, the remainder apparently came from homes where they were permitted greater independence and self-expression. Although some, like Thorne, had a highly developed – perhaps burdensome – sense of empathy from an early age, many seemed less preoccupied with the emotional needs of family and friends, freeing them to interact with the environment in a more creative, explorative manner.

One way in which the family of origin most clearly influenced the career choice was in imparting a sense of specialness to our future psychotherapists. Nearly all of our contributors, particularly Mahoney and Karp, had a sense of destiny from an early age, often echoed by family members and friends who recognized and fostered their exceptional talents. One privilege of this volume is the ability to trace the impact of off-handed remarks and casual gestures on the eventual career outcomes of such individuals. Each of our clinicians was able to identify one or more individuals in their biological family or childhood community who had a major influence on their later work in ways that only a retrospective view of this nature can illuminate.

Having considered 'who' influenced this career choice, it is time to determine 'what' motivated our sample to enter the field. In response to our survey, five of the ten indicated that they were motivated by a desire to gain a sense of self-understanding and identity, while one each attributed their choice to a wish to emulate an idealized sibling, answer a sense of destiny, and meet practical obligations. Our sample was less motivated by a desire to achieve self-understanding, social status, and financial security than those previously surveyed (Henry *et al.* 1971, 1973). The motivations seem more altruistic than the norm. While the lack of anonymity may have shaped their survey responses, the narratives indicate that our psychotherapists were quite socially concerned and politically active, in tune with the needs of both individuals and the larger society prior to entering this career. This, no doubt, provided added incentive to pursue a career which brings psychic relief and emotional wholeness to others.

Chance encounters

Traditional psychology has neglected the prominent role that chance plays in shaping the course of human lives. Some fortuitous encounters touch us only lightly, others leave more lasting effects, and still others branch people into new trajections of life (Bandura 1982). Apparent continuity of life paths often mislead us to focus entirely on early and deliberate forces in career development. However, we would be remiss in this section were we to address solely familial and conscious determinants (as we have to this point) without reflecting on the impact of, in the words of Sir Walter Scott, 'the happy combination of fortuitous circumstances'.

Chance, perhaps capricious, encounters of import run throughout these chapters. Mahoney writes tellingly of his 'randomly selected', one session therapeutic encounter with Milton Erickson. Strupp tells of his unintended meeting with Frieda Fromm-Reichman at a summer resort, which heightened his interest in psychoanalysis and led to his own analysis. Heppner attributes substantial credit for his aspirations to his therapy with Joseph Jesseph, who happened to be a therapist at the university counselling centre at the right time. Karp emphasizes the 'pure chance or divine ordinance' of her studying at the student library with the books of Jacob Moreno inexplicably perched in front of her.

But these psychotherapists were also predisposed towards, if not psychologically prepared for, encounters to propel them in this direction. They were obviously not influenced equally by all unintended meetings: surely Strupp met more than one stranger while on holiday that year and certainly Karp saw more than a few unknown titles in the library. Situational imperatives *and* personal proclivities converge as interdependent shapers of life paths.

Wounded healers

In a number of societies healers have been associated with a weakness to which valuable properties are assigned. The mythological image of the 'wounded healer' is widespread: not only does the patient have a therapist within him or herself but there also lies a patient within the therapist. Primitive shamans, for instance, had a mixture of priestly and healing powers, but a requirement for the role was that they posses some defect, which, in Western society, would be recognized as an illness or disability (Bennet 1979; Rippere and Williams 1985). Guggenbuhl-Craig (1971) cites many other examples of wounded healers: Chiron, Aesculapius' instructor in the healing arts, himself suffered from incurable wounds; the Babylonian dog-goddess who was both death (Gula) and healing (Labartu); the Indian goddess Kali was simultaneously the pox and its curer; and, in the highest sense, Jesus Christ. He, as a psychological symbol, bore all the sins and was destined to die while, at the same time, healed the world and offered eternal redemption. Chaplin (chapter 11) also evokes the image of the wise old woman, Hecate, who governs the crossroad – both dark and light, destruction and construction.

Many psychotherapists, we believe, choose the profession partly due to their affinity with the healer–patient archetype. Practitioners, medical and psychological alike, are accused of being more interested in pathology than health, abnormal than normal. This is a half-truth. Psychotherapists are attracted to the health–sickness polarity in others and in themselves. The image of the wounded healer thus symbolizes a painful awareness of our own limitations and the counterpole to health (Guggenbuhl-Craig 1971).

The majority of these ten therapists allude to early personal vulnerabilities which predisposed them to a career as a psychotherapist. For Chaplin 'helping to "heal" other people's souls is intimately connected with the healing and development of my own'. Street alone, however, explicitly invokes the self-view of a wounded healer. We suspect that the incidence of this dynamic constellation in psychotherapists is much greater than recognized here and elsewhere; moreover the possibility can be, and should be, fruitfully considered by each and every clinician.

Training experiences

Life and informal training experiences consistently exerted more influence on these ten therapists than did formal coursework. This pattern parallels Chaplin's (chapter 11) belief that formal training is only a small part of becoming a psychotherapist. In fact, many of the authors point to their non-traditional or circuitous training paths to the profession. Fransella (chapter 8), to take an extreme example, categorically states that, 'I have no formal training as a psychotherapist whatsoever.' She cites three enabling factors in its place: a wealth of clinical experience with psychiatric patients (as an occupational therapist), a theory deeply congruent with her self (Kelly's personal construct theory), and the inspiration of a fellow therapist (Don Bannister).

Although formal opportunities for training in clinical psychology and psychotherapy are evidently less available in England than in the United States (Remington and Green 1988), most American psychotherapists also value experiential over didactic learning. When asked to evaluate the significance of various aspects of their training experience for their career, Henry et al.'s (1971) sample produced a list of twenty specific training experiences. The most frequent responses are reproduced in Table 4 (under Comparison Sample) along with percentages for our sample. Most commonly recognized as important were clinical supervision, followed by work experience, field experience, and personal therapy. The influence of faculty members and coursework on becoming a psychotherapist was rated relatively low.

One distinction germane to the education of mental health professionals is that between training and socialization. Training is course and practical experiences designed to produce technical expertise and specified knowledge. Socialization is a broader consequence of formal training, an impact of that substantial segment of one's life upon professional values, identification, and attitudes (Feshbach 1987). Interestingly, those training aspects most frequently mentioned all fall within the realm of socialization: they offer social interaction, role-modelling, and self-awareness.

We conclude, as have those before us, that the process of becoming a psychotherapist is only loosely organized by the training system on several counts. First, many of the experiences that are strongly emphasized in formal training, such as core knowledge and research design, are seen by graduates

227

John C. Norcross and James D. Guy

Table 4 Most important aspects of training for career

| Training Aspect | First Choice | | Present in Three Choices | |
	Present Sample	Comparison Sample*	Present Sample	Comparison Sample*
Clinical supervision	25%	21%	22%	53%
Work experience	12.5%	16%	19%	30%
Field work	12.5%	13%	4%	17%
Personal therapy	12.5%	9%	15%	21%
Patients	12.5%	9%	15%	20%
Formal training	12.5%	7%	11%	14%
Faculty members	0%	7%	0%	11%
Course work	12.5%	4%	7%	13%
Professional colleagues	0%	3%	7%	7%

* Adapted from Henry *et al.* (1971).

to be of only minimal importance. Second, the informal socialization considered to be very important by most psychotherapists, such as personal psychotherapy and mentoring experiences, are not fully incorporated into the training structure of many programmes (Henry *et al.* 1971, 1973).

In closing this section, we would point out that the lifelong process of education should not be confused with a period of formal, post-baccalaureate training. The editors and contributors have surely not done so. They have uniformly preserved this critical distinction by separating the social and physical recognition of the psychotherapist role, as reflected in receipt of a degree, diploma, or licensure, from the individual and emotional acceptance of the calling. The latter typically occurs many, many moons after the former. This process is in keeping with Ernst Kris' (1952) conception of the formative decade in career development. It hardly seems possible to become a sophisticated therapist in less than ten years; these therapists' odysseys poignantly attest to the gradual process of professional maturation.

Stresses and satisfactions

A better title for this section might be 'the agony and the ecstasy'. It is not uncommon for psychotherapists to alternate between sleep-deprived nights fraught with recollections of treatment failures and clients' projected hostility and fleeting moments of realization that they have genuinely helped a fellow being. We will try to present a balance of these polarities (from the emotionally draining to the personally fulfilling), the agonies (stresses) and the ecstasies (satisfactions), as have the contributors.

Stresses

While it is obvious that psychotherapists are 'normal' human beings who face the same trials and tribulations encountered by their patients, this is no less true of our exceptional clinicians. Their personal narratives make it painfully clear that they have experienced many of the same personal tragedies, failures, and stressors as the rest of us. Despite our secret fantasy that these prominent therapists have found a way to inoculate themselves against the sources of distress encountered by their patients and less experienced colleagues, a careful reading of their autobiographical chapters proves otherwise.

The results of our survey further drive home this point. At a rate nearly identical to that reported by a larger sample of practitioners (Guy *et al.* 1988), seven of the ten indicated that they had experienced identifiable personal distress during the previous three years. Job stress and burn out were cited as the primary sources of difficulty for four of the seven, twice the rate of the national sample. Whether this is the result of sampling error or the possibility that master clinicians are under greater performance pressure is difficult to determine. Equally puzzling is the finding that 29 per cent cited 'legal problems' as a primary source of distress, compared to less than 7 per cent of the national sample. Do notoriety and success bring bigger headaches? Our psychotherapists also experienced distress related to personal illness and marital problems at twice the rate reported by the larger group. While it would be foolish to make unfounded conclusions based on such a small and select sample, the possible implications of these findings are interesting to ponder. At the very least, it appears that our practitioners are just as vulnerable, if not more so, to life's exigencies as those with less talent in treating similar problems in others.

We asked our master clinicians whether their personal distress had decreased the quality of patient care that they provided. Fully six of the seven said that it had not. While this response pattern may have reflected concern over the lack of anonymity involved in signing their name to our survey, it may also be that more experienced and/or talented psychotherapists are able to keep most of their personal problems from negatively impairing their professional work. Unfortunately, this was not as true of the larger national sample. A total of 37 per cent reported that their personal distress decreased their quality of patient care (Guy *et al.* 1988).

When considering job-related sources of stress, several interesting patterns emerge. Table 5 compares our therapists and a larger American sample of clinicians. It appears that our practitioners encounter problems related to time pressures, organizational politics, excessive workload, emotional depletion, and excessive paperwork at a rate very similar to that of average clinicians. This certainly makes sense and is almost reassuring – in a perverse sort of way.

The differences in sources of job-related distress, on the other hand, are intriguing. Our psychotherapists report that professional conflicts are a much

Table 5 Sources of stress in psychotherapy work

Stress	Present Sample Mean Rating	Rank	Comparison Sample* Rank
Time pressures	4.1	1	NR
Organizational politics	4.0	2(Tie)	3
Excessive workload	3.8	2(Tie)	1
Professional conflicts	3.7	4	14
Physical exhaustion	3.5	5	9
Emotional depletion	3.2	6(Tie)	4(Tie)
Economic uncertainty	3.2	6(Tie)	NR
Excessive paperwork	3.0	8	6
Responsibility for patients' lives	2.8	9(Tie)	4(Tie)
Difficulty leaving 'psychodynamics' at office	2.8	9(Tie)	13
Doubts regarding efficacy of therapy	2.7	11(Tie)	10
Social difficulties after work	2.7	11(Tie)	15
Difficulty in working with disturbed people	2.5	13	2
Controlling one's emotions	2.4	14(Tie)	7(Tie)
Constraints of the '50-minute hour'	2.4	14(Tie)	12
Difficulty in evaluating progress	2.3	16	7(Tie)
Inevitable need to relinquish patients	1.9	17	11
Monotony of the work	1.4	18	16

Ratings were made on a seven-point, Likert-type scale where 1 = not at all a source of stress, 4 = moderate source of stress, and 7 = major source of stress, NR = not reported.
* Adapted from Farber and Heifetz (1981).

greater source of distress than is typical of 'average' practitioners. Strupp speaks of his struggle as a non-medical therapist to gain parity with organized psychiatry and his revolt against the 'cultist aspects of psychoanalysis'. Bloomfield tells of her encounters with many divisive polarizations – the experimental approach versus the social context, the behaviourists versus the psychoanalysts – which resembled warring factions of political parties. Again, it appears that success and notoriety come with a price.

Another issue of concern mentioned was the inability to leave 'psychodynamics' at the office. This phenomenon is experienced by many therapists (Guy 1987), but our sample found it more difficult to set aside their interpretive skills than the average practitioner. Perhaps their notable passion for psychotherapeutic endeavours, as well as their exceptional ability, have shaped their world-view to the point that it has become inappropriate, if not nearly impossible, to cease thinking 'therapeutically' about their experiences and relationships. Karp writes that 'being an everyday citizen can be anti-climatic after working with the concentrated emotion of the psycho-therapist'.

Relatedly, our sample reports greater stress from 'social difficulties after work' than that noted by the larger sample. Karp makes the all-too-often-heard admission that 'Too often I give more to my patients than to my family.' She, Chaplin, and Bloomfield relate how being a therapist exerts considerable strain on their intimate relationships; more than one contributor acknowledged that psychotherapy occupied their emotional resources and available time to the exclusion of their significant others. Relationship problems are *the* most frequent precipitant of psychotherapists' psychological distress – accounting for 30 per cent to 40 per cent of those surveyed (Deutsch 1985; Norcross and Prochaska 1986).

The psychotherapist who denies that clinical work is gruelling and demanding is, in Thorne's terms, 'mendacious, deluded, or incompetent'. Our master therapists experience the same personal and professional problems encountered by 'average' practitioners. However, the pattern of differences between the two groups suggests that exceptional ability and therapeutic notoriety exacerbate some sources of distress while effectively reducing others.

A case in point of the latter may be that our therapists encounter much less stress from working with 'disturbed people' than the average clinician. Indeed, the narratives suggest that they are quite comfortable with even the most troublesome of patients, enabling them to be both successful clinicians and effective supervisors. Their survey responses depicted in Table 5 indicate that the depth of their self-knowledge and understanding makes the control of personal emotions less problematic. They are better able to relinquish their patients at the end of the treatment, and they find it easier (but not easy) to evaluate treatment progress.

Satisfactions

Despite the agonies and the burdens, psychotherapists make the best of their lot. But we can do more than passively adjust: we can be informed by the *malaise,* indeed can transcend it and use it for self-renewal. Paradoxically, a new health, a new freedom can be discovered through the vicissitudes we are subjected to (Sacks 1985). Psychotherapists can achieve what Nietzsche liked to call great health: unhostile humour, interpersonal courage, and resilience of spirit.

Somewhat unexpected as a recurring satisfaction was the diversity and synergy of professional activities. This was most apparent in the writings of the three psychologists whose principal employment was in academia (Mahoney, Strupp, and Heppner), though certainly not limited to them. We found ourselves smiling knowingly as we read these sections since both of us have made similar decisions to combine small clinical practices with an academic career. It does raise a fascinating paradox: one of the gratifications of psychotherapy is not having to do it full time!

Mahoney, for one, values the balance between realities of actual practice and more abstract endeavours. Academia affords generous freedom and opportunities seldom offered elsewhere. Heppner concludes, 'In short, being an educator has not only stimulated new learning about the therapy process, but also facilitated the development of my identity as a therapist.' All speak of the mutual facilitation of their psychotherapy practice and psychotherapy research. Heppner shows how research/writing can be 'a major stimulus', providing new insights into clients' worlds and pushing him towards greater specificity. Strupp's lifelong fascination with the problem of how psychotherapy works has, he writes, 'absorbed and gratified' him second only to his family. Fransella informs us that the assumptions of personal construct therapy and the unquenchable curiosity of its practitioners will mean that they will 'nearly always have other work to do along with therapy', e.g. research, supervision, and teaching.

Turning to sources of satisfaction in psychotherapy *per se*, we see in Table 6 that enhancing growth in patients is by far the most highly rated gratification for these ten therapists. Chaplin calls psychotherapy 'a great privilege'; Rowan states that his greatest satisfaction is 'just of seeing people blossom and come forth'. Others speak of 'awe' when describing the therapy process. This special form of therapeutic ecstasy, rarely experienced in normal interpersonal relationships, is derived from being involved with the ontic birth of a new being – assisting in definition, reformation, and expansion (Burton 1972).

Although the primary objective and ethical mandate of psychotherapy is patient improvement, the needs of the therapist obviously come into play. Self-knowledge and self-growth were tied in our small sample for the second major source of satisfaction. Writing in *Twelve Therapists*, a distantly related ancestor of the present compendium, Arthur Burton (1972: 2) puts the therapist's needs directly at the fore: 'When some of his own growth needs are met, the therapy prospers; when they are not, the therapy languishes.' In like fashion, Thorne is 'positively nourished' by his clinical work, allowing him 'to love and be loved'.

Personal therapy

In 'Analysis terminable and interminable', Freud (1937/1964: 246) asked, 'But where and how is the poor wretch to acquire the ideal qualifications which he will need in this profession? The answer is in an analysis of himself, with which his preparation for his future activity begins.' The majority of psychotherapists, following Freud's exhortations, have obtained personal treatment for themselves.

Indeed, one of the most firmly held and cherished beliefs among psychotherapists is that personal treatment is a desirable, if not a necessary, prerequisite for clinical work. Fromm-Reichman (1950: 42) wrote that 'any attempt at intensive psychotherapy is fraught with danger, hence unacceptable'

Table 6 Sources of satisfaction in psychotherapy work

Satisfaction	Mean Rating	Present Sample Rank	Comparison Sample* Rank
Enhancing growth in patients	6.7	1	2
Self-knowledge	5.7	2(Tie)	5
Self-growth	5.7	2(Tie)	4
Using therapeutic expertise	5.2	4(Tie)	1
Professional autonomy	5.2	4(Tie)	NR
Learning about many types of people	5.1	6	3
Being socially useful	5.0	7	6
Professional independence	4.4	8	NR
Achieving intimacy	3.9	9(Tie)	8
Status of a professional career	3.9	9(Tie)	8
Learning intimate details	3.7	11	9
The 'mystique' of the therapist	3.2	12	10

Ratings were made on a seven-point, Likert-type scale where 1 = not at all a source of satisfaction, 4 = moderate source of satisfaction, and 7 = major source of satisfaction, NR = not reported.
* Adapted from Farber and Heifetz (1981).

when not preceded by personal analysis. Likewise, Chessick (1974: 86) argued that without personal treatment the psychotherapist is 'endangering himself and his patients'.

These ten therapists follow strongly in this tradition. When asked to rate the importance of personal therapy as a prerequisite for clinical work, one replied unimportant, four said important, and five very important. These results are in keeping with American clinical psychologists (Norcross and Prochaska 1982b) and psychotherapists (Prochaska and Norcross 1983), who rated personal therapy very important half of the time and not at all important or unimportant less than 10 per cent of the time.

Consistent, too, is the fact that nine of these ten therapists had undergone personal psychotherapy at least once themselves. Ninety per cent slightly exceeds previous incidence rates of American psychologists (75%–76%), psychiatrists (67%), and clinical social workers (65%–72%; Henry et al. 1971; Norcross, Strausser, and Missar 1988).

The incidence of personal therapy varies systematically with one's own treatment history and theoretical orientation (Garfield and Kurtz 1976b; Greenberg and Staller 1981; Guy and Liaboe 1986). Behaviour therapists do seek personal treatment – somewhere between 44 per cent and 59 per cent – but less frequently and for a shorter duration on average than their non-behavioural colleagues (Lazarus 1971; Norcross and Prochaska 1984; Gochman, Allgood, and Geer 1982; Norcross and Wogan 1983). Practically all psychoanalytically-orientated practitioners, on the other hand, report intensive personal therapy. Having had personal treatment obviously influences one's subsequent attitude towards its desirability; a case in point is that the only author not reporting therapy herself (Fransella) was the only one to rate it an unimportant prerequisite.

The number of personal treatment experiences in our sample of ten ranged between one and 'many'. What is impressive is that all but one of the nine therapists sought therapy on more than one occasion, paralleling a national average of 2.3 discrete treatment 'episodes'. We say impressive because the profession's collective silence on the topic has created an illusion that most clinicians do not feel the need for personal therapy once they are in practice (Guy and Liaboe 1986). The accumulating evidence rebuts any such illusions; most clinicians do in fact utilize the very services they provide. Eight of the nine contributors who had personal therapy appear to have received it after receipt of their academic degrees. 52 per cent of psychoanalysts in one study (Goldensohn 1977) and between 55 per cent (Grunebaum 1986) and 62 per cent (Guy *et al.* 1987) of practising psychotherapists in two other studies obtained personal psychotherapy following training.

Although we did not inquire specifically into the outcomes of therapy, the chapters leave no doubt but that the experience was potent and constructive. Rowan makes it crystal clear that 'the most important influence on any therapist is the personal therapy they have experienced themselves on themselves and for themselves.' Chaplin characterizes her Jungian analysis as 'extremely useful'; Heppner relates his first as a 'productive counselling experience'; Bloomfield expresses gratitude towards her 'kind and gentle' analyst 'for not being like the proverbial blank screen'. Strupp writes of a lengthy analysis which, as he came 'to appreciate only much later, was a very constructive experience'. Mahoney, similarly, entered personal therapy which 'so effectively paved the way for much of my later personal and professional development'. These retrospective views are congruent with psychotherapists' positive evaluations of personal treatment outcome; over 90 per cent indicate improvement in terms of behaviour/symptomatology, cognitions/insight, and emotions/relief (Buckley *et al.* 1981; Norcross, Strausser, and Missar 1988). Satisfactory results are probably achieved in personal therapy more regularly than is suggested by the impression lingering in the literature and in private conversations (Shapiro 1976).

Nevertheless, as with all psychotherapy (Mays and Franks 1985), a vocal minority report negative outcomes and/or actual harm as a result of personal work. When asked 'Was your therapy/analysis harmful in any way?' between 8 per cent and 21 per cent of surveyed psychotherapists respond in the affirmative (Buckley *et al.*, 1981; Grunebaum 1986; Norcross, Strausser, and Faltus 1988). Amongst our ten therapists, we were able to locate only one therapy experience which might fall into this category: Strupp's second analysis which was 'less than successful'. Interestingly, he attributed this outcome to an authoritarian and cold analyst, whom Strupp later realized cared little for him as

Table 7 Lasting lessons from personal therapy

Lesson	Present Sample	Comparison Sample*
Importance of the personal relationship, warmth and empathy	18%	12%
Importance of transference/countertransference	6%	8%
Need for more patience and respect/avoid value judgements	12%	7%
Therapist's use of self is essential	6%	4%
Need for personal treatment among therapists	0%	4%
Importance of unconscious motivations and material	0%	4%
Change is gradual and painful albeit possible	12%	3%
Psychotherapy is effective/growth producing	6%	3%
Inadequacy of insight alone/need for emotional experience	6%	2%
Other	34%	53%

* Adapted from Norcross, Strausser, and Faltus (1988).

a person. This reason – a rigid, distant, and uninvolved therapeutic relationship – is advanced as the most frequent cause of harmful treatment experiences among psychotherapists (Grunebaum 1986; Norcross, Strausser, and Faltus 1988).

The goal of the psychotherapist's personal treatment is to alter the nature of subsequent therapeutic work in ways that enhance its effectiveness. The actual mechanism of this process is as complex and individualized as the number of psychotherapist-patients. We asked these ten therapists – and hundreds of others previously – to reflect on their personal treatment in order to describe briefly any lasting lessons they acquired concerning the practice of psychotherapy. Four blank lines were provided for this purpose. Their multifarious responses were content-coded and the most frequent response categories are presented in Table 7.

The modal enduring lessons these psychotherapists took from their own treatment all concerned the interpersonal relationship – warmth and empathy, transference and countertransference, patience, and respect. The importance of caring, respect, being totally present, and recognizing our common humanness underscored these responses. This heightened awareness may well translate into clinical practice. Personal therapy has been positively associated with the clinician's ability to display empathy, warmth, and genuineness (Peebles 1980), and his or her increased emphasis on the personal relationship in therapy (Wogan and Norcross 1985). The trend holds true for general samples of psychotherapists (e.g. Sundland and Barker 1962) as well as psychoanalytic (Strupp 1955) and behaviour (Norcross and Wogan 1983) therapists.

The harvest of clinical acumen here is a *desideratum* of psychotherapeutic practice. The most frequent responses correspond closely to the recurring commonalities in the literature on how the therapist's therapy should theoretically improve his or her performance (e.g. Fleischer and Wissler 1985; Fromm-Reichman 1950; Garfield and Kurtz 1976b; Nierenberg 1972; Shapiro 1976; Wampler and Strupp 1976). To wit, personal therapy: improves the emotional and mental functioning of the psychotherapist; provides a more complete understanding of personal dynamics, interpersonal elicitations, and conflictual issues; alleviates the emotional stresses and burdens inherent in this 'impossible profession'; serves as a profound socialization experience; places therapists in the role of the client, and thus sensitizes them to the needs of their clients; and provides a first-hand, intensive opportunity to observe clinical methods. Isn't it delightful when the fruits of theoretical analysis approximate the results of clinical experience?

And what of future personal therapy for these ten therapists? At least two relate that they are currently engaged in ongoing work, Rowan being the most vocal proponent of this self-renewing endeavour. The comments of the remaining authors portend a return to treatment as desired or needed. Freud, as is so often the case, anticipated the issue many years ago. He recommended that the analyst reinitiate personal treatment on the recognition that intense therapy continually exposes the clinician to the impact of patients' unconscious processes.

> Every analyst should periodically – at intervals of five years or so –
> submit himself to analysis once more, without feeling ashamed of taking
> this step. This would mean, then, that not only the therapeutic analysis
> of patients but his own analysis would change from a terminable into an
> interminable task.
>
> (1937/1964: 249)

In closing, we – like these master therapists and our clients – should expect a lifetime of struggling for awareness. Ever repeated confrontations with our personal and public selves are necessary for fulfilment. We cannot, like the biblical Isaac, spend just one night wrestling with the angel to win his blessing (Guggenbuhl-Craig 1971). The struggle will last a lifetime.

Be comforted by the knowledge that the process, as opposed to the outcome, is the gift of self-renewal. Bloomfield assures us that it is 'not so much the arrival but the journey' that is nourishing. Mahoney, speaking of his own development and that of his clients, reminds us of Ram Dass' contention that the purpose of the dance is not to finish. The purpose of the dance is to dance! May we all dance 'til we drop.

References

Bandura, A. (1982) 'The psychology of chance encounters and life paths',

American Psychologist 37: 747–55.

Bennet, G. (1979) *Patients and Their Doctors: The Journey Through Medical Care*, London: Bailliere Tindall.

Bruce, W. E. and Sims, J. H. (1974) 'Birthorder among psychotherapists: a see-saw phenomenon', *Psychological Reports* 34: 215–20.

Buckley, P., Karasu, T. B. and Charles, E. (1981) 'Psychotherapists view their personal therapy', *Psychotherapy: Theory, Research and Practice*, 18: 299–305.

Burton, A. (ed.) (1972) *Twelve Therapists: How They Live and Actualize Themselves*, San Francisco: Jossey-Bass.

Chessick, R. D. (1974) *The Technique and Practice of Intensive Psychotherapy*, New York: Jason Aronson.

Deutsch, C. J. (1985) 'A survey of therapists' personal problems and treatment', *Professional Psychology: Research and Practice* 16: 305–15.

Farber, B. A. and Heifetz, L. J. (1981) 'The satisfactions and stresses of psychotherapeutic work: a factor analytic study', *Professional Psychology* 12: 621–30.

Feshbach, S. (1987) 'Trends and issues in clinical psychology', *The Clinical Psychologist* 40(1): 4–5.

Fleischer, J. A. and Wissler, A. (1985) 'The therapist as patient: special problems and considerations', *Psychotherapy* 22: 587–94.

Ford, E. S. C. (1963) 'Being and becoming a psychotherapist: the search for identity', *American Journal of Psychotherapy* 17: 472–82.

Freud, S. (1905/1963) 'Fragment of an analysis of a case of hysteria', in *Collected Papers of Sigmund Freud* (volume III), London: Hogarth Press.

Freud, S. (1937/1964) 'Analysis terminable and interminable', in J. Strachey (ed.) *Complete Psychological Works of Sigmund Freud*, London: Hogarth Press.

Fromm-Reichman, F. (1950) *Principles of Intensive Psychotherapy*, Chicago: University of Chicago Press.

Garfield, S. L. and Kurtz, R. (1976a) 'Clinical psychologists in the 1970s', *American Psychologist* 31: 1–9.

Garfield, S. L. and Kurtz, R. (1976b) 'Personal therapy for the psychotherapist: some findings and issues', *Psychotherapy: Theory, Research and Practice* 13: 188–92.

Gochman, S. I., Allgood, B. A., and Geer, C. R. (1982) 'A look at today's behavior therapists', *Professional Psychology* 13: 605–11.

Goldberg, C. (1986) *On Being a Psychotherapist*, New York: Gardner.

Goldblank, S. (1986) 'My family made me do it: the influence of family therapists' families of origin on their occupational choice', *Family Process* 25: 309–19.

Goldensohn, S. S. (1977) 'Graduates' evaluation of their psychoanalytic training', *Journal of the American Academy of Psychoanalysis* 5: 51–64.

Greenberg, R. P. and Staller, J. S. (1981) 'Personal therapy for therapists', *American Journal of Psychiatry* 138: 1467–71.

Grunebaum, H. (1986) 'Harmful psychotherapy experiences', *American Journal of Psychotherapy* 40: 165–76.

Guggenbuhl-Craig, A. (1971) *Power in the Helping Professions*, Dallas: Spring Publications.

Guy, J. D. (1987) *The Personal Life of the Psychotherapist*, New York: Wiley.

Guy, J. D. and Liaboe, G. P. (1986) 'Personal therapy for the experienced psychotherapist: a discussion of its usefulness and utilization', *The Clinical*

Psychologist 39(1): 20–3.

Guy, J. D., Stark, M. J. and Poelstra, P. L. (August 1987) 'Personal therapy for psychotherapists before and after entering professional practice', paper presented at the 95th Annual Convention of the American Psychological Association, New York, NY.

Guy, J. D., Poelstra, P. L., and Stark, M. J. (1988) 'Personal distress and therapeutic effectiveness', *Professional Psychology: Research and Practice*, (in press).

Guy, J. D., Poelstra, P. L., and Tamura, L. (1988) 'Birth order and the practice of psychotherapy: a national survey of psychologists practicing psychotherapy'. Manuscript under review.

Henry, W. E. (1966) 'Some observations on the lives of healers', *Human Development* 9: 47–56.

Henry, W. E., Sims, J. H., and Spray, S. L. (1971) *The Fifth Profession: Becoming a Psychotherapist*, San Francisco: Jossey-Bass.

Henry, W. E., Sims, J. H., and Spray, S. L. (1973) *Public and Private Lives of Psychotherapists*, San Francisco: Jossey-Bass.

Holt, R. R. and Luborsky, L. (1958) *Personality Patterns of Psychiatrists*, volume I. New York: Basic Books.

Kottler, J. A. (1986) *On Being a Therapist*, San Francisco: Jossey-Bass.

Kris, E. (ed.) (1952) *Psychoanalytic Explorations in Art*, New York: International Universities Press.

Lazarus, A. A. (1971) 'Where do behavior therapists take their troubles?' *Psychological Reports* 28: 349–50.

McNair, D. M. and Lorr, M. (1964) 'An analysis of professed psycho-therapeutic techniques', *Journal of Consulting Psychology* 28: 265–71.

Mays, D. T. and Franks, C. M. (eds.) (1985) *Negative Outcome in Psychotherapy and What to Do About it*, New York: Springer.

Miller, A. (1981) *Prisoners of Childhood*, New York: Basic Books.

Nash, J., Norcross, J. C., and Prochaska, J. O. (1984) 'Satisfactions and stresses of independent practices', *Psychotherapy in Private Practice* 2(4): 39–48.

Nierenberg, M. A. (1972) 'Self-help first', *International Journal of Psychiatry* 10: 34–41.

Norcross, J. C. (1985) 'In defense of theoretical orientations for clinicians', *The Clinical Psychologist* 38(1): 13–17.

Norcross, J. C. and Prochaska, J. O. (1982a) 'A national survey of clinical psychologists: affiliations and orientations', *The Clinical Psychologist* 35 (3): 1, 4–6.

Norcross, J. C. and Prochaska, J. O. (1982b) 'A national survey of clinical psychologists: views on training, career choice, and APA', *The Clinical Psychologist* 35 (4): 1–6.

Norcross, J. C. and Prochaska, J. O. (1983) 'Clinicians' theoretical orientations: selection, utilization, and efficacy', *Professional Psychology* 14: 197–208.

Norcross, J. C. and Prochaska, J. O. (1984) 'Where do behavior and other therapists take their troubles?: II', *The Behavior Therapist* 7: 26–7.

Norcross, J. C. and Prochaska, J. O. (1986) 'Psychotherapist heal thyself I: the psychological distress and self-change of psychologists, counselors, and laypersons', *Psychotherapy* 23: 102–14.

Norcross, J. C. and Wogan, M. (1983) 'American psychotherapists of diverse persuasions: characteristics, theories, practices, and clients', *Professional Psychology: Research and Practice* 14: 529–39.

Norcross, J. C., Prochaska, J. O., and Gallagher, K. M. (1989) 'The clinical psychologist in the 1980s', *The Clinical Psychologist*.

Norcross, J. C., Strausser, D. J., and Faltus, F. J. (1988) 'The therapist's therapist', *American Journal of Psychotherapy* 42: 53–66.

Norcross, J. C., Strausser, D. J., and Missar, C. D. (1988) 'The processes and outcomes of psychotherapists' personal treatment experiences', *Psychotherapy* 25: 36–43.

Orlinsky, D. and Howard, K. I. (1977) 'The therapist's experience of psychotherapy', in A. S. Gurman and A. M. Razin (eds.) *Effective Psychotherapy: A Handbook of Research*, New York: Pergamon.

Peebles, M. J. (1980) 'Personal therapy and ability to display empathy, warmth and genuineness in psychotherapy', *Psychotherapy: Theory, Research and Practice* 17: 252–62.

Prochaska, J. O. and Norcross, J. C. (1983) 'Contemporary psychotherapists: a national survey of characteristics, practices, orientations, and attitudes', *Psychotherapy: Theory, Research, and Practice* 20: 161–73.

Racusin, G. R., Abramowitz, S. I., and Winter, W. D. (1981) 'Becoming a therapist: family dynamics and career choice', *Professional Psychology* 12: 271–9.

Ragan, C., Maloney, H. N., and Beit-Hallahmi, B. (1980) 'Psychologists and religion: professional factors and personal belief', *Review of Religious Research* 21: 208–17.

Remington, B. and Green, P. (1988) 'Teaching psychology in American and British universities: some personal impressions', *Teaching of Psychology* 15: 26–30.

Rippere, V. and Williams, R. (eds) (1985) *Wounded Healers: Mental Health Workers' Experiences of Depression*, New York: Wiley.

Sacks, O. W. (1985) *The Man who Mistook his Wife for a Hat and Other Clinical Tales*, New York: Summit.

Schultz, D. (1981) *Theories of Personality*, Monterey, CA: Brooks-Cole.

Shapiro, D. (1976) 'The analyst's own analysis', *Journal of the American Psychoanalytic Association* 25: 5–42.

Sharaf, M. R. (1960) 'An approach to the theory and measure of intraception', unpublished doctoral dissertation, Harvard University.

Strupp, H. H. (1955) 'The effect of the psychotherapist's personal analysis upon his techniques', *Journal of Consulting Psychology* 19: 197–204.

Sundland, D. M. and Barker, E. N. (1962) 'The orientations of psychotherapists', *Journal of Consulting Psychology* 26: 201–12.

Viscott, D. (1972) *The Making of a Psychiatrist*, New York: Pocket Books.

Wampler, L. D. and Strupp, H. H. (1976) 'Personal therapy for students in clinical psychology: a matter of faith?' *Professional Psychology* 7: 195–201.

Wogan, M. and Norcross, J. C. (1983) 'Dimensions of therapeutic activity: a replication and extension of earlier studies', *Psychotherapy: Theory, Research and Practice* 20(1): 67–74.

Wogan, M. and Norcross, J. C. (1985) 'Dimensions of therapeutic skills and techniques: empirical identification, therapist correlates, and predictive utility', *Psychotherapy* 22: 63–74.

Appendix

On becoming a psychotherapist: Chapter structure

We would like you to structure your contribution according to these headings:

1. *Why* did I become a psychotherapist?
2. *How* did I become a psychotherapist?
3. *When* did I become a psychotherapist?
4. *What* sustains me as a psychotherapist?
5. Implications for other psychotherapists

Please give each of these five headings sufficient weight to ensure that no one heading is neglected.

(1) Why did I become a psychotherapist?

This is an invitation to explore what motivated your desire to become a psychotherapist.

You might find it helpful to consider these issues (amongst others):

- how would you trace the origins of your desire to become a psychotherapist?
- describe any sort of family tradition in this area
- did your desire to be a psychotherapist meet with encouragement, disapproval or indifference from family and friends, and how important were these reactions both in forming and carrying through your choice of profession?
- were there particular examples of being helped – or not being helped – at times of crisis which might have been significant in influencing your desire to become a therapist?
- describe how you might have been influenced by a significant person or event in your wish to become a psychotherapist
- what kinds of fantasies, ideals, longings or myths were associated with becoming a psychotherapist (e.g. Freud's identification with the figures of Oedipus and Moses)?

- on what kind of figure or model did you base your notion of being a psychotherapist (i.e. did you think a psychotherapist would be most like a doctor, psychologist, guru, priest, educator, reformer, revolutionary philosopher, etc.)?
- what did you imagine it would be like being a therapist (e.g. exciting, painful, romantic, uplifting, depressing, morbid, voyeuristic, frightening...)?
- what kind of person did you think would make a good therapist and in what ways did you consider that you might or might not measure up to this?
- what doubts and dilemmas did you experience in your desire to become a psychotherapist?
- what price did you expect to pay in choosing to become a therapist?

(2) How did I become a psychotherapist?

This question addresses your training, how you learnt the art or science of psychotherapy.

You can reflect on this under the following sub-headings:

(a) How and why did you choose one particular school or type of therapy?
e.g. through recommendation, chance encounter, reading...?

- what professional transition did you have to make in order to become a psychotherapist (e.g. were you involved in one of the helping professions or did you come from outside the field? What accounted for your professional transition?)?
- what drew you to one particular school or orientation or repelled you from the others?
- with what personal beliefs and aspects of your character did your choice of a particular school or orientation resonate?

(b) Formal training

- what impact did your formal training have on your emerging career as a therapist?
- what weight and significance would you give to the different aspects of your training? e.g.
  - learning a theory or body of knowledge
  - your 'training therapy' or 'working on yourself'
  - working with patients* under supervision as an apprentice or trainee
  - being inspired by or attached to one or more of your trainers
  - colleagueship with your peers or trainers

- being initiated into a particular institute/group/tradition
- what did your training teach you and what did it not teach you (how far do you think psychotherapy can be taught)?
- how much did your training nourish, change or do violence to your ideas and ideals about becoming a therapist?

(c) Informal training

How far do you think you learnt how to become a psychotherapist from events and relationships outside of your formal training?

(3) When did I become a psychotherapist?

We would like you to try and identify the point at which you ceased being someone interested in therapy or learning about therapy and *became a psychotherapist*. When did you suspect or know 'this is what (or who) I am'?

You might consider:

- what discrepancies, connections or resonances were there between being a psychotherapist in your own eyes, and in the eyes of other people (especially your patients and teachers, but also colleagues, friends, family, etc.)?
- what marked the transition from being a student or trainee psychotherapist to becoming a 'proper' psychotherapist (e.g. an encounter with one particular patient or several patients, your relationship with a teacher or another significant person, a particular development in your own thinking or style of working...)?
- how far did this transition coincide with the ending of your formal training?
- what changes in both thinking and practice have characterized the period from the end of your formal training to the present, and what has occasioned them?

(4) What sustains me as a psychotherapist?

In other words, how would you answer the question: 'How can you stand, day in and day out, listening to other people telling you their troubles?'

In particular, what is it about the presence of your patients that sustains you as a therapist?

You might consider:

- what does it mean to you to be a psychotherapist? e.g. does it make you proud, uncomfortable, diffident, wary, embarrassed, overwhelmed, awed, gratified...?

- what kinds of patients nourish your sense of being a psychotherapist and what kinds do most violence to it or call it most into question?
- how far are you in this business for yourself? In particular, how far are you conducting or continuing your own therapy through your work with your patients, and how far is this legitimate?
- how far do relationships with colleagues, family, friends, etc. sustain your sense of yourself as a therapist, and how far do they put a strain on your being a therapist? How important, in this regard, are other activities (professional and non-professional)?
- how do you see your future career? e.g. do you see yourself being a therapist for the rest of your life?
- do you think, on reflection, you made the right choice in becoming a psychotherapist? What doubts do you have? If you had your time again would you still choose psychotherapy as a profession?

(5) Implications for other psychotherapists

What would you like other psychotherapists, or therapists in training, to learn from your experiences?

As you consider this, pick out what you take to be the main themes of your contribution.

What has writing about yourself in this way revealed to you about your own desire to be a psychotherapist?

Note

For reasons of economy we will use the term 'patient' rather than the clumsy 'patient/client', but in your contribution use whichever term you feel is most appropriate.

Author index

Adams, B. 116
Adcock, C.J. 137
Allgood, B.A. 233
Allport, G.W. 137
Armistead, N. 158

Balint, M. 214
Bandura, A. 225
Bannister, D. 121
Barker, E.N. 235
Beck, J. 153
Bennet, G. 226
Binder, J.L. 108
Bowen, M. 142
Bruce, W.E. 222
Buckley, P. 234, 235
Burton, A. 215, 232

Casement, P. 45
Chaikin, J. 152
Chaplin, J. 184
Chertok, L. 209
Chessick, R.D. 233

Deutsch, C.J. 231
Dryden, W. 11

Eagle, M. 9
Ellenberger, H. 3,5
Elliott, R. ix
Ellis, A. 6
Ernst, S. 158

Farber, B.A. 230
Feshbach, S. 227
Field, J. 157
Fleischer, J.A. 236
Flugel, J.C. 36
Ford, E.S.C. 221, 222
Franks, C.M. 234
Fransella, F. 116, 119, 121

Freud, S. 50, 101, 217, 232, 236
Fromm-Reichman, F. 232, 236

Gabriel, T.J. 9, 10
Garfield, S.L. 233, 236
Geer, C.R. 234
Gilbert, P. 10, 12
Gochman, S.I. 233
Goldberg, C. ix, 215
Goldblank, S. 222
Goldstein, A.P. 6
Goldstein, H. 9, 10
Goldensohn, S.S. 234
Gomes-Schwartz, B. 112, 113
Goodison, L. 158
Green, P. 227
Greenberg, L.S. 9
Greenberg, R.P. 233
Greenson, R. 197
Groesbeck, C. 195
Grunebaum, H. 234, 235
Guggenbuhl-Craig, A. 226, 236
Guy, J.D. ix, 215, 222, 229, 230, 234

Hadley, S.W. 112, 113
Haley, J. 140
Hampden-Turner, C. 156
Heifetz, L.J. 230
Henry, G.W.3
Henry, W.E. 218, 221, 222, 223, 224, 225, 227, 228, 233
Heron, J. 167
Herzberg, A. 35
Hinkla, D. 129
Holt, R.R. 218, 223
Howard, K.I. 215

James, J. 167
Jung, C.G. 68, 172

Karasu, T.B. 10, 11

Kelly, G. 116, 122, 123, 127–8, 137
Kottler, J.A. ix, 4, 5, 12, 167, 215
Kris, E. 228
Kurtz, R. 234, 236

Lazarus, A.A. 234
Levi, P. 193, 207
Liaboe, G.P. 234
London, P. 3
Luborsky, L. 218, 223

McConnaughty, E.A. 4, 7, 12
Mahoney, M.J. 9, 10
Mahrer, A.R. 157, 160
Mair, M. 7–8
Malina, J. 153
Marmor, J. 166, 202
Margulies, A. 9
Maslow, A.H. 137, 157
Mays, D.T. 234
Michaels, G.Y. 6
Miller, A. 164, 222
Minuchin, S. 140
Missar, C.D. 233, 234
Mor, B. 162

Napier, A.Y. 142
Nierenberg, M.A. 236
Norcross, J.C. 219, 220, 231, 233, 234, 235

Orlinsky, D. 215

Peebles, M.J. 236
Perls, F. 155
Pilgrim, D. 4
Prochaska, J.O. 219, 231, 233

Racusin, G.R. 224, 225
Ragan, C. 218
Raphael-Leff, L. 10
Reason, P. 158

Remington, B. 227
Rippere, V. 226
Rogers, C. 139, 167
Rostagno, A. 152
Roustang, F. 208
Rowan, J. 154, 155, 156, 158, 159, 162, 164, 166
Russell, G.A. 11
Rutter, M. 7

Sacks, O.W. 221, 231
Safran, J.D. 9
Schultz, D. 223
Shapiro, D. ix, 234, 236
Sharaf, M.R. 222
Shorter, B. 174
Sjöö, M. 162
Spence, D. 213
Staller, J.S. 233
Starhawk 176
Stein, D. 176
Stiles, W.B. ix
Strausser, D.J. 233, 234
Strupp, H.H. 104, 105, 112, 113, 235
Sundland, D.M. 235
Suzuki, S. 141

Thorne, B.J. 54, 66
Turner, V. 213

Wampler, L.D. 236
Whittaker, C.A. 142
Wilber, K. 166
Williams, R. 6, 226
Winnicott, D.W. 195
Wissler, A. 236
Wogan, M. 235

Yalom, I.D. 5

Zilboorg, G. 3

Subject index

Adler, Alfred 5
Anna Freud Clinic 41
Association for Humanistic Psychology 153–4, 159, 163
astrology 170

Bandura, Albert 22, 23, 24
Bannister, Don 125, 126, 138
Beck, Aaron 9
behavioural self-control 23, 24
behavioural therapy 9, 26, 60, 109; and anorexia 25; dangers of 25, 132; vs. personal construct theory 121, 123
behaviourism 220; radical 22
Bierer, Joshua 42
Blake, William 188
British Association for Counselling 163

client-centred therapy 58-60, 64, 109; see also Rogers, Carl
clients in therapy: cultural differences of 46; level of education of 50; old-aged 50; psychotic 45; resistances of 50; self-empowerment of 31, 154; suicide of 45–6; young 65
co-counselling 157-8, 161, 164
confrontation 11
consumer research 150–1
containment 11, 178, 181
Council of Group Studies 157
counselling (psychology) 62, 72, 74–7 passim
countertransference 7, 8
creativity 157

Dass, Ram 237
Dichter, Ernest 150
Doron, Giora 159
double-blind experiments 119

empathy 54, 59, 80, 196-8 passim, 236
Erickson, Milton 22

facilitators 10–11
family therapy 140–2
feminist therapy 170, 175, 178–9, 183–5
Follett, Mary Parker 150
Foucault, Michel 30
Frank, Jerome 32, 104
Freud, Sigmund 8, 103, 108, 109, 112, 122; and Marx 149
Fromm, Erich 173

gestalt therapy 155; see also Perls, Fritz
Gibson, Sara 174
Goethe, J.W. von 102, 216
Gosling, Bob 41–2
grieving 9, 59, 76
group work 41-2, 43–4, 151-61 passim, 165–6, 173; B NOW group 152-4, 173

healing 3, 5, 176, 213, 226–7; homoeopathic 195–6, 199
Hegel, G.W.F. 149
Heron, John 163
humanistic psychology 154–5

infant–mother interaction 10
Institute of Group Analysis 42
Institute of Psychiatry 120
International Congress of Social Psychiatry 44
International Primal Association 163
interpretation 51, 113
intimacy 160
intuition 178

Jackins, Harvey 157
Jesseph, Joseph 72, 73, 83
Jung, C.G. 5, 57–8, 60

Keller, Fred 22
Kelly, George 120, 121-9 passim, 133;see also personal construct theory
Kohut, H. 9

246

Laing, Ronald D. 42
Levious, Mildred 174
Lyward, George 55–6, 61

Marxism 149, 151, 183
Mesmer, Franz Anton 3
Moreno, Jacob Levy 91–2, 94–5
Moreno, Zerka 94–5
mythology 37, 175, 179–80, 226–7

New Paradigm Research Group 158
Nietzsche, F.W. 231

occupational therapy 117–19
Oedipus: myth of 37; complex 159

pastoral care 44
Perls, Fritz 151, 180;see also gestalt therapy
personal construct theory 116, 121-33
    passim; and diagnosis 128; and laddering
    129; reflexivity of 132-3; and stuttering
    121, 122, 126, 127; and weight problems
    127
phenomenological research 30
Popplestone, Ruth 174
positive unconditional regard 11, 59
positivism 10
primal integration therapy 159
Proctor, Brigit 181
programmed self-instructional (PSI) courses
    22
psychoanalysis 103, 107–9 passim, 207–8;
    and self-psychology 9
psychodrama 91–5 passim; and stammering
    92
psychotherapists (see also psychotherapy):
    academic backgrounds of 21–6, 36, 43,
    54, 71–3, 91–3, 103, 120, 137–8, 150,
    173; background motivations of 4, 18–21,
    39, 70–4, 81, 87–90, 102, 116, 134–6,
    144–5, 148–52, 169–79, 192–9, 223–5,
    231–2; career determinants of 223–5; and
    chance encounters 226; complacency of
    167; conflicts with psychiatrists 106–7;
    expression of feelings by 51: family
    origins of 18, 33–5, 53–4, 70–1, 87–90,
    102, 116–17, 134–5, 148–9, 221–3; inner
    worlds of 199–200; isolation of 196–8;
    neutrality of 113; in personal therapy
    7–8, 27, 36, 103, 108, 164, 232–7;
    political orientations of 217–18;
    professional experience of 28–9, 44–9,
    62–6, 77–83, 97–9, 106–9, 117–19, 121,
    126–9, 140–4, 161–2, 182–7; professional
    training of 6–8 passim, 30, 40–4, 56,
    58–62, 74–7, 93–5, 104–5, 125–6,
    138–40, 179–81, 227–8; projections of 6,
    7, 180; and recognition 200–1;
    relationship experiences of 27–8, 49,

56–7, 64, 66, 76, 82–3, 98–9, 100, 145,
159–60, 164, 186, 231; religious
orientations of 217–18; resistances of
165; satisfactions of 231–7; and the self
200–10, 214n; and self-observation 204;
social origins of 4; social support for 84,
186; stresses of 229–31; and suitability
6–7; teaching experiences of 79, 84–5,
143–5, 161–2, 177, 187–8; theoretical
orientations of 219–20; and therapy
choice 5–6, 121–5, 129, 183, 187; as
wounded healers 195, 226–9; and writing
34, 184, 213
psychotherapy (see also behavioural therapy;
    clients in therapy; client-centred therapy;
    co-counselling; confrontation;
    containment; counselling (psychology);
    countertransference; family therapy;
    feminist therapy; gestalt therapy; group
    work; healing; humanistic psychology;
    interpretation; intuition; positive
    unconditional regard; primal integration
    therapy; psychoanalysis; psychodrama):
    and Buddhism 145; dangers of technique
    8–10, 31, 203, 215; diagnosis in 128;
    dogmatism in 43; eclecticism in 132;
    empathy in 54, 59, 80, 196–8 passim;
    and energy flow 183; and the feminine
    169–70, 178–9, 183–5, 187; in history
    3–4; humanistic 153–4; humour in 51;
    intuition in 178; and jargon 51; Jungian
    analysis 162, 174, 179; love in 64–5, 68,
    176; and narrative tradition 213; and the
    NHS 4, 146; and paganism 162; politics
    of/and 166, 184, 188, 211–13; and
    religion 59–60, 65–6, 145, 183, 210–11;
    Rogerian 73, 75, 139; silences in 182–3;
    and spirituality 60, 65–6, 162, 166–7,
    174–6, 183–4; and stigma 30; style in
    10–11, 12, 187; and Taoism 183;
    technique in 8, 12, 31; theory in 50,
    131–2, 206–8, 219; transpersonal 162;
    and wholeness/integration 198–9
psychotic patients 45

Quaesitor 158

radical psychology 155–6, 158, 188
Raimy, Victor 32
real self (the) 154–5, 164
Red Therapy 158
regulators 10–11
Reich, Wilhelm 173, 174
resistance 50
Rogers, Carl 58–60, 73, 85, 109; see also
    client-centred therapy; positive
    unconditonal regard; psychotherapy,
    Rogerian
Rowan, John 173

Samuels, Andrew 174
Sartre, J.P. 201
Schutz, Will 151
self-empowerment 31, 154
Senft, Paul 43–4
sexual politics 164
Shertzer, Bruce 58, 59, 60
Society for the Exploration of Psychology
   Integration 32
Society for Psychotherapy Research 32
Southgate, John 157
speech impediments 89; see also stammering
Spinoza (Baruch) 149
spirituality 60, 65–6, 162, 166–7, 174–6,
   183–4, 210–11
stammering 91–2, 121, 122, 126, 127
Strupp, Hans 32
stuttering see stammering
suicide of clients 45–6
Sullivan, Harry Stack 108, 109, 113
supervision 45, 50, 64, 139, 140, 181; and
   countertransference 50; peer 181

Swartley, Bill 159, 163
Szasz, Thomas 30

Taoism 183
Tavistock Clinic 41
teleological philosophy 10
therapeutic relationship (the) 110–12
transference 7, 8, 45, 51, 108–9
Turquet, Pierre 41

unconscious (the) 122

van der Heydt, Vera 42

weight problems 25, 127
Weimer, Walter 26
Westminster Pastoral Foundation 174,
   179–81 passim
Wilber, Ken 162
working through 9
wounded healer 195, 226–9

Grieve. 9.59-76